IMAGES
of America

ST. GEORGE

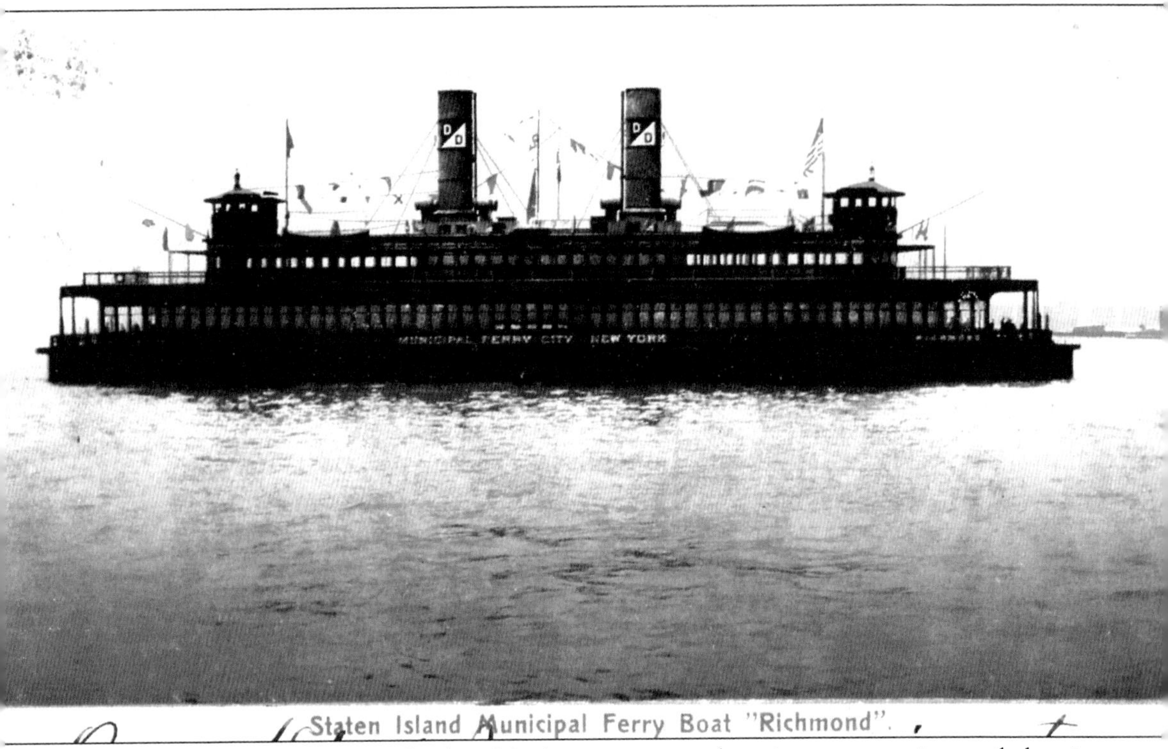

Ferry service from Staten Island to Manhattan was run by private companies until the city took over the service early in the 20th century. In 1906, New York City commissioned four new ferries, all named for one of the outer boroughs. This postcard, postmarked October 24, 1906, shows the new ferry boat *Richmond*, named for Richmond County, Staten Island. (Collection of David Goldfarb.)

On the cover: Please see page 17. (Courtesy of Staten Island Historical Society.)

IMAGES
of America

ST. GEORGE

David Goldfarb and James G. Ferreri

ARCADIA
PUBLISHING

ISBN 978-0-7385-6252-0

Published by Arcadia Publishing
Charleston SC, Chicago IL, Portsmouth NH, San Francisco CA

Printed in the United States of America

Library of Congress Control Number: 2008932145

For all general information contact Arcadia Publishing at:
Telephone 843-853-2070
Fax 843-853-0044
E-mail sales@arcadiapublishing.com
For customer service and orders:
Toll-Free 1-888-313-2665

Visit us on the Internet at www.arcadiapublishing.com

Contents

ACKNOWLEDGMENTS

The authors would like to thank the following individuals and organizations: the Staten Island Historical Society for their help in assembling many of the photographs used in this book, Carlotta DeFillo for her time and expertise and Maxine Friedman for her kindness and support; the archivist, Patricia Salmon, at the Staten Island Institute of Arts and Sciences for her assistance with information and photographs; the Staten Island Advance for permission to use images; Marjorie Decker Johnson for sharing her knowledge as well as her photographs; John Kilcullen for sharing his collection of St. George images; and Cindy Voorspuy and Daniel Kusrow for information on the Copp House, the Benziger family, and for sharing Daniel's collection of photographs and post cards.

We would also like to acknowledge the efforts of the St. George Civic Association and the Preservation League of Staten Island in obtaining the designation of the St. George-New Brighton Historic District.

Jim Ferreri acknowledges the following: my parents, Ann and Ernest M. Ferreri, for teaching me about Staten Island history, and for allowing me to grow up in a c. 1850 Gothic Revival home that set me on the road to preservation; Marie Lynn LaForte, my sister, for her patience in educating me in the "computer sciences," so that I was able to work on this book; and Sandra Zummo, the features editor at the Staten Island Advance, for leading this neophyte columnist securely down the road to journalistic respectability. For her help and friendship I will forever be grateful.

David Goldfarb would like to thank his wife Elizabeth K. Goldfarb for her patience while he worked on this book as well as his son Daniel K. Goldfarb for his time and effort to photograph modern St. George.

Unless otherwise noted, all images are from the collection of the Staten Island Historical Society.

INTRODUCTION

"God might have made a more beautiful place than Staten Island, but He didn't." Those are the words of 19th-century orator, editor, abolitionist, and Staten Island resident George William Curtis, spoken about one of the five boroughs that comprise greater New York City today—the borough that historically is the most isolated and least populated of the five.

Staten Island grew at a slower pace than its neighbors Manhattan and Brooklyn due to its relative isolation from the rest of the country. The lack of a transportation network across and off the island gave rise to a more agrarian society of landowners and well-to-do families engaged in the oyster-harvesting, ship-building, and fishing industries.

The town located at the northeastern tip of the island has a long and varied history; once an industrial center, it was at other times one of the most gracious residential neighborhoods in New York City.

Though bearing the name St. George today, the area was called by different names over the years, including Camp Washington during the Civil War, and New Brighton beginning in the 1830s.

During the Revolutionary War, some 30,000 British soldiers occupied the island. The town that would go on to become St. George played an important role during this occupation; the forces set up a lookout point to observe New York Harbor from an earthen work fort on a high point of land known today as Fort Hill. From this vantage point, the British were able to monitor the harbor, Manhattan, and Long Island.

Revolutionary War hero the Marquis de Lafayette visited former New York governor and vice president Daniel D. Tompkins at his home on Fort Hill on August 15, 1824, the day before his triumphant arrival at the battery in New York.

By the 1830s, developers finally grasped the potential for Staten Island to become a resort community for wealthy New Yorkers and visiting Southern plantation owners seeking to escape the heat of summer.

New Brighton, named for the famous English resort town favored by the Prince Regent early in the 19th century, was founded in the 1830s by Manhattan developer Thomas E. Davis, as one of the first suburban communities in the United States. Davis built a grand home for himself and a series of homes as grand for other wealthy residents, on the shore of the Kill Van Kull. His Greek Revival–style home would be expanded to create the Pavilion Hotel, a venue that would go on to host the great and near-great in American politics and entertainment, as well as members of polite society in 19th-century America.

It was during these years that Staten Island's northeastern shore became the site of other glittering hotels and large estates, as well as the location of cricket matches, major league baseball competitions, and the first games of lawn tennis played on American soil.

On November 29, 1817, the first steam ferry began service between Manhattan and Staten Island. Because of the "high" price—the then-astronomical cost of 12.5¢ each way—the commute attracted only wealthy New Yorkers, who ultimately settled on Staten Island's north shore after becoming captivated by the borough's beauty.

New Brighton resident Daniel D. Tompkins, who led a protracted and eventually successful fight to end slavery in New York State, joined other entrepreneurs like Cornelius Vanderbilt, Erastus Wiman, and, after the consolidation of greater New York in 1898, Staten Island's first borough president, George Cromwell, in working toward the creation of a transportation network that would connect Staten Island to the outside world. Eventually a successful network of rail and ferry service was established that, for the first time, connected most parts of the island with ferries leaving from most shores across the island, with the main terminus at St. George.

The town of St. George came into being in order to facilitate the area's development as a transportation hub and an attraction for visitors from other areas of the city and the country.

Legend has it that local developer Wiman promised local investor George Law that he would "canonize him" if Law would allow Wiman to develop his lands for the consolidation of rail connections in an area near today's Staten Island Ferry Terminal. And so was born the town of St. George.

There were problems along the way to developing the region, however. One of the more notorious incidents in Staten Island and New York State's history took place in this town that would become St. George. A group of upstanding men of the community gathered on the evening of September 1, 1858, near the quarantine station, with one intention; they would burn the complex down in order to finally cease the landing of ships carrying passengers with infectious diseases, who were then transferred to the quarantine.

After nearly five decades of attempts to rid the community of this irritant, which was responsible for the deaths of countless Staten Island residents outside its grounds, the burning of the quarantine station finally forced the government to relocate the station to two small islands offshore.

By the early 20th century, St. George was on its way to becoming the center of municipal activity and the great transportation hub of rail and ferry service for Staten Island's thousands of commuters. It was at this time that John Carrere and Thomas Hastings' beautiful Staten Island Borough Hall, county courthouse, and St. George branch of the New York Public Library were erected as part of the new municipal complex.

Because of its proximity to Manhattan, St. George has always attracted residents who work on Manhattan Island. Such future entertainment luminaries as Paul Newman, Joanne Woodward, and Martin Sheen all called St. George home early in their careers.

It was true then, and it's true today that St. George is a less-expensive alternative to Manhattan for young New Yorkers. It also is only a scenic 25-minute ferry ride away from Gotham, a mere five water-miles away. The world famous Staten Island Ferry docks at St. George to this day and the ride across Upper New York Bay remains a great attraction in a city filled with some of the greatest attractions in the world.

One

Early Settlement

Staaten Eylandt, named by the Dutch to honor the States-General in Holland, was purchased in 1626 from the Leni Lenape Indians and subsequently ceded to the English in 1664. The earliest Europeans to travel into the Narrows stopped at a location near today's Victory Boulevard at Bay Street to fill their ship's casks from a natural spring near the shore that for generations after was to be known as the "Watering Place." The area known today as St. George was part of the original Colonial land patent of Elias Duxbury known as the "Duxbury Glebe," which was subsequently ceded by St. Andrew's Church.

On July 2 and 3, 1776, British soldiers set up their headquarters in New Dorp but built an earthen work fortification overlooking New York Harbor on high land that is known today as Fort Hill.

By 1800, the New York quarantine had been moved to the area to house immigrants from Ireland and Germany arriving with contagious and incurable diseases. The quarantine was viewed by area residents as an unwelcome danger to the community. On September 1, 1858, local residents burned the buildings of the compound.

Daniel D. Tompkins, governor of New York as well as vice president of the United States, played a pivotal role in the establishment of the area as a transportation hub when he incorporated the Richmond Turnpike Corporation in 1816, located near his ferry slip, which at the time was near the Watering Place, in the village that he founded and named Tompkinsville. The Richmond Turnpike, originally a toll road for passengers traveling from New York City via a ferry, was advertised as the fastest route to Philadelphia at the time.

In 1834, Thomas E. Davis acquired from Daniel Tompkins's estate the property he named New Brighton. It is believed to have been laid out by English architect John Haviland (in New York to design the prison known as the Tombs). But because of a change in the economy, aside from a few model homes, the plan was not developed.

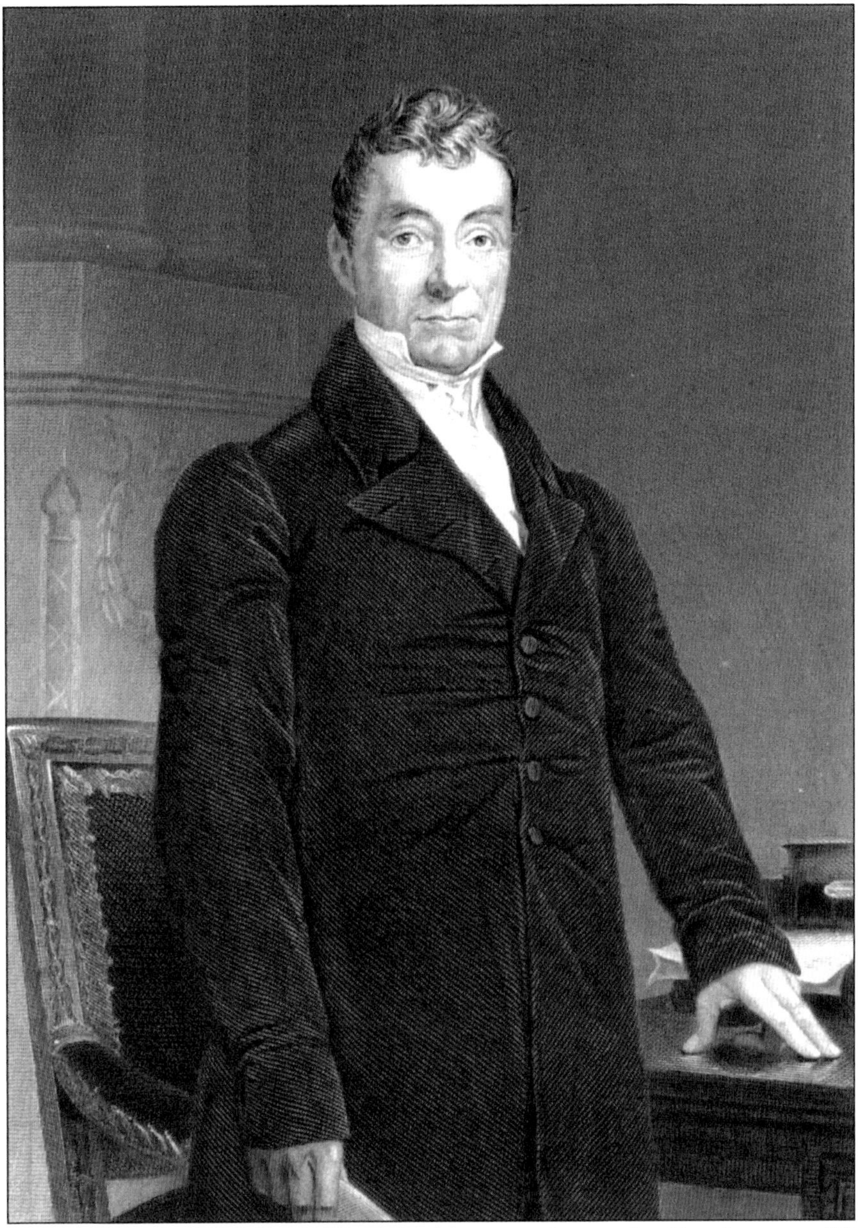

Marquis de Lafayette, who came to the aid of America during the Revolutionary War, was assigned to the staff of George Washington and was responsible for several major victories against the British. He returned to France in 1779 and convinced the French government to send further aid to the Americans. Lafayette was considered a national hero when he visited Daniel D. Tompkins at his large home on the hill in St. George in 1824, on his farewell trip across America. Tompkins's home stood near the intersection of today's Fort Place and Sherman Avenue. On his visit to Tompkins, Lafayette's ship sat anchored offshore as the general traveled up the hill to be hosted by Tompkins, who would die one year later in 1825. Lafayette attended the memorial service for Vice President Tompkins at the Dutch Reform Church. The engraving is from 1874 by Johnson Wilson and Company from a painting by Alonzo Chappel. (Collection of David Goldfarb.)

Daniel D. Tompkins was governor of New York from 1807 to 1817. He was elected vice president of the United States on the ticket with James Monroe in 1816 and was reelected in 1820, serving from March 4, 1817, to March 4, 1825. This is a steel engraving portrait of Tompkins, engraved by T. Woolnoth from a painting by J. W. Jarvis. (Collection of David Goldfarb.)

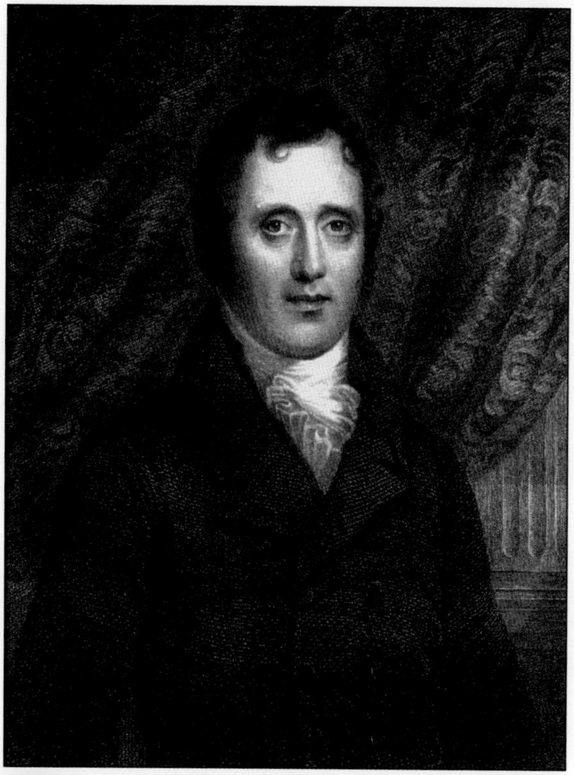

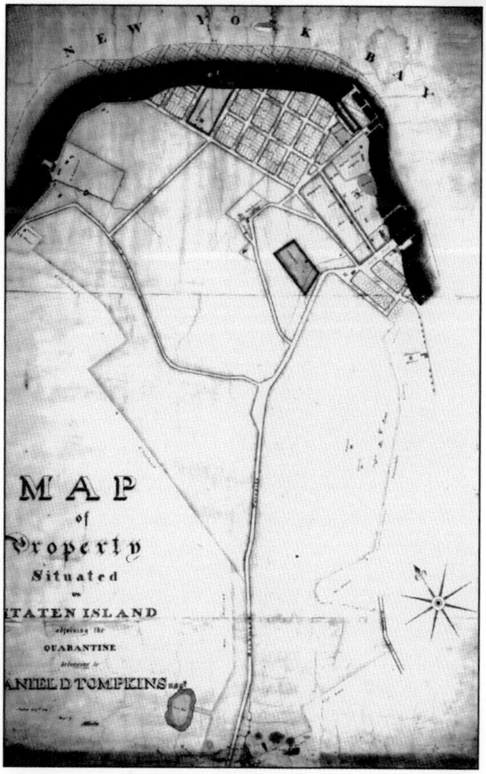

This early map of Staten Island's northeastern shore shows both the quarantine station and the lands belonging to Governor Tompkins. Tompkins played a pivotal role in the establishment of the area as a transportation hub when he incorporated the Richmond Turnpike Corporation in 1816, located near his ferry slip, which at the time was near the Watering Place, in the village that he founded and named Tompkinsville.

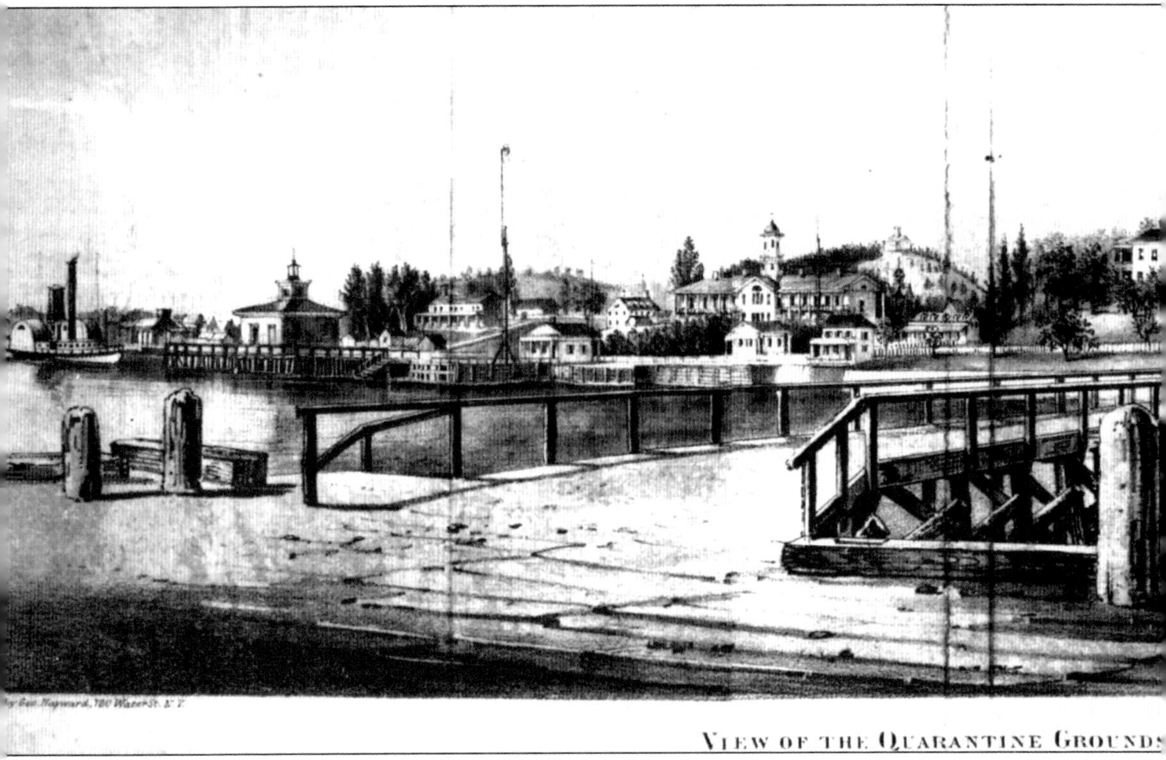

Here is a view of the quarantine grounds and buildings. The land on which the quarantine was located was originally part of the Duxbury Glebe, which was granted to St. Andrew's Church by Elias Duxbury in 1718. New York State took 30 acres of the glebe for the establishment of quarantine for "persons infected with yellow fever and other contagious diseases." Staten

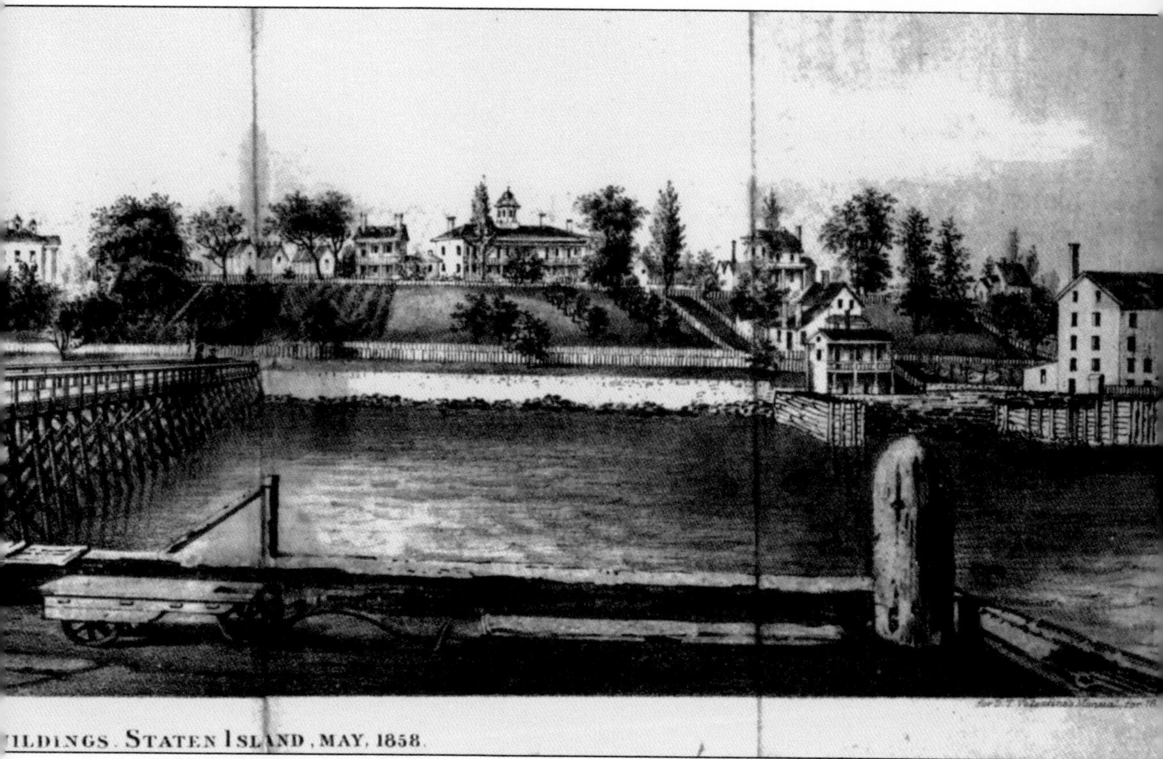

Islanders did not want persons ill with such diseases located so near the general public, but their protests fell on deaf ears. The high walls surrounding the facility did little to contain disease, and the staff was allowed to leave the grounds, further endangering the Staten Island populace. (Collection of David Goldfarb.)

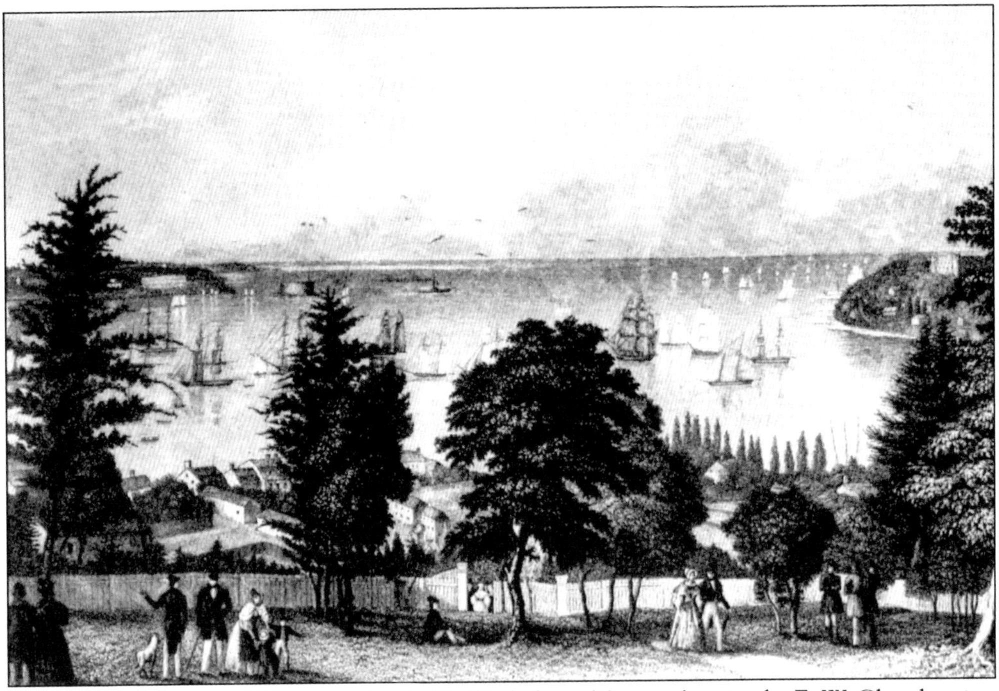

The image above is an 1835 engraving by R. Hirshelwood from a drawing by E. W. Clay showing a view of the Narrows from the pavilion near the quarantine Ground. The second image shows the burning of the quarantine. On September 1, 1858, 30 "gentlemen of prominence" assembled with the intention of ridding Staten Island's north shore of the threat of contamination. They first removed any patients from the wards then set fire to the buildings. Buildings that survived the first night were again burned the following evening. The members of the group were tried, but there were no convictions. Staten Island was required to pay to the state $133,800 for the damage. The quarantine hospitals moved to two artificial islands—Hoffman and Swinborne—off Staten Island's southern shore. The engraving is from Frank Leslie's *Illustrated Newspaper* of September 18, 1858.

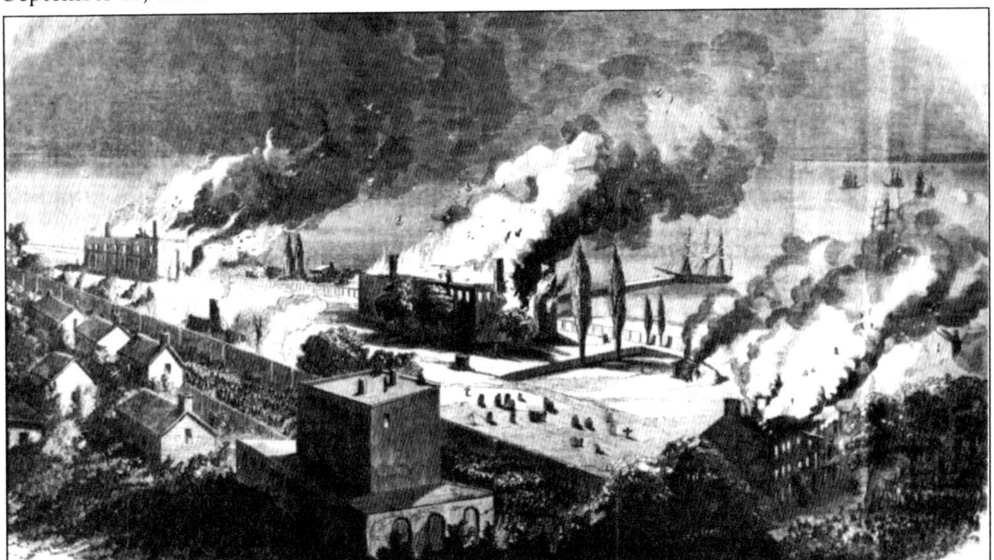

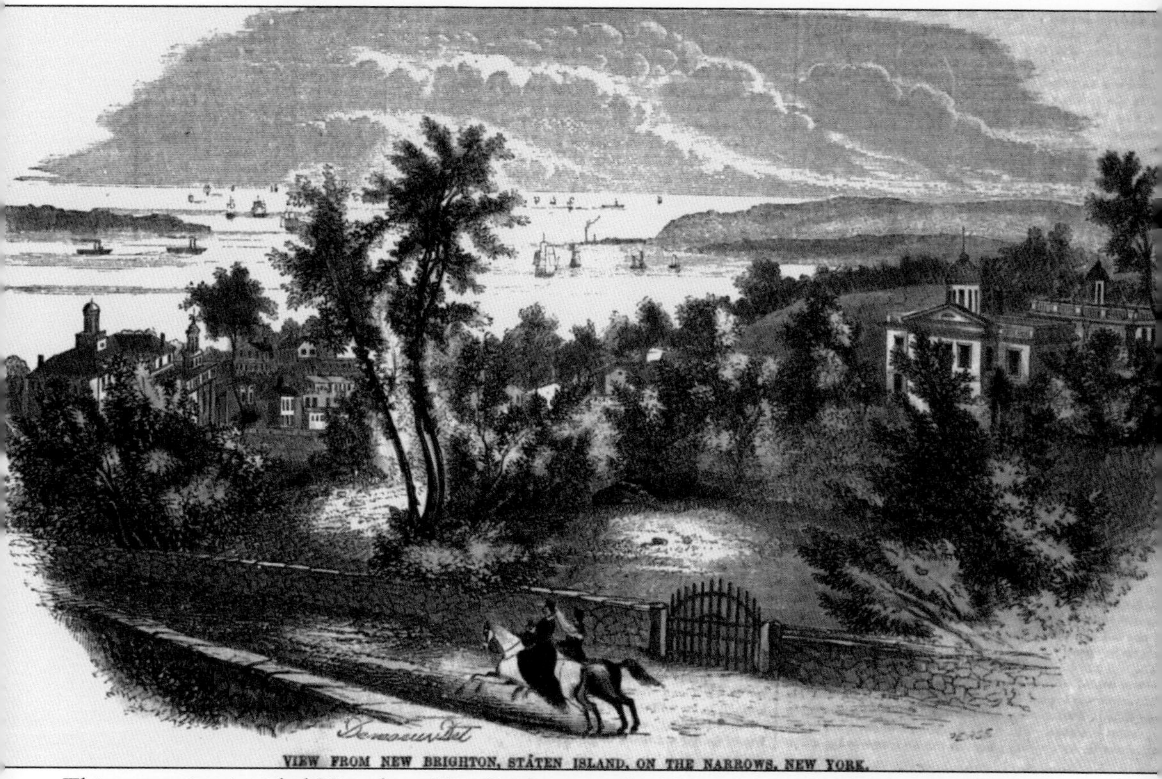

This engraving is titled *View from New Brighton, on the Narrows, Staten Island, New York* and appeared in *Gleason's Pictorial* on September 30, 1854. "It is a chosen spot during the summer months, of thousands from the city, for relaxation from the dust and turmoil of the crowded thoroughfares of the city." (Collection of David Goldfarb.)

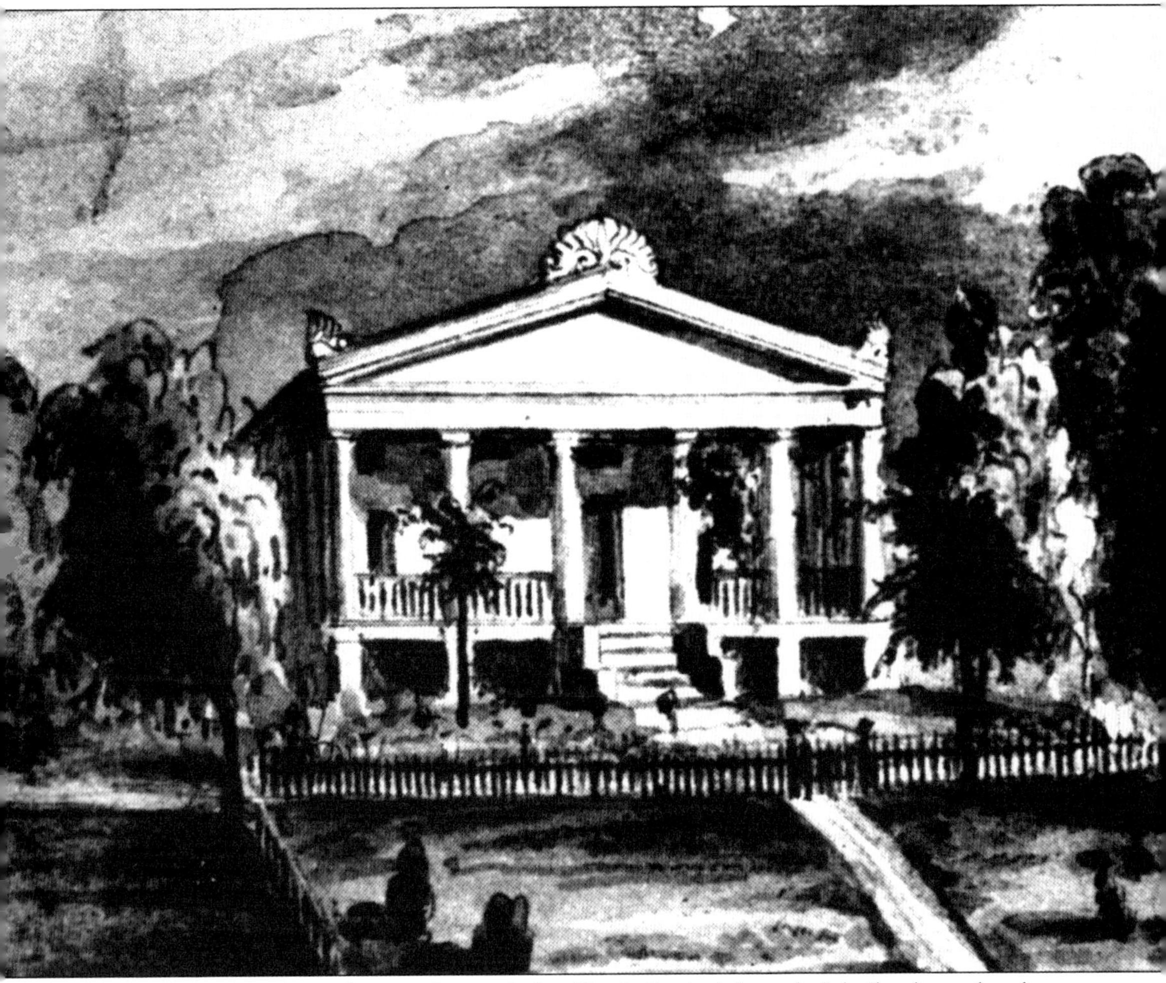

This is an artist's rendering of one of the Greek Revival "temples" built along the shore as the first buildings of the development known as New Brighton, which was one of the earliest suburban planned communities in New York City. Between 1834 and 1835, Manhattan developer Thomas E. Davis acquired the triangle of land extending along the North Shore from the quarantine station and Richmond Turnpike to Sailors' Snug Harbor, initiated planning for an exclusive and fashionable summer retreat named New Brighton, after the famous English resort favored by the Prince Regent. The earliest buildings in New Brighton were five Greek Revival houses along the shore road, renamed Richmond Terrace, that were built in 1835. Davis's home was the first to be built in the Greek Revival style, and it set the tone for the remaining development.

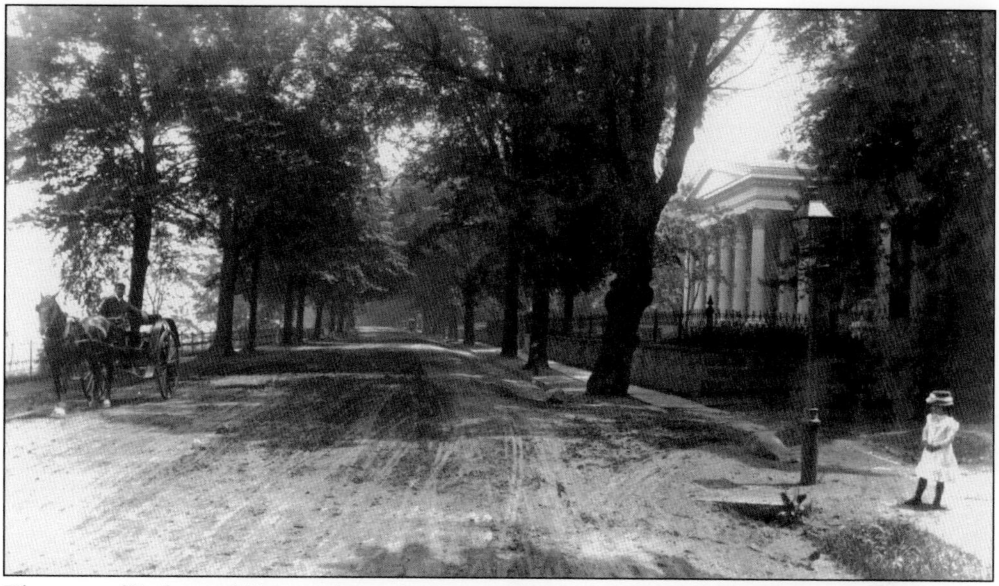

The view of Richmond Terrace shows the original homes built in New Brighton. The photograph was taken around 1885 looking east.

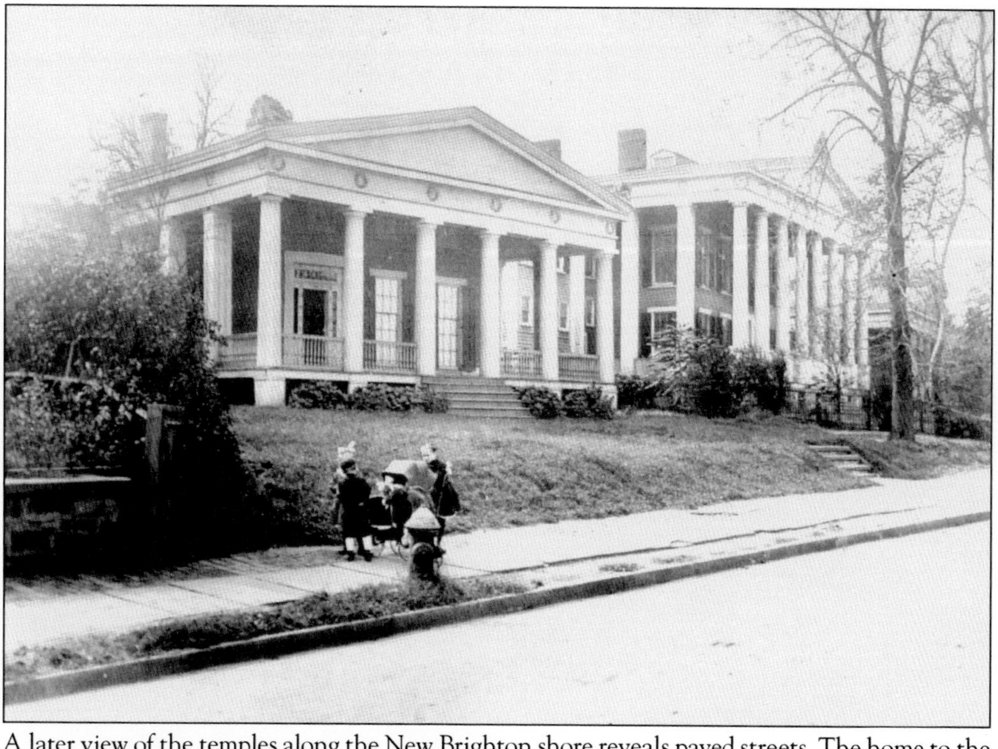

A later view of the temples along the New Brighton shore reveals paved streets. The home to the left is the Pendleton House, since demolished.

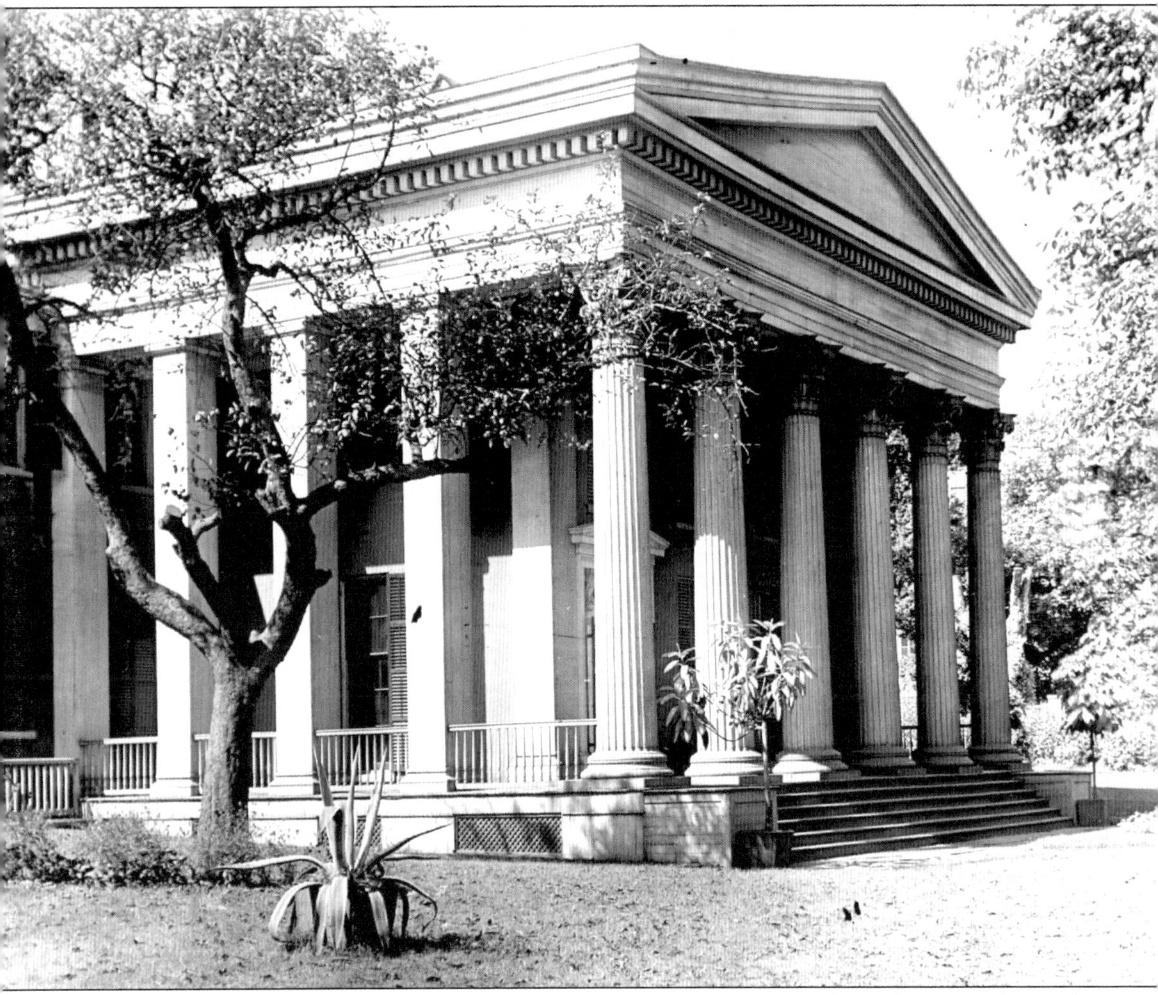

This c. 1910 photograph of another of the Greek Revival homes built in the 1830s shows the home of the Harding family. Note the very ornate Corinthian capitals on the columns.

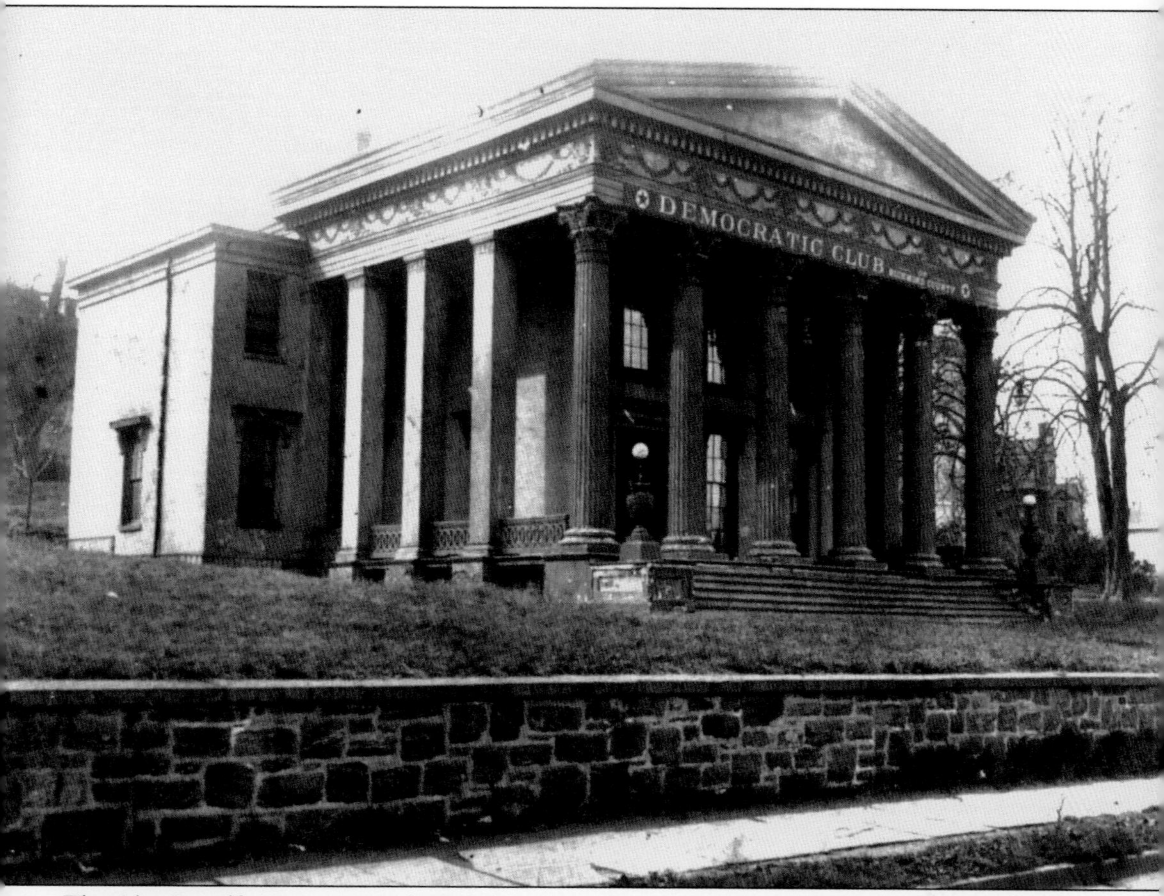

The Alex Proudfit House, around 1912, shows that the grand home has been converted for use as the Democratic Club of Richmond County. This and other of the original temples from 1835 were demolished in the early 1960s to make way for the Richmond Terrace Houses of the New York City Housing Authority.

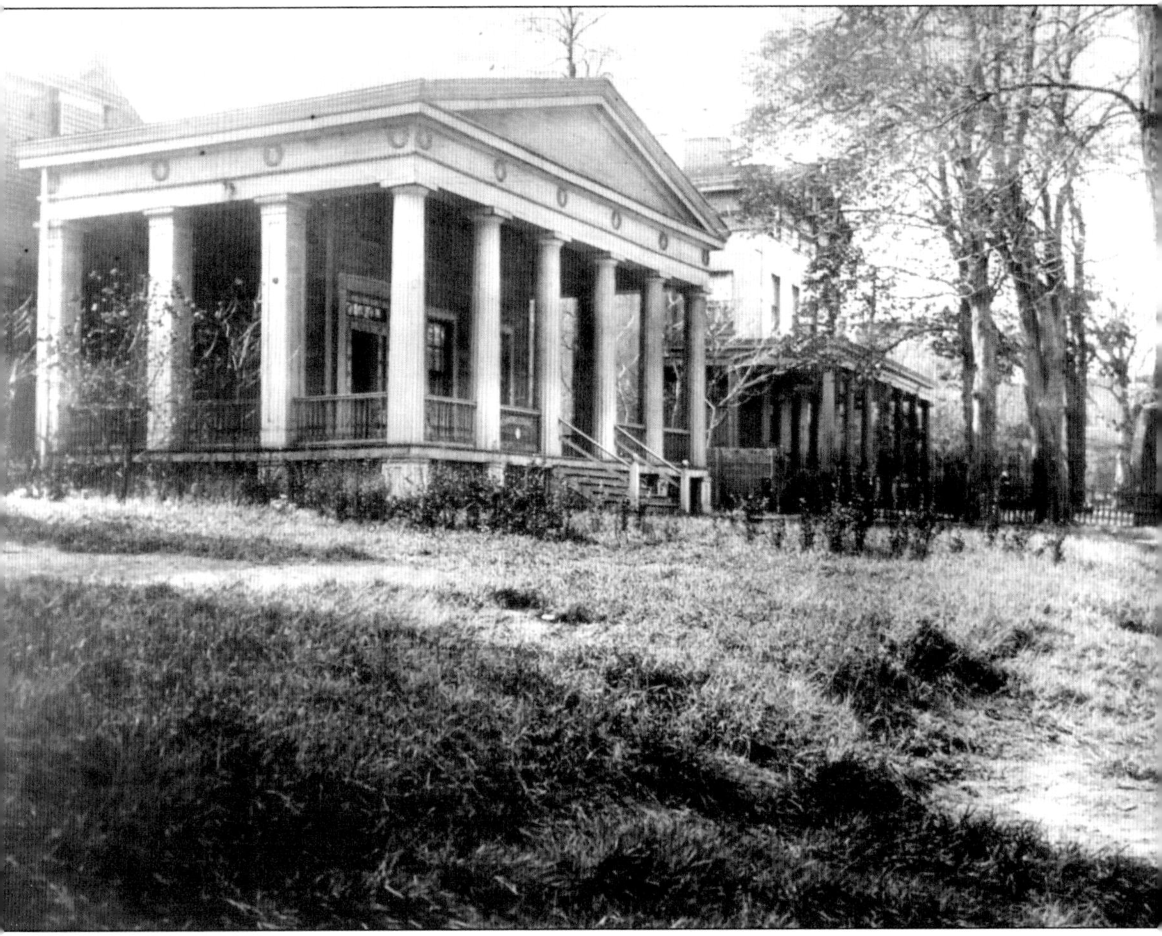

The home to the left belonged to the Wilkinson family, who were active in a factory nearby that produced colorful silk handkerchiefs. This photograph is dated October 13, 1912, and shows that the old homes were not receiving the care they needed, with overgrown lawns and shrubs.

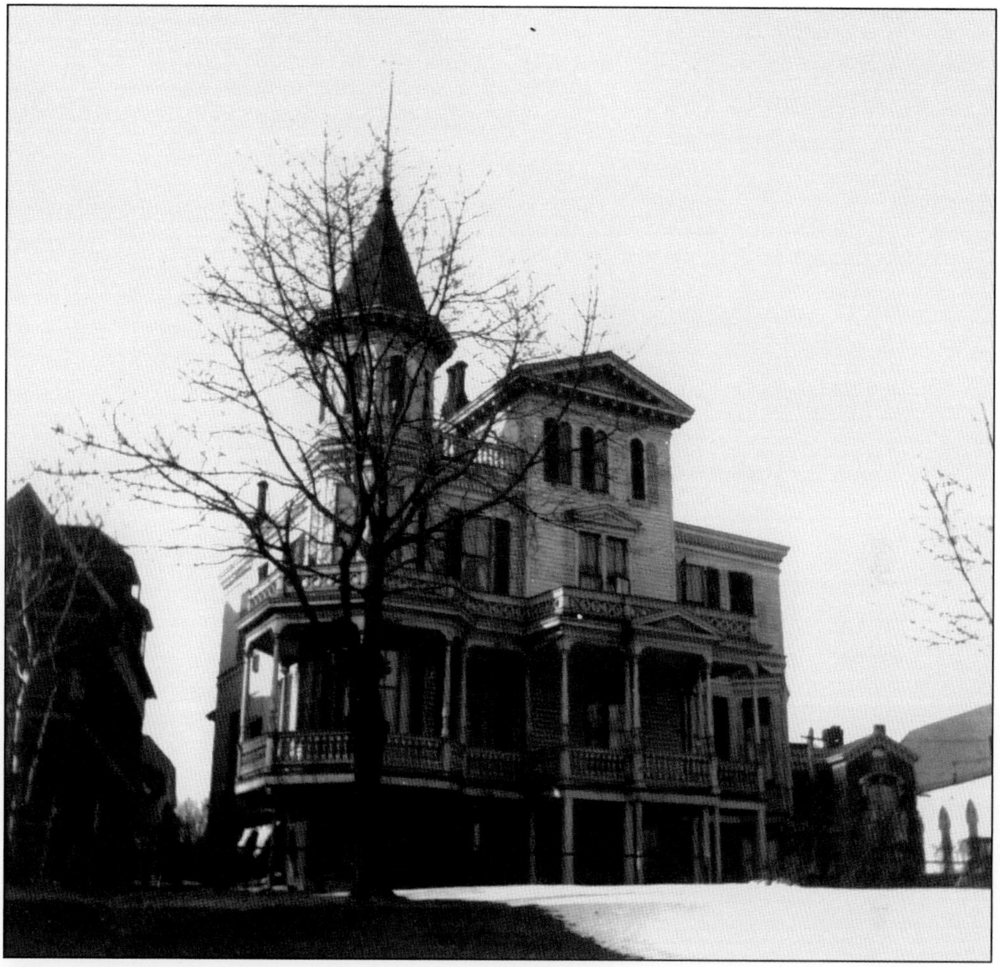

This spectacular late-19th-century home was built on the burial grounds for immigrants who died at the nearby quarantine station. The long-forgotten graveyard was located between St. Mark's Place, Hyatt Street, and Central Avenue, where there is a municipal parking lot today, and where soon there will be a skyscraping courthouse building. Test excavations in 2007 found hundreds of bones from the unfortunate victims who were quarantined because of the virulent illnesses they contracted aboard ships coming to America, only to die in the New World.

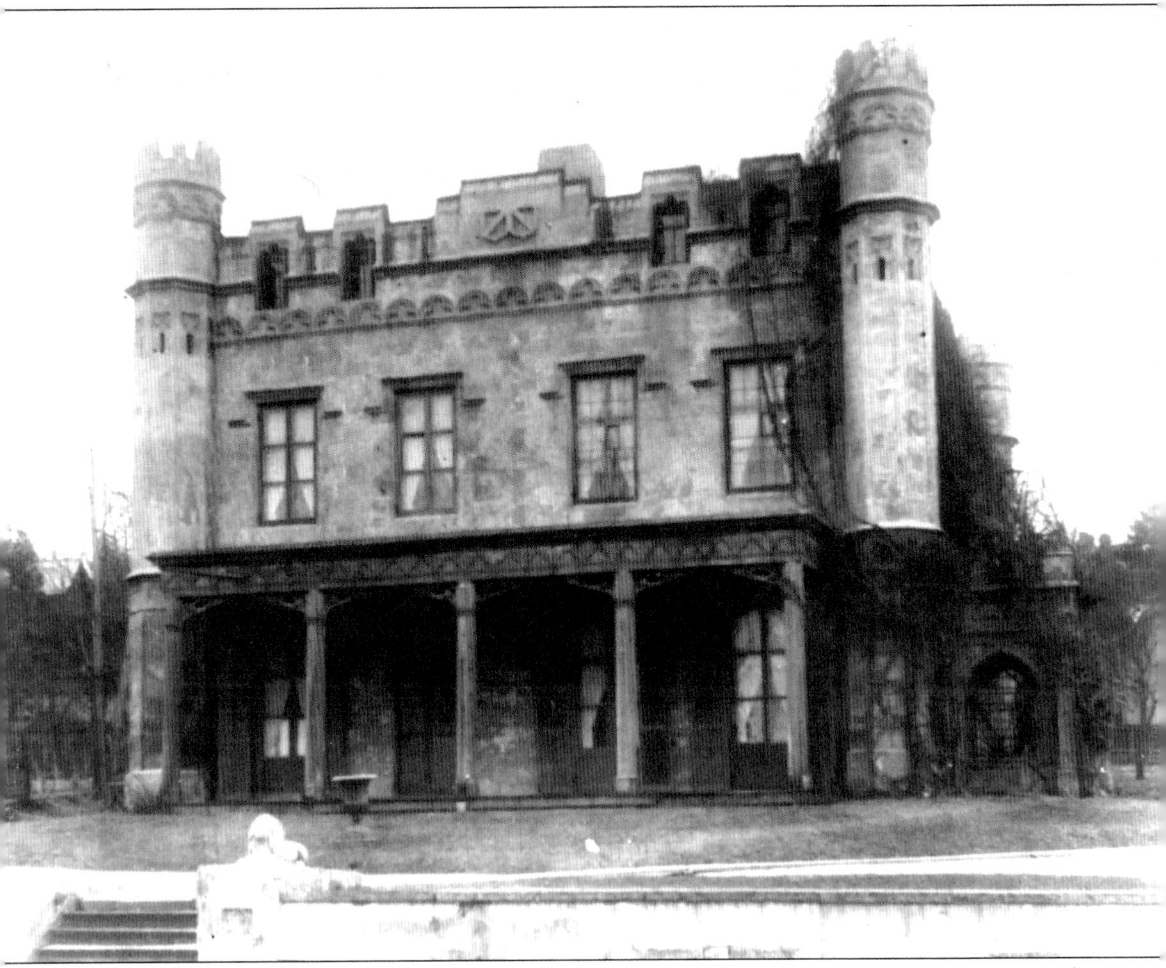

This New Brighton residence was built of concrete blocks around 1830 and was known as the Ward Mansion. It is perhaps related to the Caleb Ward Mansion on Ward Hill, also constructed of concrete.

Two

Houses of Worship

Daniel D. Tompkins, governor of New York State, became an active member of the Staten Island Reformed Church and secured permission from the U.S. Health Service to conduct religious services in the hall of the Fever Hospital (a part of the quarantine) in 1817. It was located at about the present site of Staten Island Borough Hall. When this arrangement proved inadequate, then–vice president Tompkins gave a plot of ground where a cornerstone for a new church was laid on October 18, 1818. The location today is the area between Bay Street and Van Duzer Street fronting on Victory Boulevard.

The next home of the Brighton Heights Reformed Church was at the corner of St. Mark's Place and Fort Place. The new church was designed by architect John Correja and built in 1863. In 1996, this church building burned and was immediately demolished. A new church was built on the site.

The nucleus of the present St. Peter's Roman Catholic Church met in a gun factory in New Brighton on the southeast corner of Lafayette Street and Richmond Terrace, for weekly mass beginning in 1839. The gun factory soon became unsuited for church services, and ground on Carroll Place in New Brighton was donated for the new church by the New Brighton Association. The gun factory was used until the church was opened in 1844. The building, a small, sturdy brick edifice, was nestled into a hill that descended from the street now known as St. Mark's Place, and faced the harbor. The front door of the structure was reached by precipitous steps leading to the steep incline on Carroll Place.

A fire destroyed the first St. Peter's Roman Catholic Church building during the 1890s. The present neo-Romanesque structure was designed in 1900 by the architectural firm of Harding and Gooch. In 1901, the cornerstone of the brick church edifice was laid, and in 1902, work was started on the upper portion. On Thanksgiving Day in 1903, the church was dedicated and is still considered one of the most magnificent edifices on Staten Island.

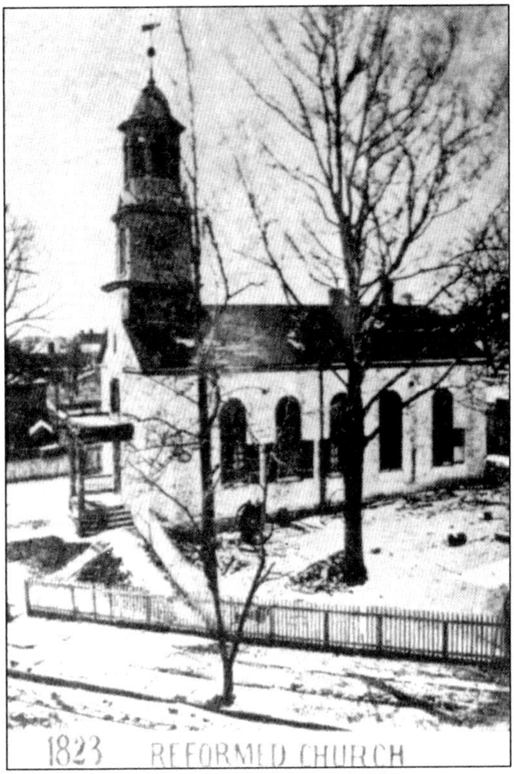

This is the first church building for the Brighton Heights Reformed Church; Vice President Daniel D. Tompkins donated the plot of ground on which it stood. The cornerstone was laid in 1818, and the church was dedicated in 1820. This church was located on land that is now the area between Bay Street and Van Duzer Street, fronting on Victory Boulevard. Marquis de Lafayette attended the memorial service for Tompkins at this church.

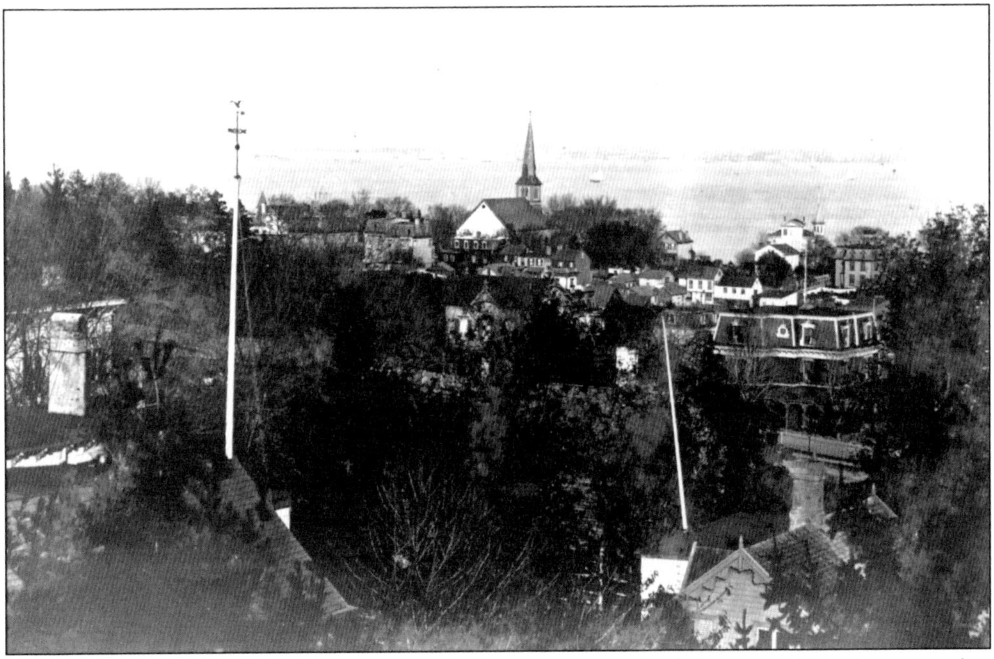

A view towards New York City from Fort Hill shows the back of the second Brighton Heights Reformed Church at the corner of St. Mark's Place and Fort Place. Fort Hill was named for the earthen work fortifications built by the British soldiers who occupied Staten Island during the Revolutionary War.

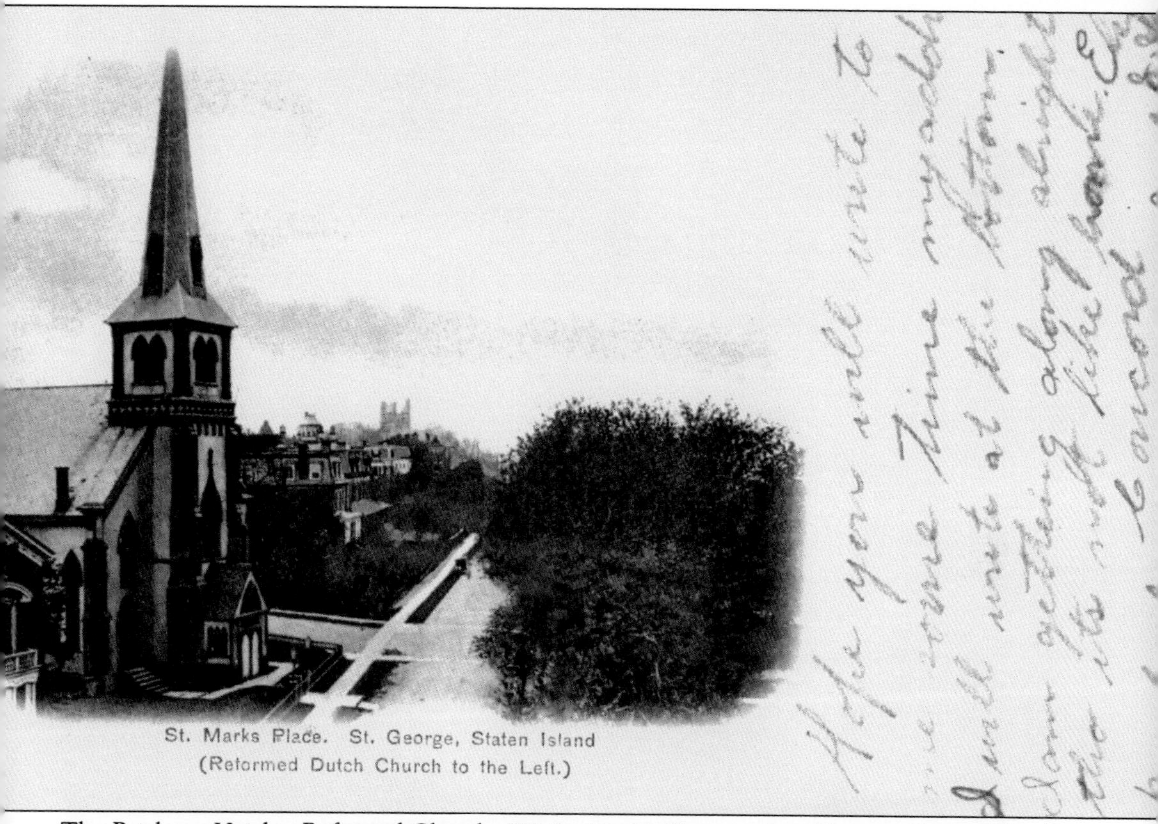

The Brighton Heights Reformed Church, 320 St. Mark's Place, at Fort Place on Staten Island was designed by architect John Correja and built in 1863. When the Reformed Protestant Dutch Church in Tompkinsville outgrew its original building, it acquired this property in nearby Brighton Heights and commissioned the Manhattan architect John Correja to design a stone structure. The cost of building the Gothic Revival design proved high, and Correja eventually adapted the form to allow for the construction of a less expensive wooden building. With its prominent spire, the church was highly visible along the northeast shore of Staten Island. It was designated a city landmark in 1967. This old postcard view of St. Mark's Place clearly shows some of the significant buildings in St. George such as the Brighton Heights Reformed Church, Curtis High School in the distance, as well as the dome of St. Peter's Roman Catholic Church. (Collection of David Goldfarb.)

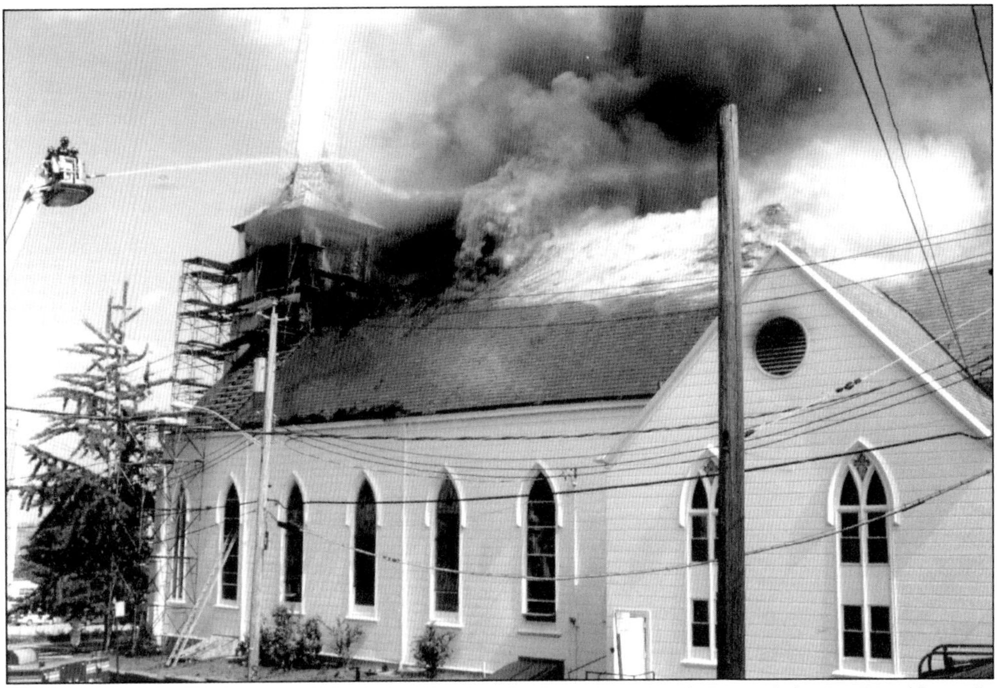

These dramatic photographs show the 1996 three-alarm fire that destroyed the roof and heavily damaged the steeple of the 133-year-old Brighton Heights Reformed Church. (Collection of David Goldfarb.)

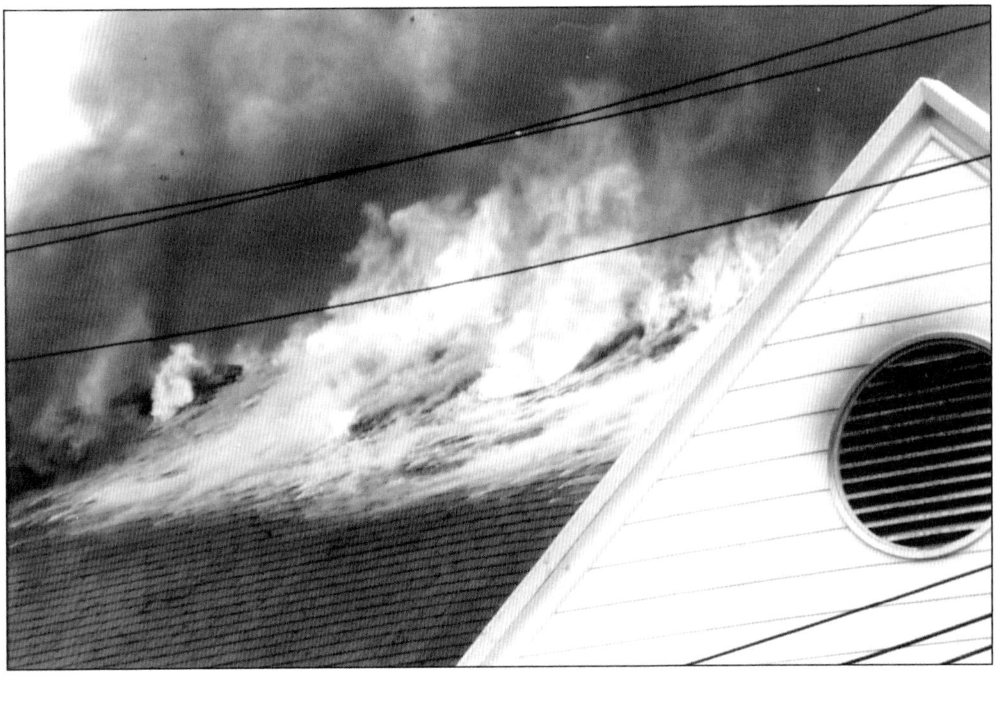

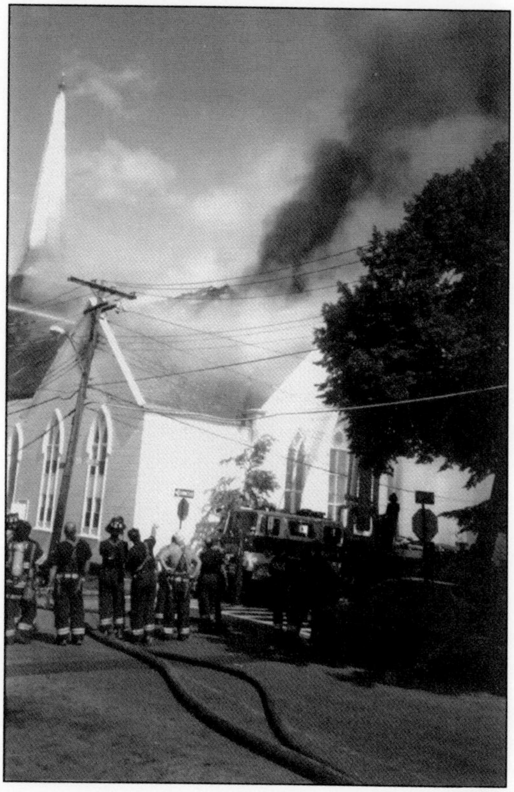

The fire began at about 3:30 p.m. and required upwards of 200 firefighters from Staten Island and Brooklyn to subdue it later that evening. Firefighters stood by helplessly for a time due to a lack of sufficient water pressure to battle the blaze. Three cherry pickers were employed to blast water on the blaze from 80 feet above. (Collection of David Goldfarb.)

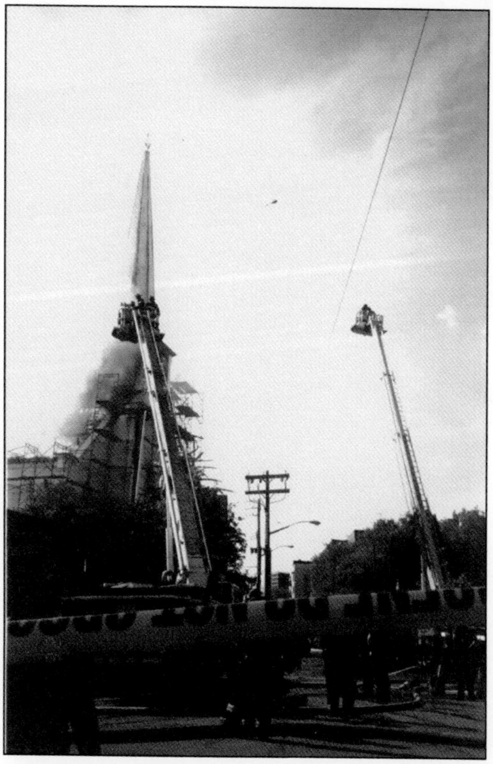

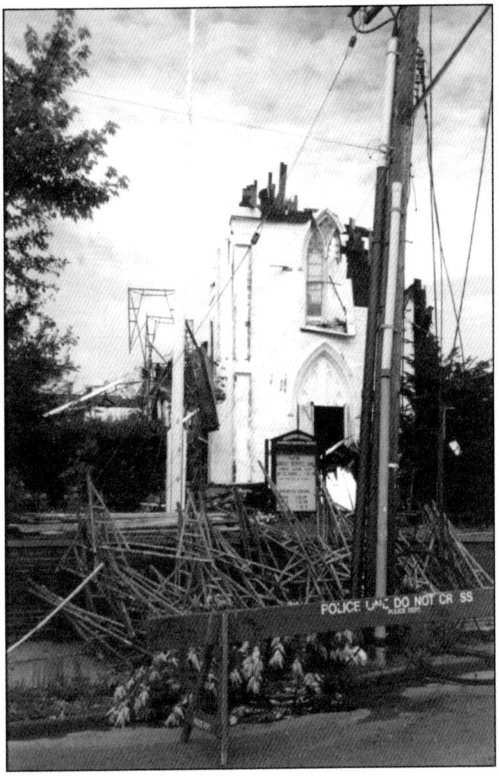

Staten Island's historic Brighton Heights Reformed Church (a designated New York City landmark) was demolished on June 29, 1996, after a fire the previous day. (Collection of David Goldfarb.)

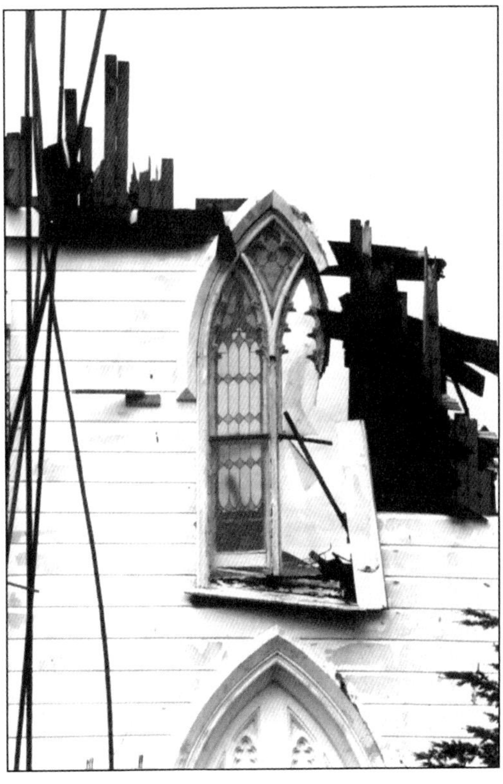

The blaze that destroyed the Brighton Heights Reformed Church, which was being repainted, was started by a worker using a heat gun to remove old paint. The church had already suffered a small fire in November 1995, which was started the same way. (Collection of David Goldfarb.)

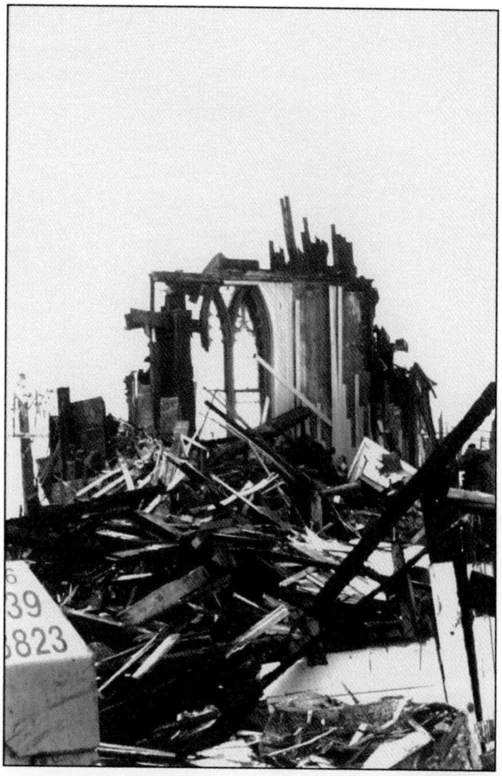

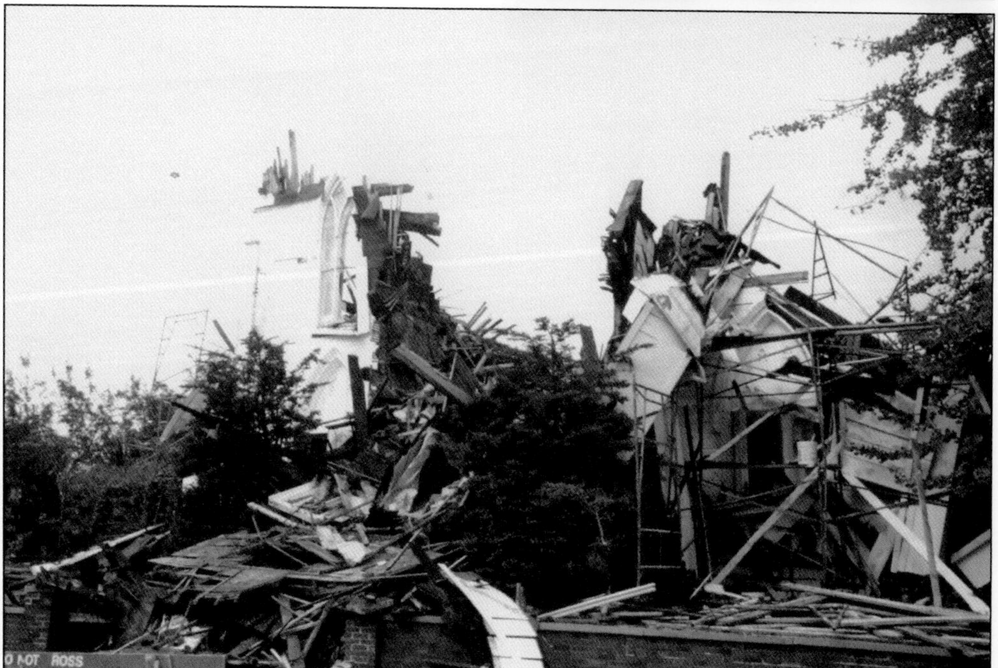

Borough President Guy Molinari was instrumental in slowing the demolition process of the church while preservationists salvaged some of the irreplaceable stained-glass windows. (Collection of David Goldfarb.)

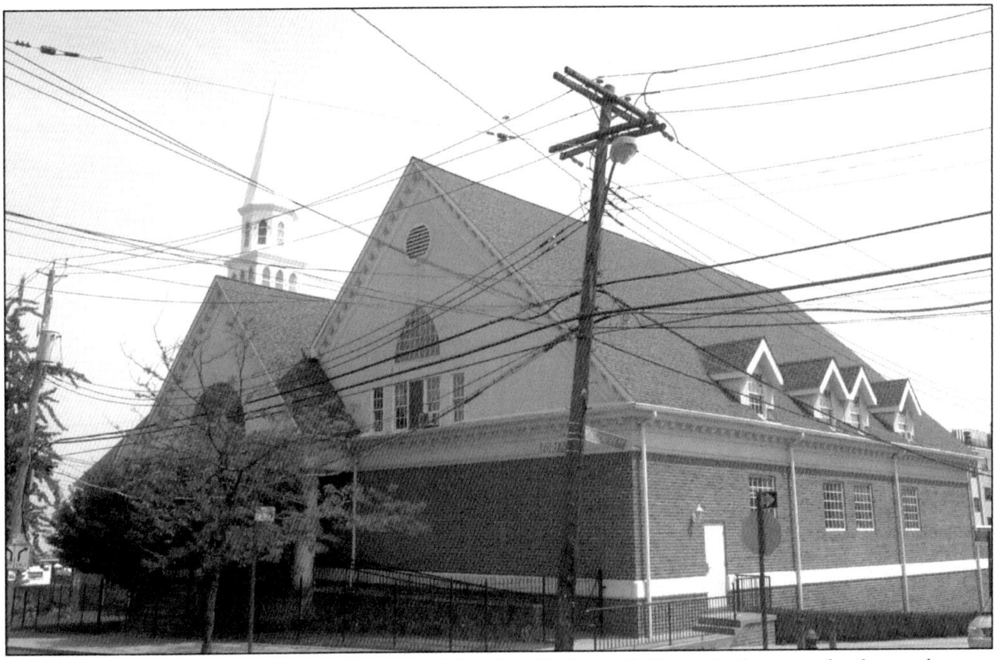

These pictures show the current Brighton Heights Reformed Church that was built on the site after the previous church was demolished. After the fire, the site was de-designated by the New York City Landmarks Preservation Commission. (Photographs by Daniel K. Goldfarb.)

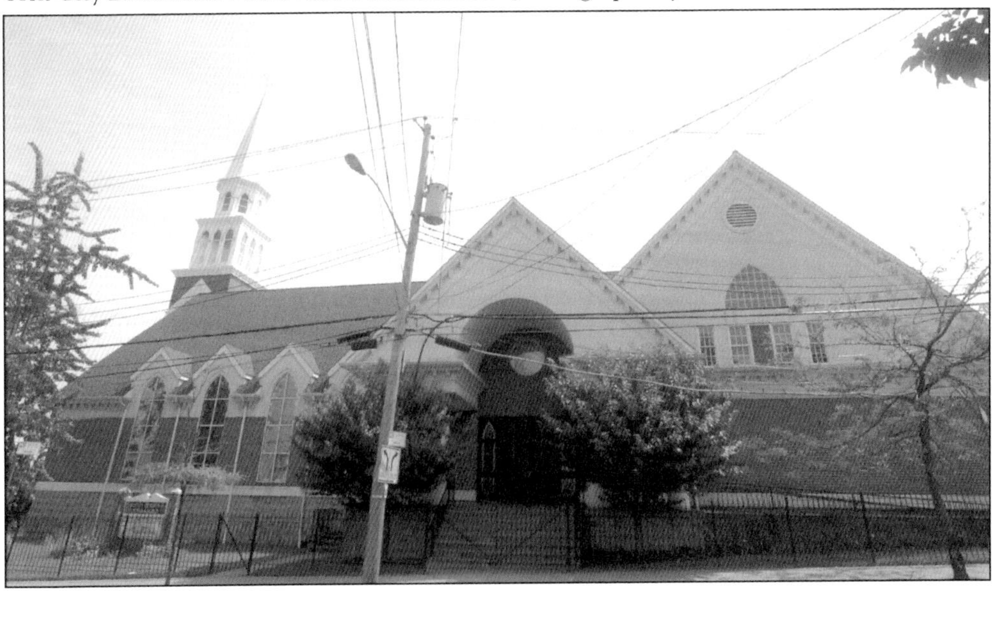

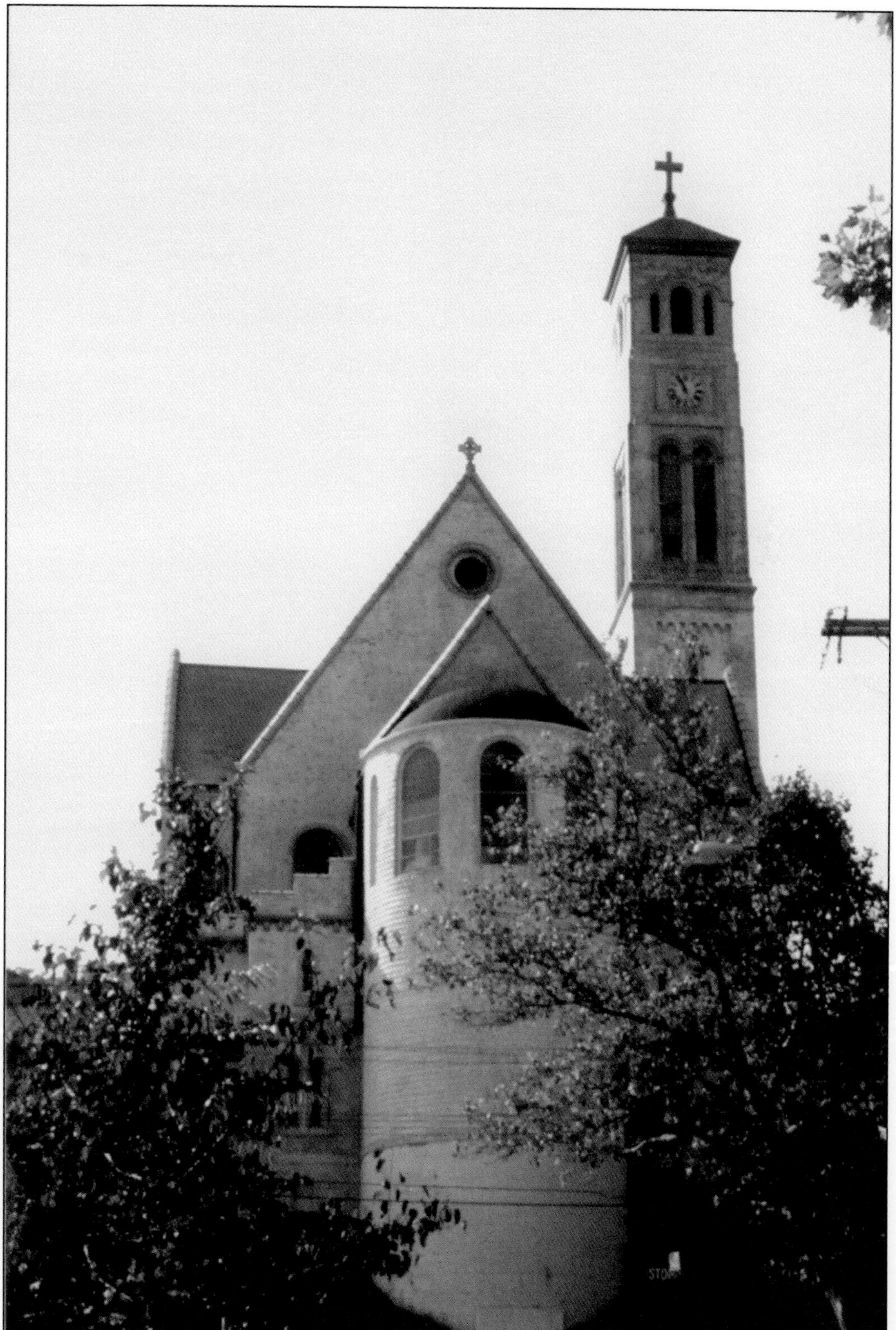

This photograph from Carroll Place shows parts of the 1844 St. Peter's Roman Catholic Church. The building, a small, sturdy brick edifice, was nestled into a hill that descended from the street now known as St. Mark's Place and faced the harbor. The front door of the structure was reached by precipitous steps leading to the steep incline on Carroll Place. In August 1853, the Sisters of Charity came to St. Peter's Roman Catholic Church and established the first parish school in the church basement. (Collection of David Goldfarb.)

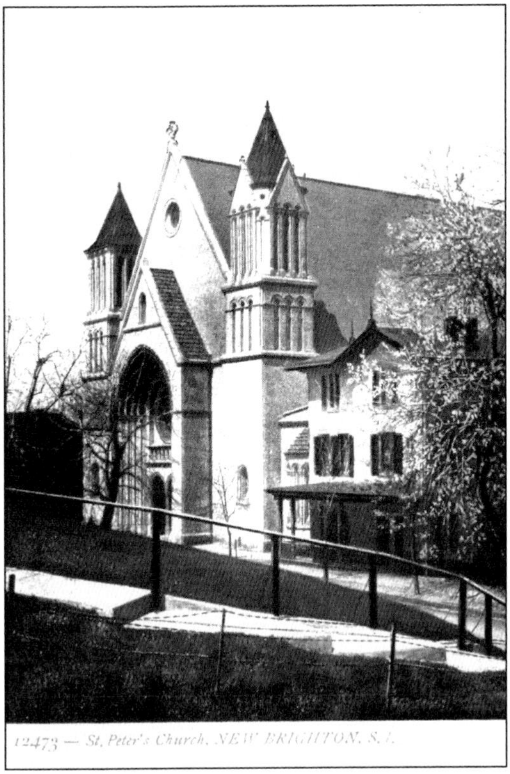

This postcard shows the present church building of St. Peter's Roman Catholic Church and the original rectory building. The present neo-Romanesque structure was designed in 1900 by the architectural firm of Harding and Gooch under the direction of the Rev. Terrence Early. In 1901, the cornerstone of the brick church edifice was laid, and in 1902, work was started on the upper portion. (Collection of David Goldfarb.)

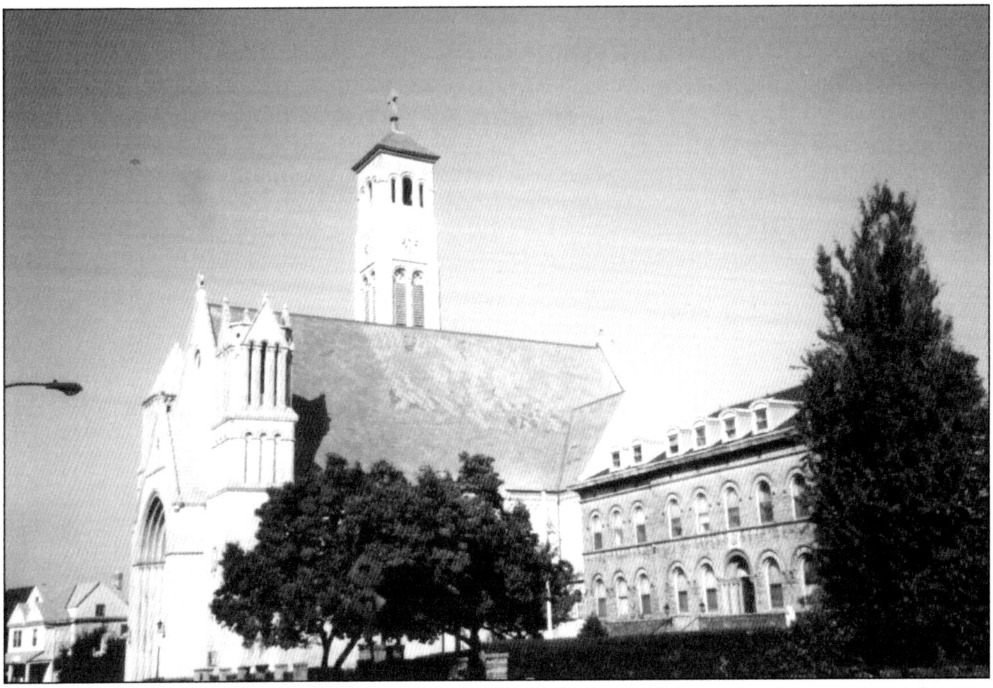

This photograph of St. Peter's Roman Catholic Church shows the new rectory on the right. On Thanksgiving Day in 1903, the church was dedicated and is still considered one of the most magnificent edifices on Staten Island. (Collection of David Goldfarb.)

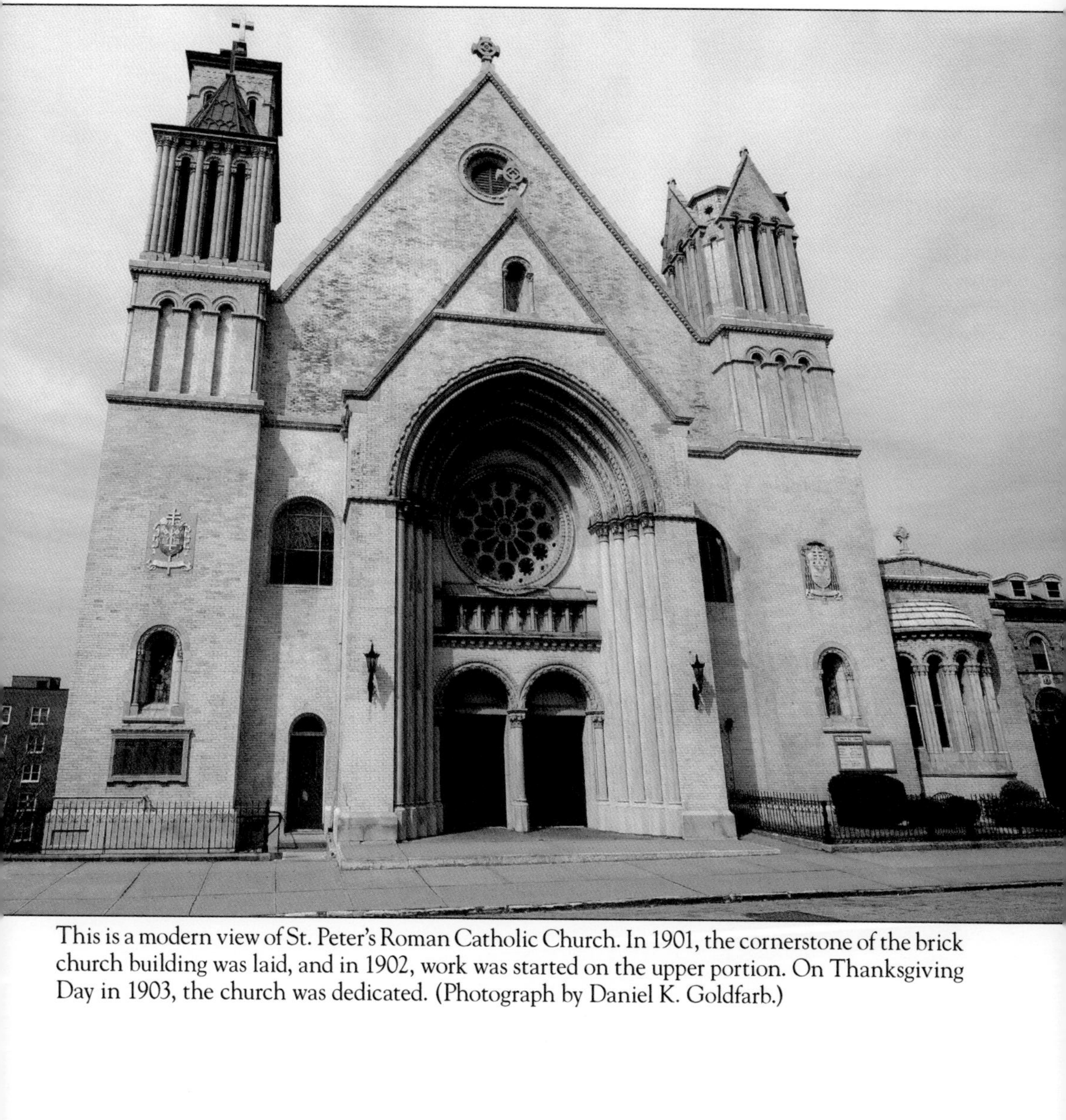

This is a modern view of St. Peter's Roman Catholic Church. In 1901, the cornerstone of the brick church building was laid, and in 1902, work was started on the upper portion. On Thanksgiving Day in 1903, the church was dedicated. (Photograph by Daniel K. Goldfarb.)

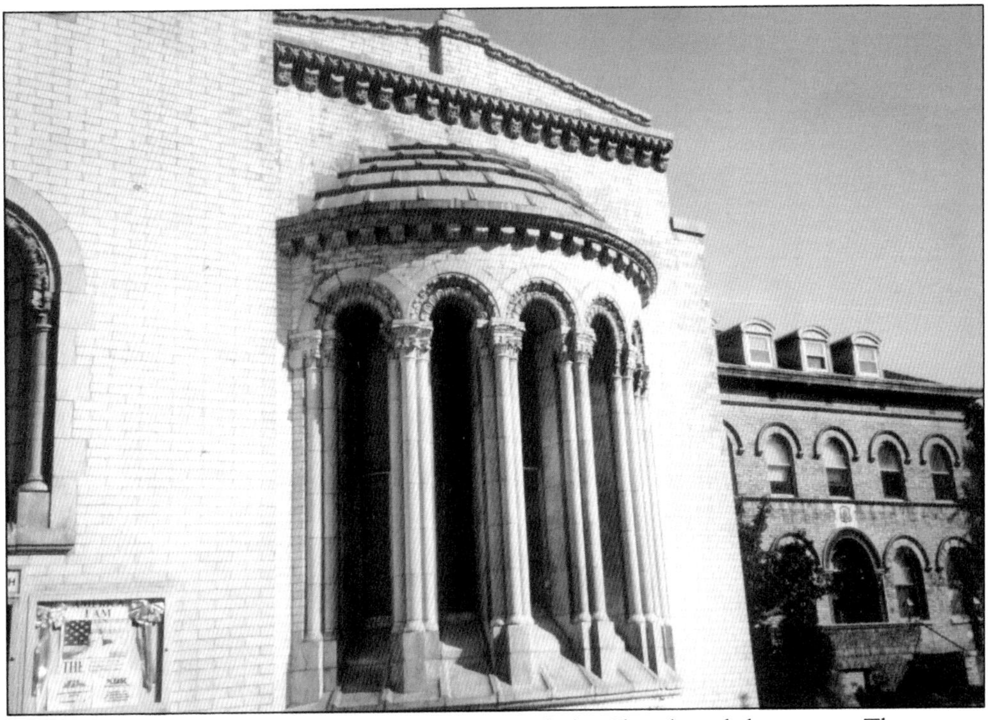

The picture shows a detail of St. Peter's Roman Catholic Church and the rectory. The rectory was designed by architect George H. Streton and draws on the form of a Renaissance palazzo and neo-Renaissance/neo-Romanesque ornament. (Collection of David Goldfarb.)

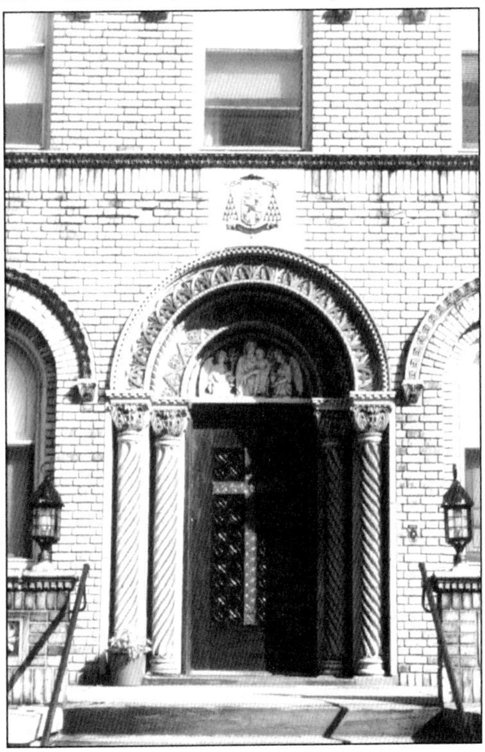

The rectory is clad with blended shades of tan brick enriched by square terra-cotta plaques with various religious symbols that have been placed along the balustrades of the porches, at the frieze below the main roof, as well as on the chimneys. (Collection of David Goldfarb.)

Three

Resort Development

During the first quarter of the 19th century, Staten Island grew and prospered, becoming a resort for the wealthy seeking to escape the increasingly crowded city. It was at this time that many hotels began to be built along Richmond Terrace, as well as in the surrounding neighborhoods.

One of the grandest, the Pavilion Hotel, was built originally as the home of the founder of New Brighton, Thomas E. Davis. The Pavilion Hotel soon was large enough to accommodate 300 to 400 patrons, hosting such luminaries as Jenny Lind and Pres. Martin Van Buren. During the Civil War years, the hotel played host to the wives and children of confederate officers escaping the war in the south.

Daniel D. Tompkins's daughter's grand home, Marble House, would eventually make way for the St. Mark's Hotel on the hillside facing the harbor. The St. Mark's Hotel would become the Hotel Castleton, a sprawling Victorian-era structure.

In the years before the area became known as St. George, the waterfront land was known by its Civil War use as Camp Washington. It was here that Mary Ewing Outerbridge, a resident of the area, introduced lawn tennis in the spring of 1874. Her brother Emilius helped her to set up a net and mark out a tennis court on the grounds of the camp, then used by the Staten Island Cricket and Baseball Club.

By the last quarter of the century, as transportation continued to be a problem on Staten Island, Canadian-born Erastus Wiman saw the island's potential and worked to solve the myriad of problems impeding Staten Island's growth. Wiman was instrumental in consolidating ferry and rail service across the Island. His vision for Staten Island also included its becoming an entertainment destination. He built a huge casino on the St. George waterfront, presenting sporting events such as baseball games. Wiman's casino also presented extravaganzas such as "The Fall of Rome," and "The Fall of Babylon." Wiman's shows often included elephants that were stabled on nearby Jersey Street; and supposedly, these became the inspiration for Staten Island resident cartoonist William Roger's symbol of the Republican Party.

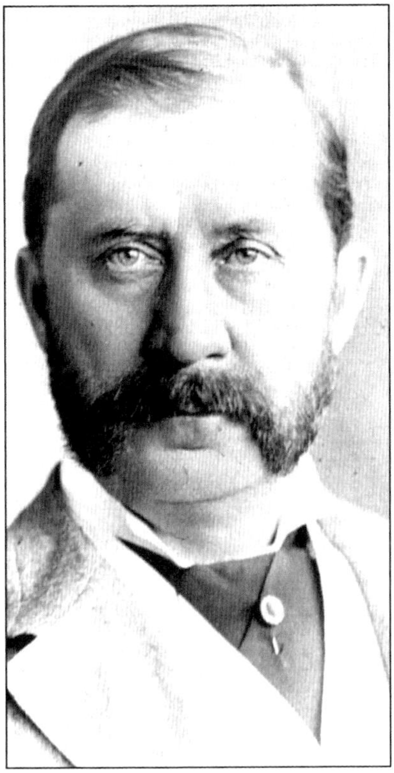

Erastus Wiman, who was born in Canada, had a tremendous impact on Staten Island. He reorganized the railroad and consolidated ferry service, creating the transit hub in St. George, as well as constructing a railroad bridge across the Arthur Kill to Elizabethport, in New Jersey. (Courtesy of the Staten Island Advance.)

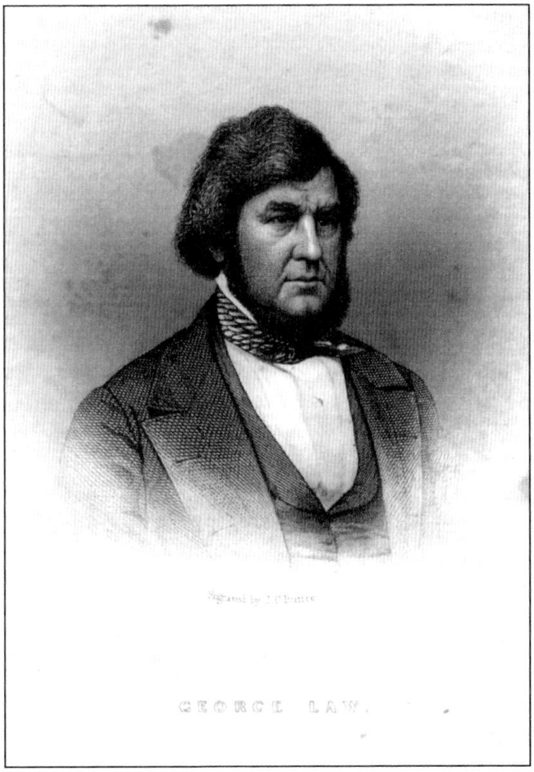

This is an engraving of George Law by J. C. Buttre. Law owned extensive land in New Brighton, which he had bought at bargain prices. When Wiman needed land in the area, Law refused to sell. Wiman finally promised to "canonize" Law if he would grant Wiman the rights to the land. So as legend has it, the town of St. George came into being. (Collection of David Goldfarb.)

This wonderful photograph, titled "View of Staten Island, October 12, 1903," was taken from Pier No. 3, Constable Hook, which was across the Kill Van Kull in New Jersey. At the center of the panorama is the Pavilion Hotel, with St. Peter's Roman Catholic Church directly behind. Curtis High School is visible to the left, while the massive Hotel Castleton sits at the extreme left of the hill, capturing the sweeping views, much as the Acropolis does in Greece.

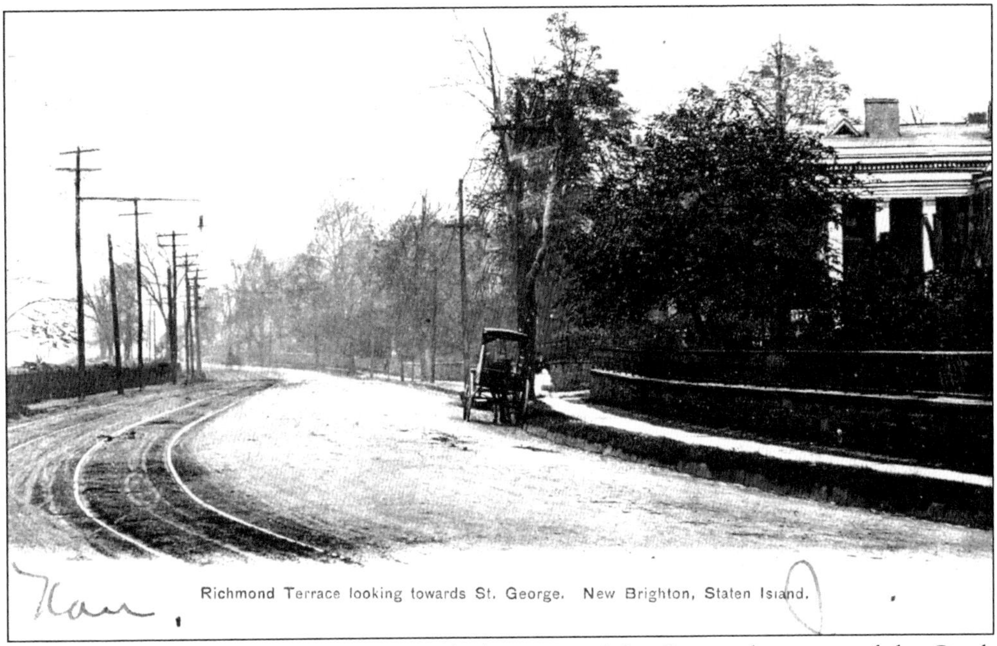

This postcard view of Richmond Terrace looking toward St. George shows one of the Greek Revival homes along the terrace. It also shows the trolley tracks, telephone poles, and a horse and buggy. The picture is from 1908 and was published by the National News Company, New York. (Collection of David Goldfarb.)

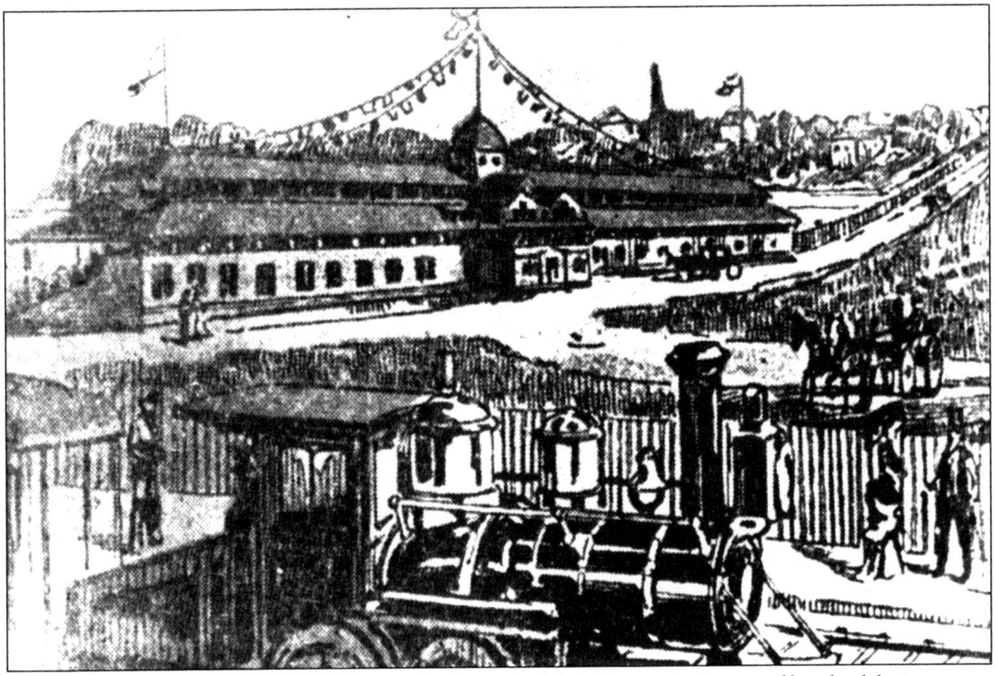

The St. George Amusement Company, the brainchild of Erastus Wiman, offered athletic events between 1886 and 1888. The bandstand in the illustration is said to have seated 6,000 spectators. Note the carriage road to the right and the Staten Island Rapid Transit train in the foreground, attesting to the convenient location of the grounds in St. George.

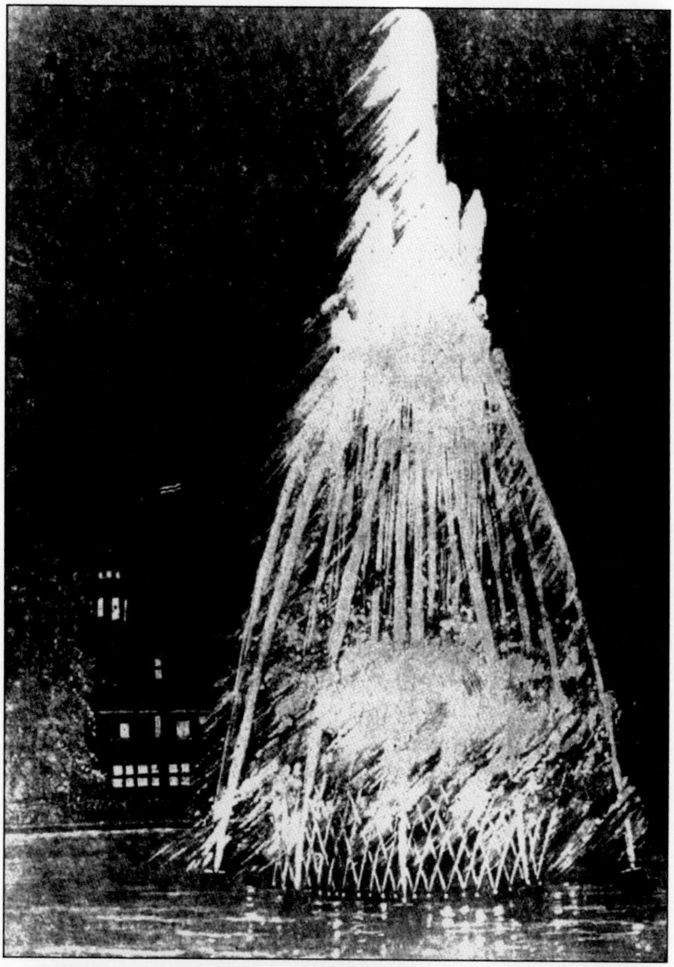

The fantastic illuminated fountain on the grounds of the Staten Island Amusement Company had its own electric generator to power the submerged colored electric lights. The building to the left was the casino on the grounds.

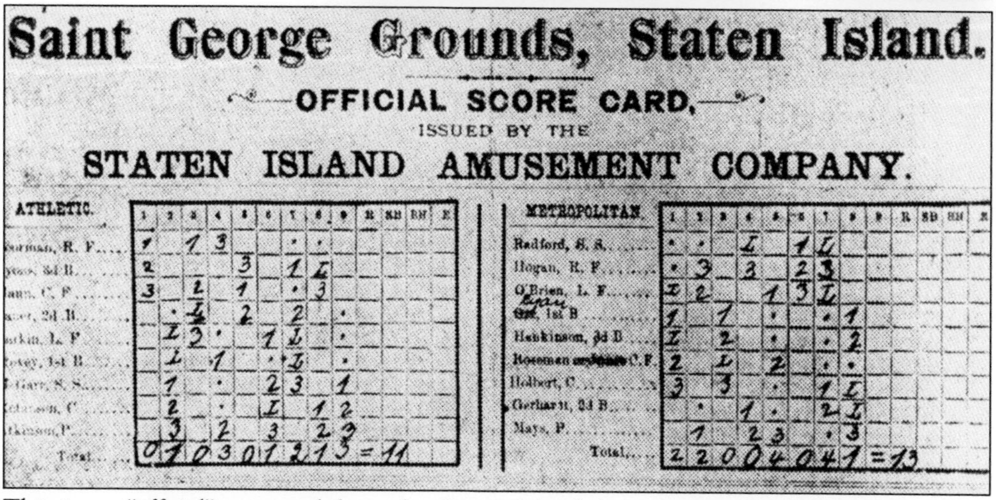

This is an "official" scorecard from the Staten Island Amusement Company on the "Saint George Grounds, Staten Island." It is said that over two million people came to the fairgrounds in 1886.

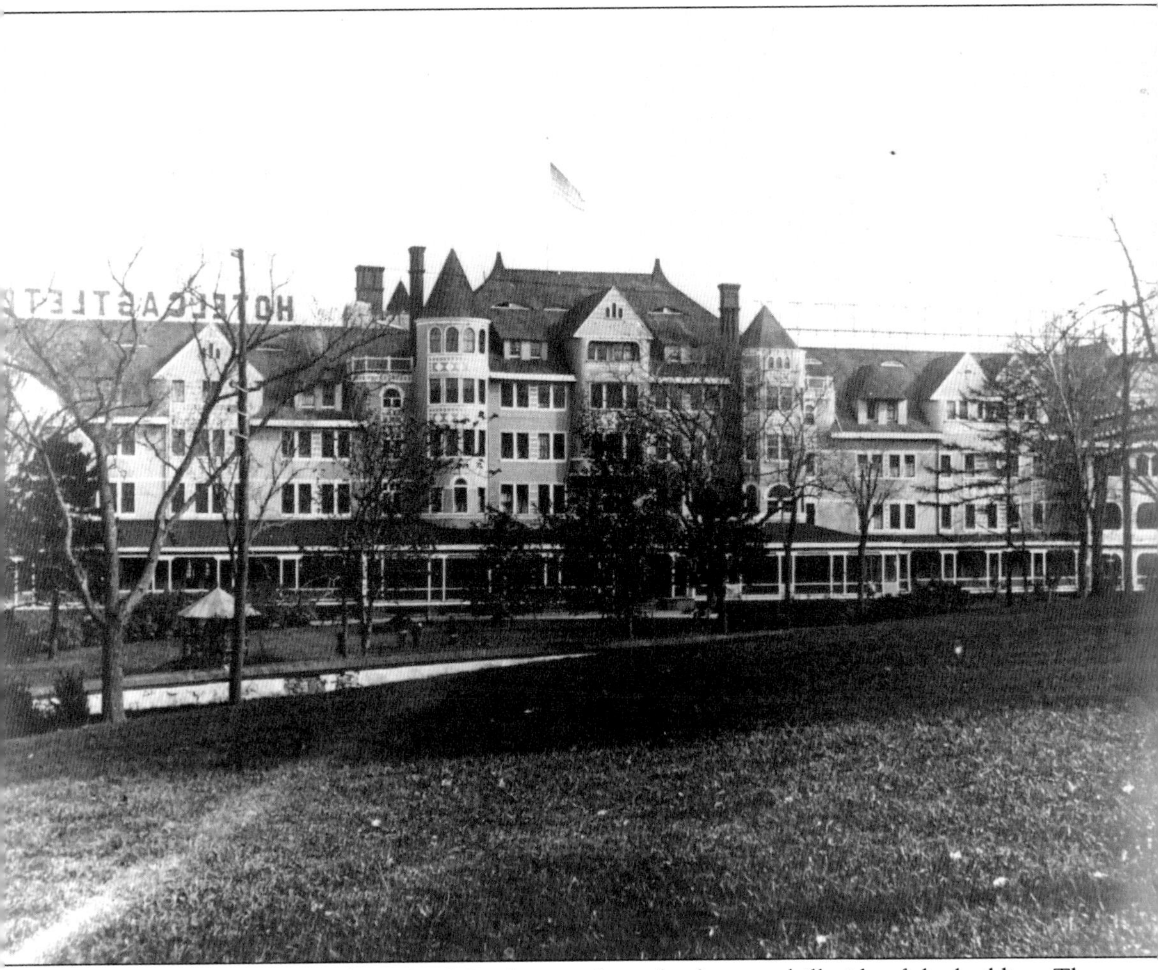

This view of the sprawling Hotel Castleton is from the front, or hill, side of the building. The sign is backward from this vantage point, allowing the lettering to be read from New York Harbor. This photograph was taken around 1900, and in 1907, the building would be destroyed in a spectacular blaze that was visible far across the bay. The hotel was never rebuilt.

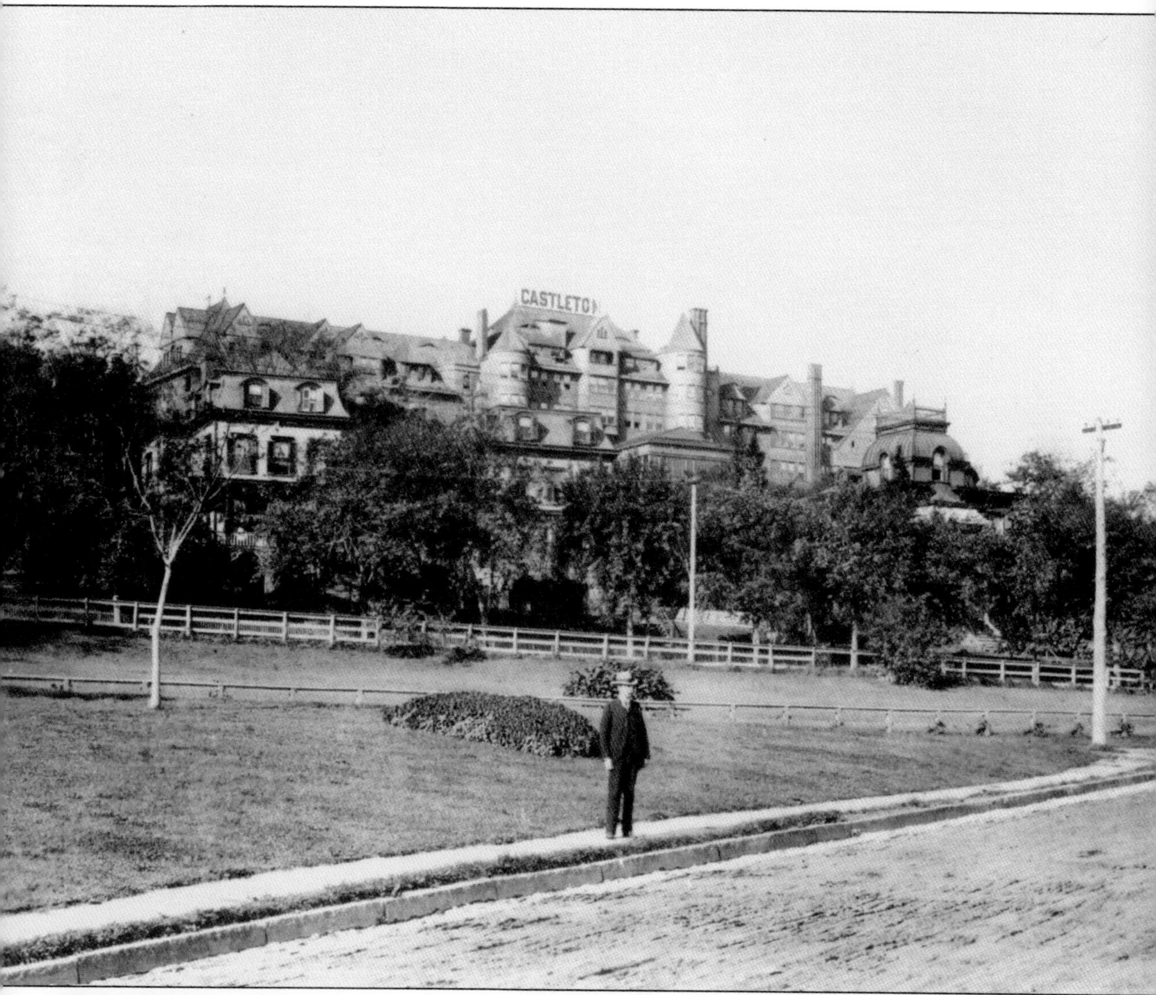

This c. 1890 view of the Hotel Castleton is interesting in that it shows the large Victorian homes that were built by the hotel's owner, Alois Petelier, along Richmond Terrace. These wonderful Italianate and Second Empire–styled homes were constructed around 1869 on the grounds of the hotel facing what was then a clean sandy beach.

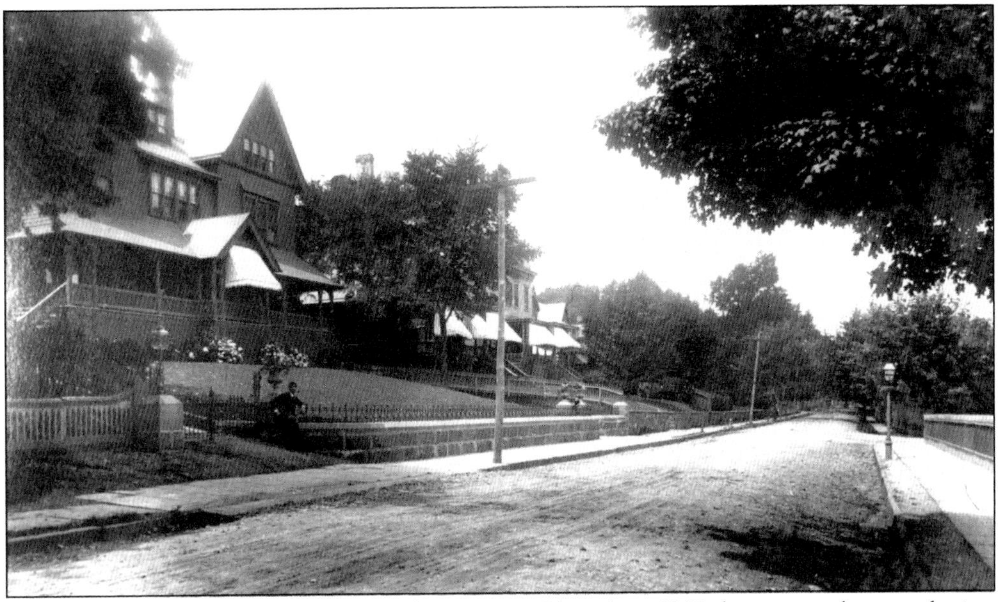

This exquisite streetscape photograph of Stuyvesant Place from 1880 shows a gentleman relaxing in front of the St. George Hotel.

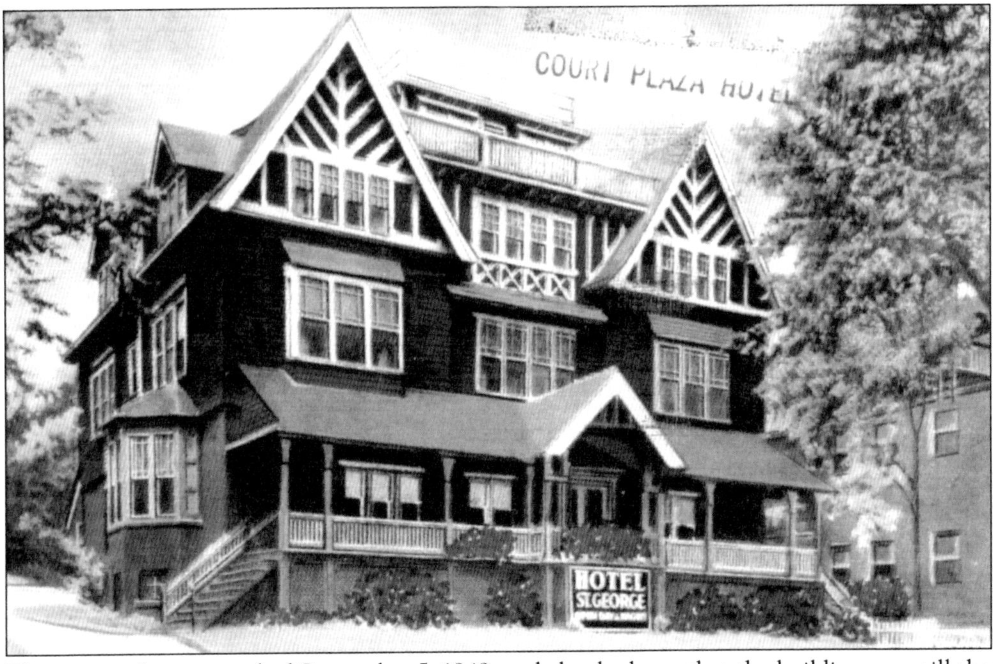

This postcard is postmarked September 5, 1949, and clearly shows that the building was still the "Hotel St. George." Comparing the postcard view with the earlier photograph from 1880, the hotel is remarkably intact some 60 years later. (Collection of David Goldfarb.)

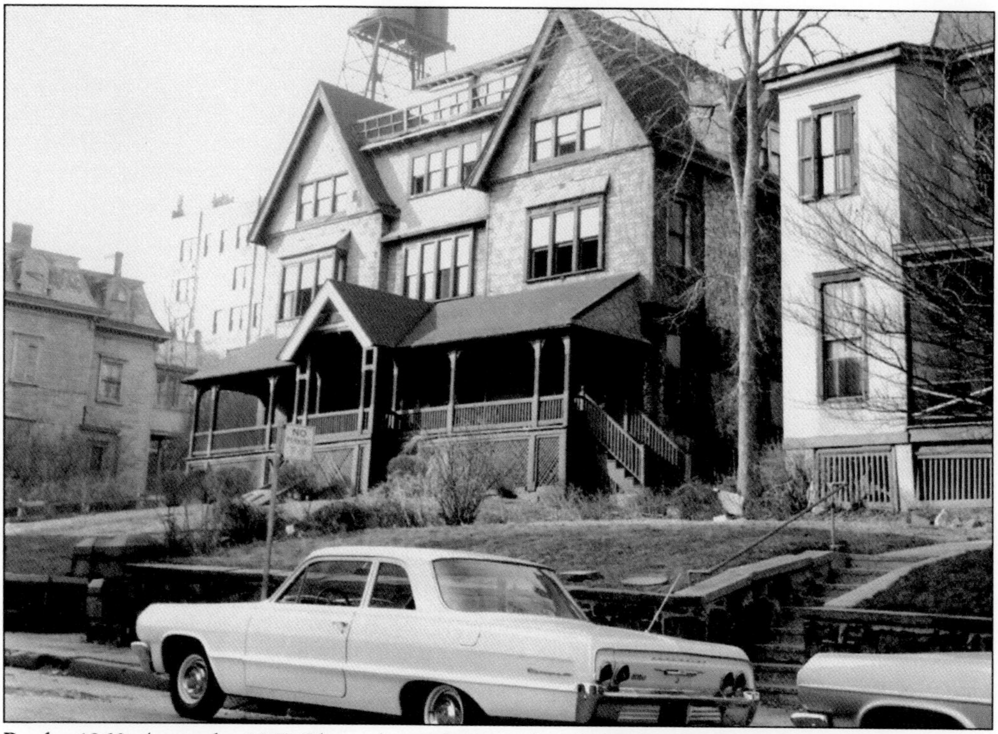

By the 1960s (note the 1962 Chevrolet parked out front) the St. George seems no longer to be a hotel. The exterior has been covered in asphalt siding covering the wonderful half-timbering in the gables, and the grounds are unkempt. The two Second Empire buildings flanking the former hotel are in similar condition. All of the buildings pictured are no longer extant.

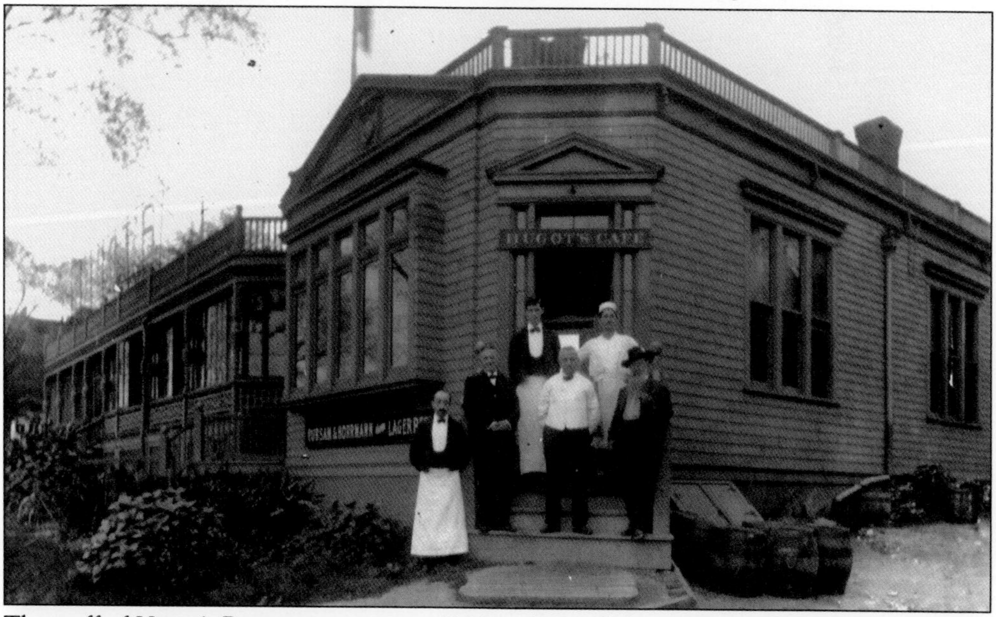

The staff of Hugot's Restaurant poses in 1900 in front of the main entrance of the sprawling restaurant, which was located at the southeast corner of Richmond Terrace and Wall Street, facing New York Harbor.

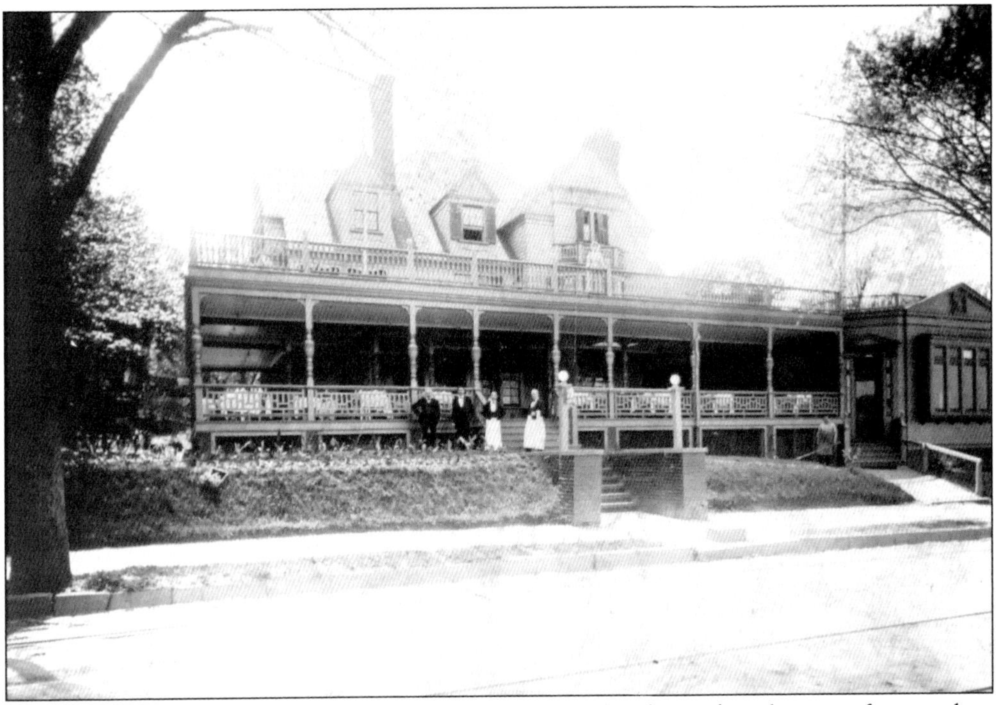

Another view of Hugot's Restaurant shows the double porches for outdoor dining in fine weather. In the years before air conditioning, what a treat it must have been to dine on the St. George shoreline, enjoying the cool breezes off the water.

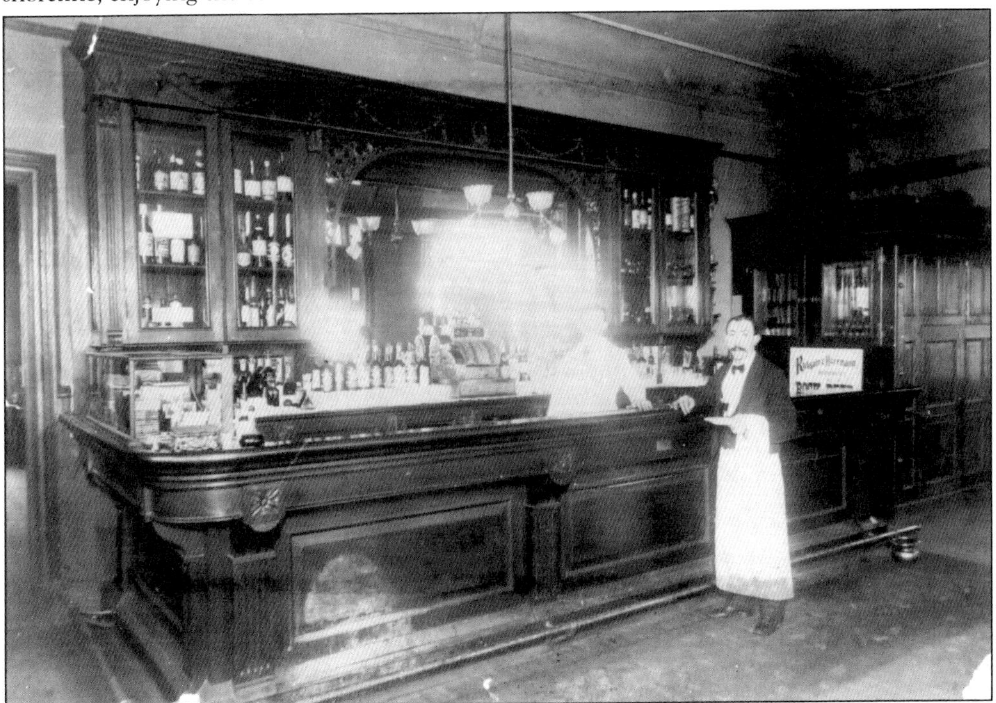

An interior photograph of the bar at Hugot's Restaurant boasts a sign announcing that Staten Island's own Rubsam and Horrmann beer is proudly served.

This photograph is of Tilley's Hotel in St. George, location unknown. Notice that the door to the right is marked "Ladies Entrance."

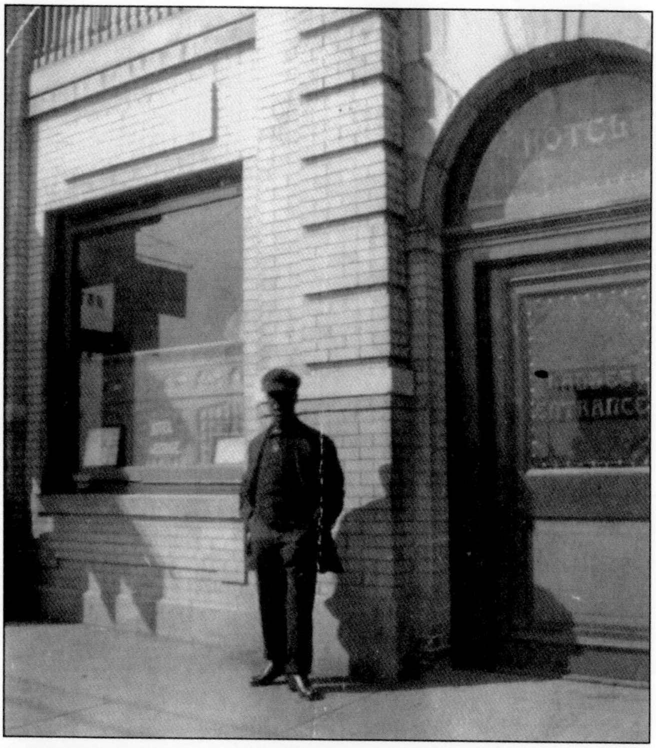

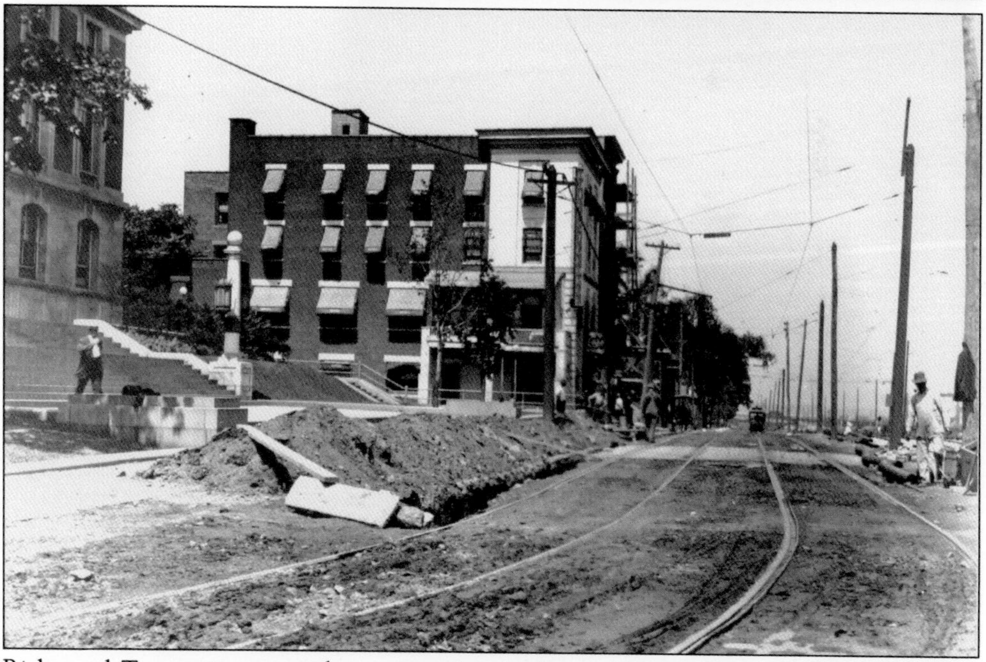

Richmond Terrace is seen under construction in front of Staten Island Borough Hall. The building to the right of borough hall was the New York Hotel, which has been demolished. The photograph was taken around 1909, so the courthouse building next to borough hall is not yet standing. Note the trolley tracks imbedded in the yet-to-be-paved roadbed, with a trolley car traveling in the distance.

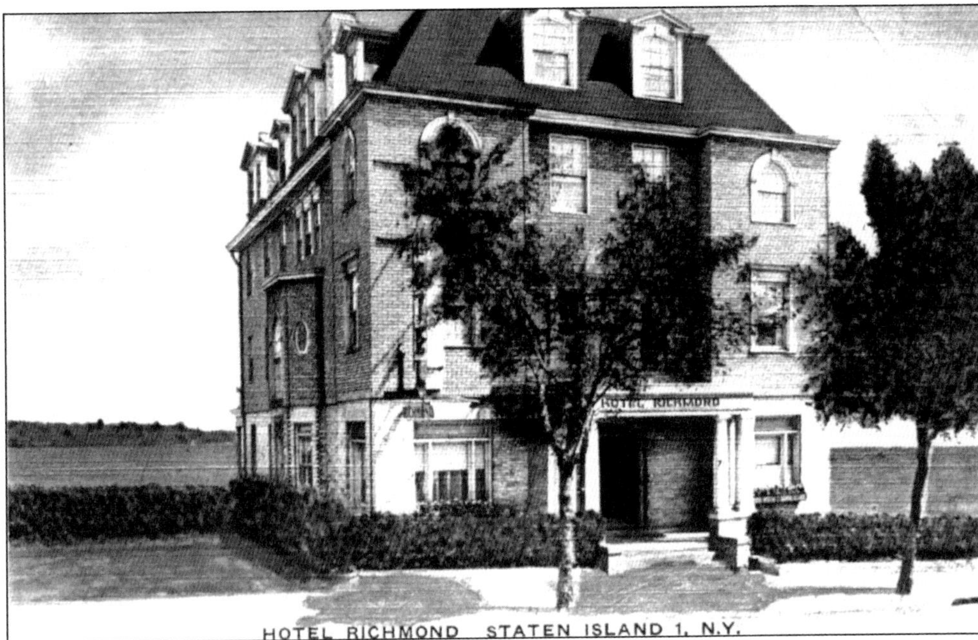

This postcard view of the Hotel Richmond, at 71 Central Avenue, has a quote on the back of the card which states, "A five minute walk from ferry terminal. Convenient to all bus lines, beaches, golf courses and resorts. Located between the main library and the medical arts center." (Collection of David Goldfarb.)

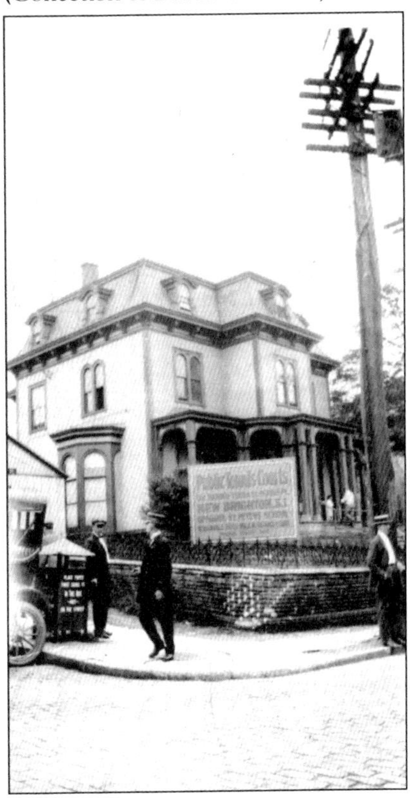

This photograph is noteworthy in that the sign on the lawn of the beautiful Second Empire home states that there were "Public Tennis Courts" opposite St. Peter's School. The sign also states that the dues were "reasonable."

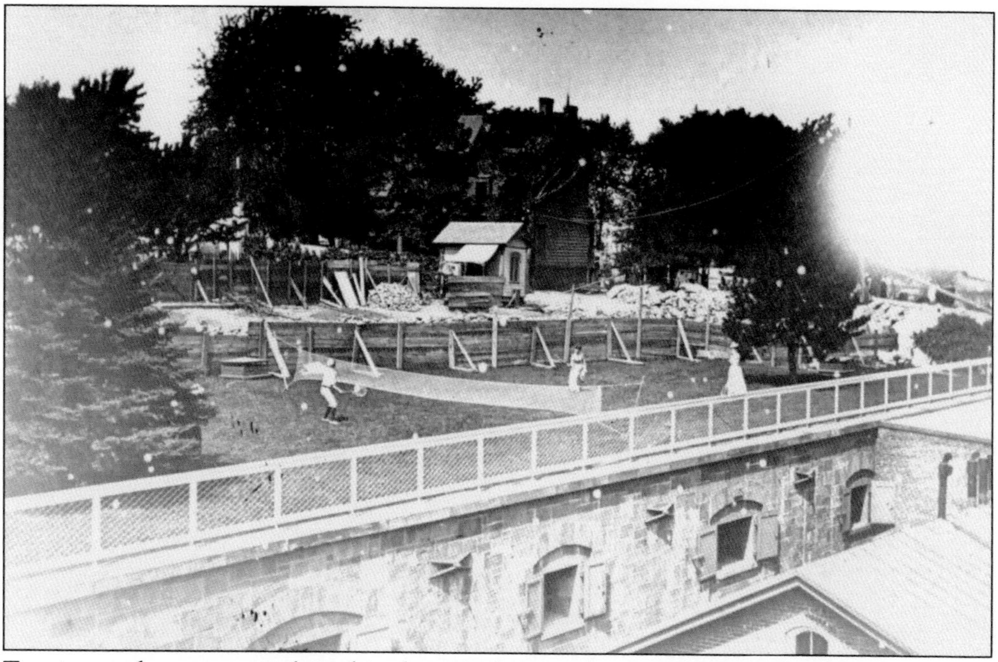

Tennis was the new rage when this photograph was taken on the grounds of the Lighthouse Depot adjacent to the ferry terminal. Here two ladies in long skirts vie with one gentleman to win their match.

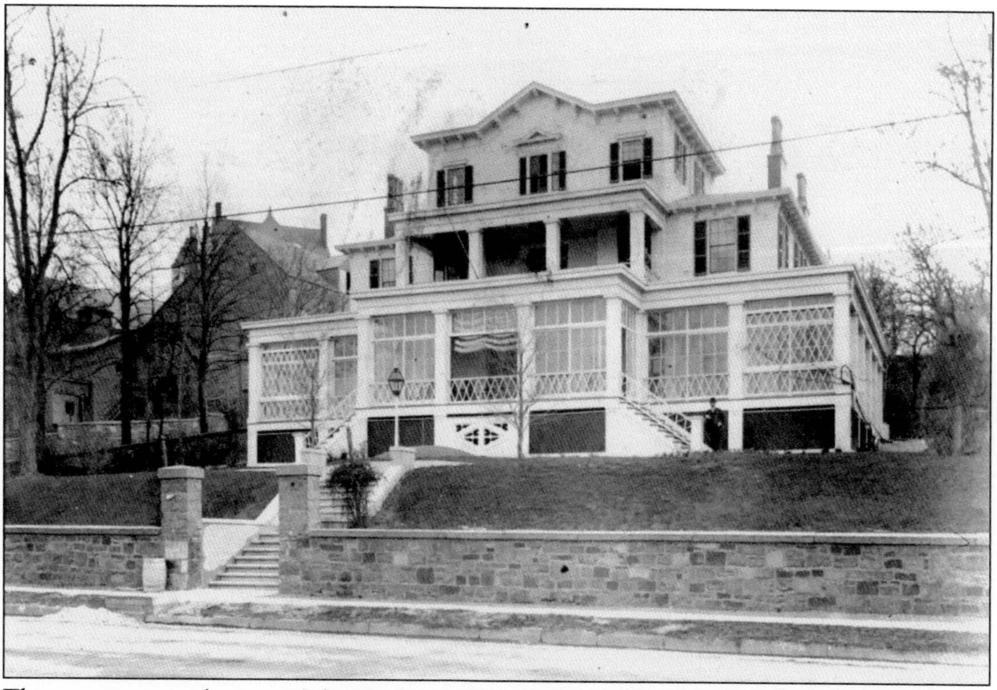

This mansion was home to John Q. Jones, who died in 1874. The large home was located at the corner of Nicholas Street and Richmond Terrace and would serve as the Staten Island Club and also the Westerleigh Collegiate Institute before it was demolished. The photograph is dated 1906.

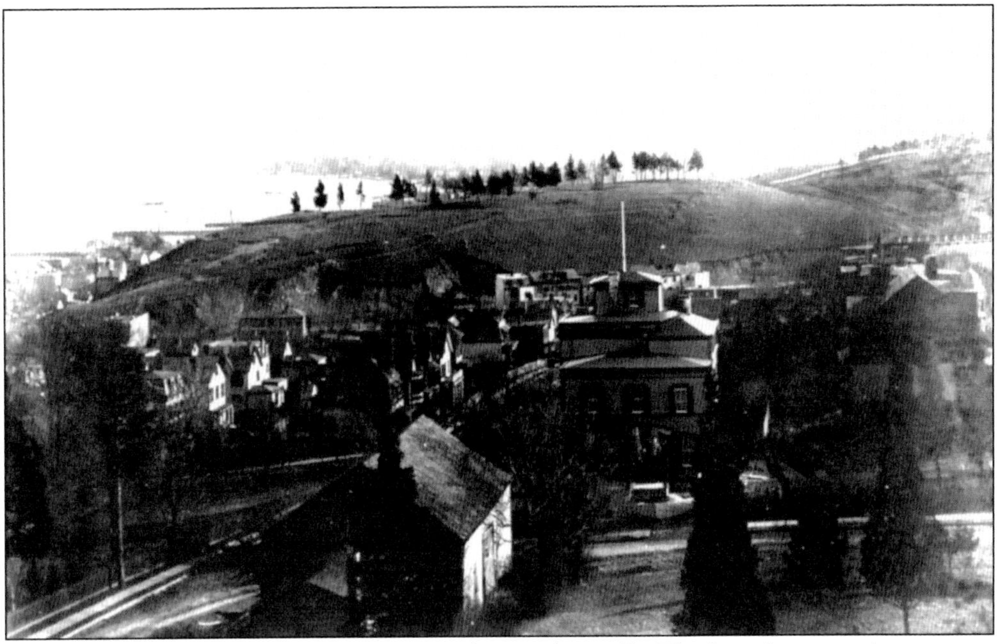

This is a view from Brighton Heights towards Tompkinsville. The large home at the center is Tate Mansion, no longer standing. The large undeveloped hill is Pavilion Hill, today Ward Hill. (Courtesy of John Kilcullen.)

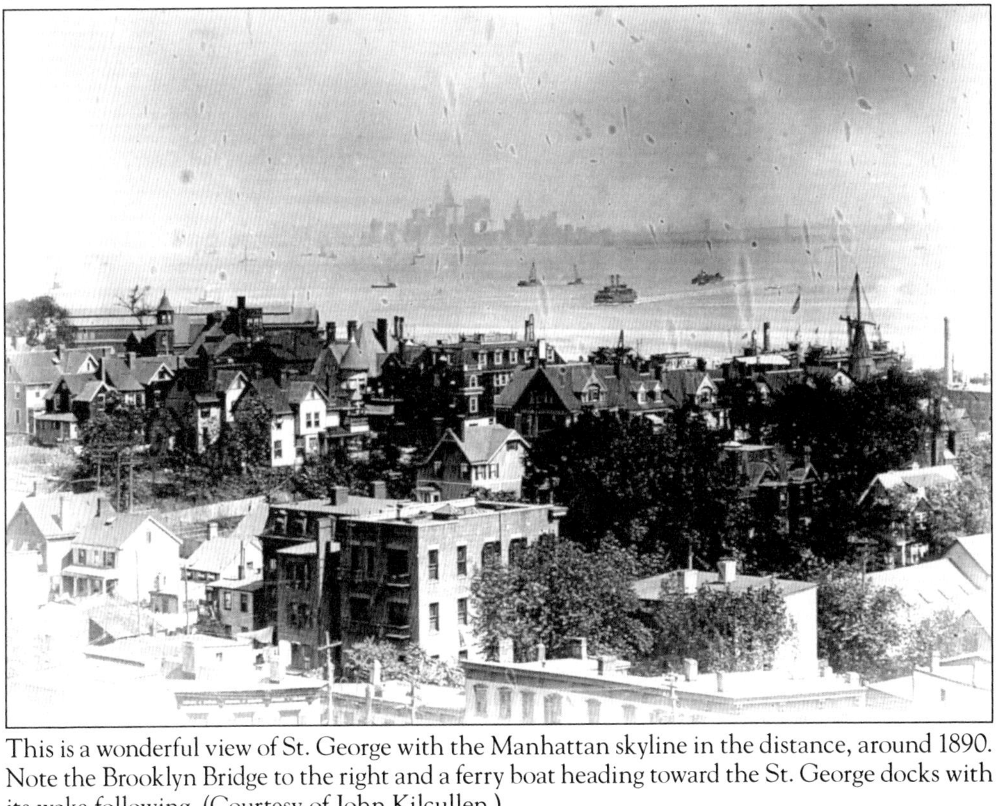

This is a wonderful view of St. George with the Manhattan skyline in the distance, around 1890. Note the Brooklyn Bridge to the right and a ferry boat heading toward the St. George docks with its wake following. (Courtesy of John Kilcullen.)

Four

A Planned Suburban Community

The original 1830s design for New Brighton, one of the earliest suburban communities in America, consisted of homes situated on winding roads along the hillside facing the Kill Van Kull. This was never completed due to the business crash and economic panic of 1837, which caused the financial ruin of thousands. By the time of the panic, Thomas E. Davis had sold his interests in New Brighton to the New Brighton Association for $660,000, and it was the association that suffered reversals during the panic. Davis was to buy back much of the property for $80,000. In January, the panic started as a result of Pres. Andrew Jackson's Bank War. During the first three weeks of April, 250 business houses failed in New York. Within two months, the failures in the city alone reached nearly $100 million. Since many of the originally planned New Brighton crescent-shaped streets had been laid out by the time of the panic, later development followed the original plans.

The village of New Brighton, which had been an independent village, was officially incorporated in 1866. It originally covered an area four miles long by two miles in width and encompassed the northeast tip of Staten Island from Tompkinsville to Snug Harbor. During the years prior to and immediately following the Civil War, some large estates were created along the crests of the hills, capitalizing on the unparalleled views of New York City and Upper New York Bay.

Development in the area remained sporadic until the late 19th century, when a building boom began and many of the homes that comprise today's St. George Historic District date from this period. The area retains many inventively styled homes by the prolific and talented Staten Island architect Edward Alfred Sargent.

In 1994, due largely to the efforts of the St. George Civic Association, the New York City Landmarks Commission designated the St. George-New Brighton Historic District. It is a small enclave comprised of 78 buildings and is part of the larger suburban development on the North Shore of Staten Island.

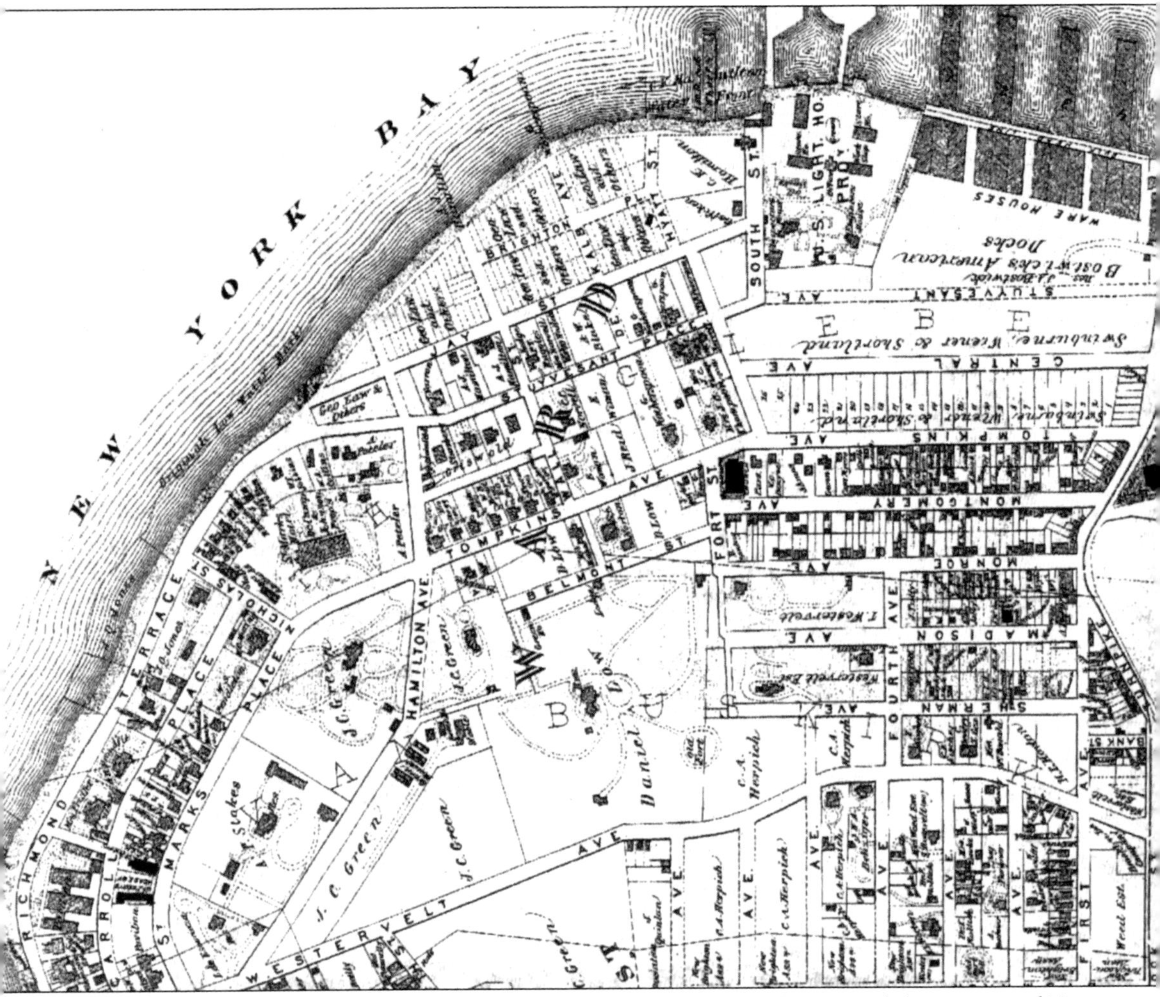

This atlas, dated 1874, clearly shows many of the most notable features of the section of New Brighton that was to become known as St. George. Note the St. Mark's Hotel, which would be renamed the Hotel Castleton, the enormous Stokes Estate, as well as the portion of St. Mark's Place overlooking New York Harbor that would form a major portion of the St. George Historic District in 1994. (Collection of David Goldfarb.)

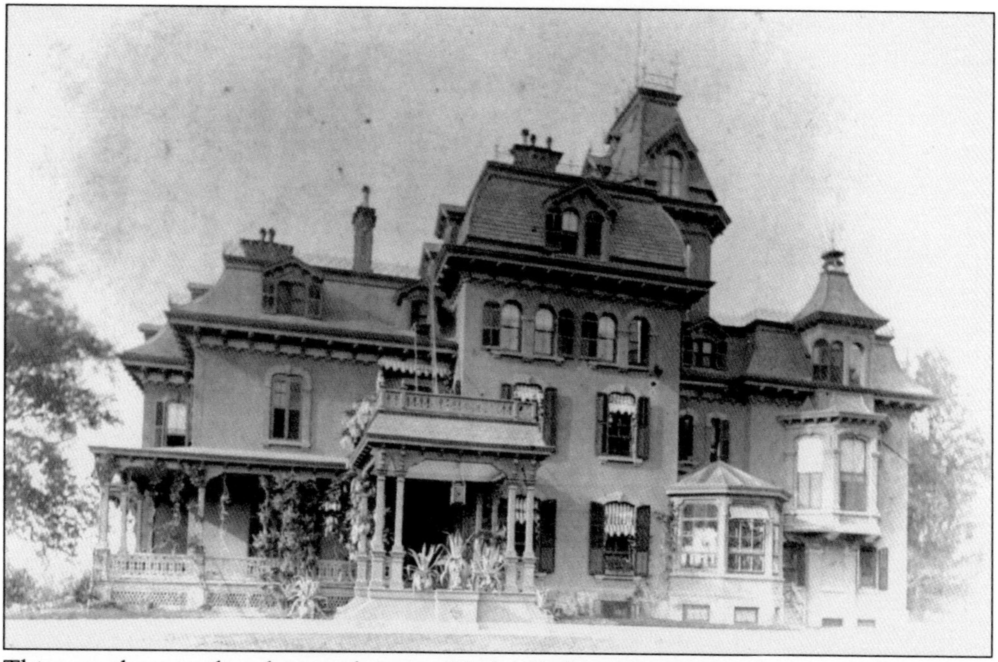

This was the sprawling home of Anson Phelps Stokes as it appeared around 1880. Stokes (1838–1913), born in New York City, was a multimillionaire merchant, banker, and publicist. His son, Isaac Newton Phelps Stokes, born in the house, was perhaps Manhattan's greatest historian. The Stokes home was razed in the 1920s to make way for an apartment complex.

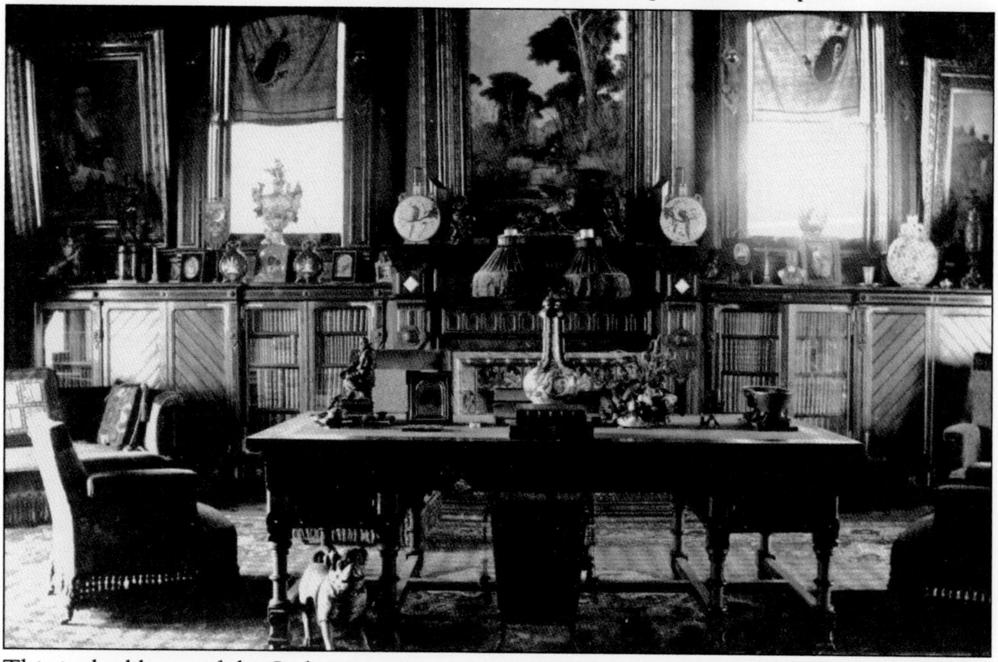

This is the library of the Stokes mansion around 1885. To the Victorian family, the home was the center unit of society and was an indication of the family's status within the community. This photograph depicts in detail the fondness of "organized clutter" that was prevalent during the last half of the 19th century.

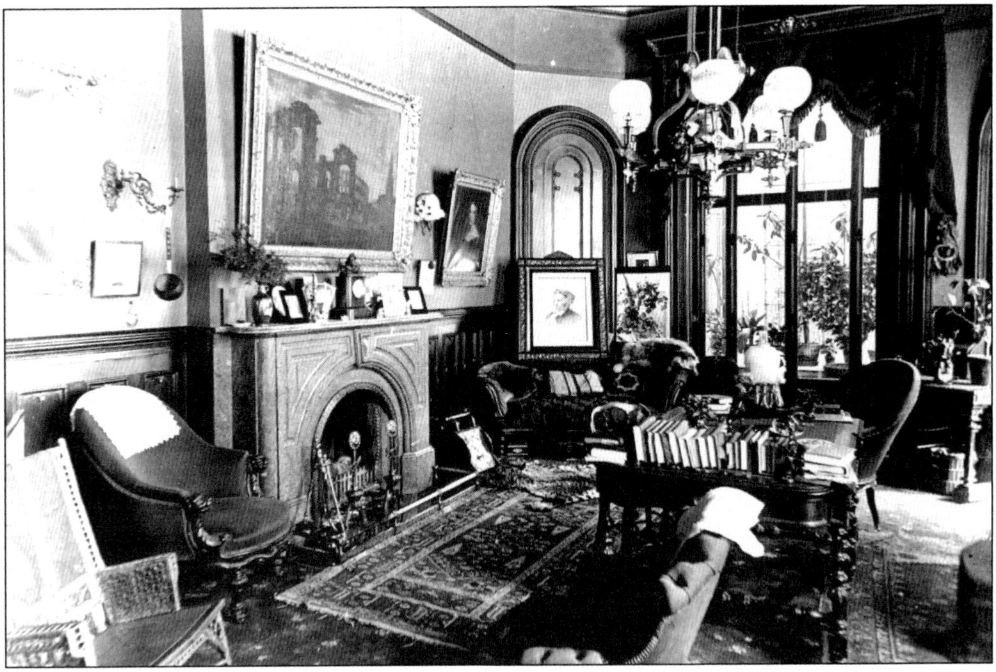

In the parlor of the Stokes mansion, note how every surface is covered with books and bric-a-brac. Animal skins cover the floors and rest atop the settee near the large window, while a gasolier hangs above a center table. An elaborate weighted pulley system allowed the lighting fixture to be raised and lowered to light or extinguish the gas jets.

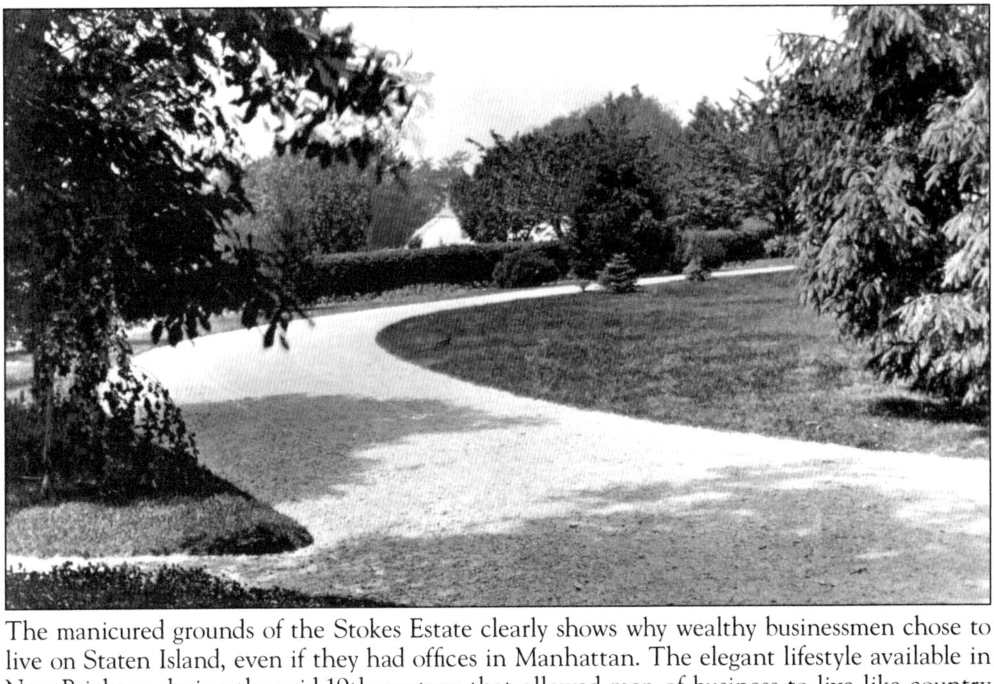

The manicured grounds of the Stokes Estate clearly shows why wealthy businessmen chose to live on Staten Island, even if they had offices in Manhattan. The elegant lifestyle available in New Brighton during the mid-19th century that allowed men of business to live like country squires on Staten Island, also allowed them to commute to business by way of a short ferry ride across the harbor.

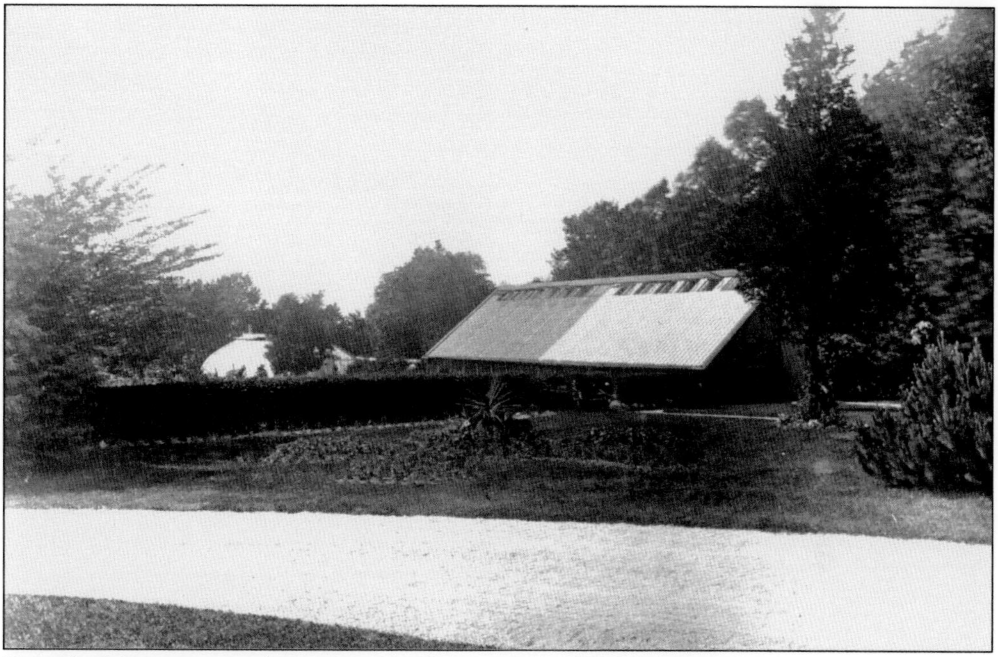

Typical of the great suburban mansions of the period, the Stokes Estate had its own greenhouses in which were grown exotic flowers and plants that would make their way inside the mansion as cut flowers or potted accents to the home's decor.

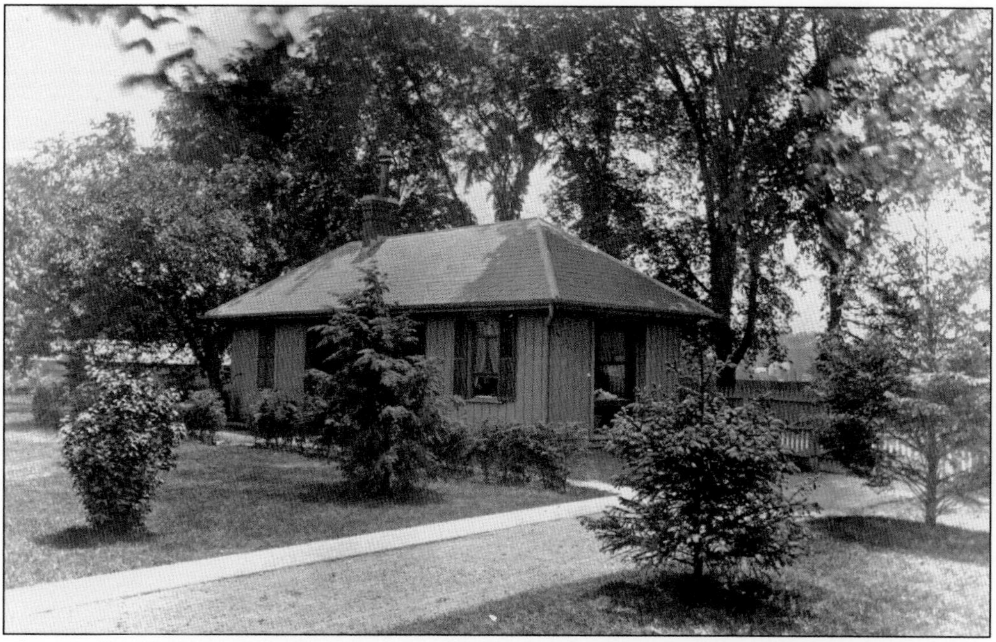

This small, at least by mid-19th century standards, out building on the Stokes Estate might have been home to the gardener or other staff that was necessary to care for the great estate.

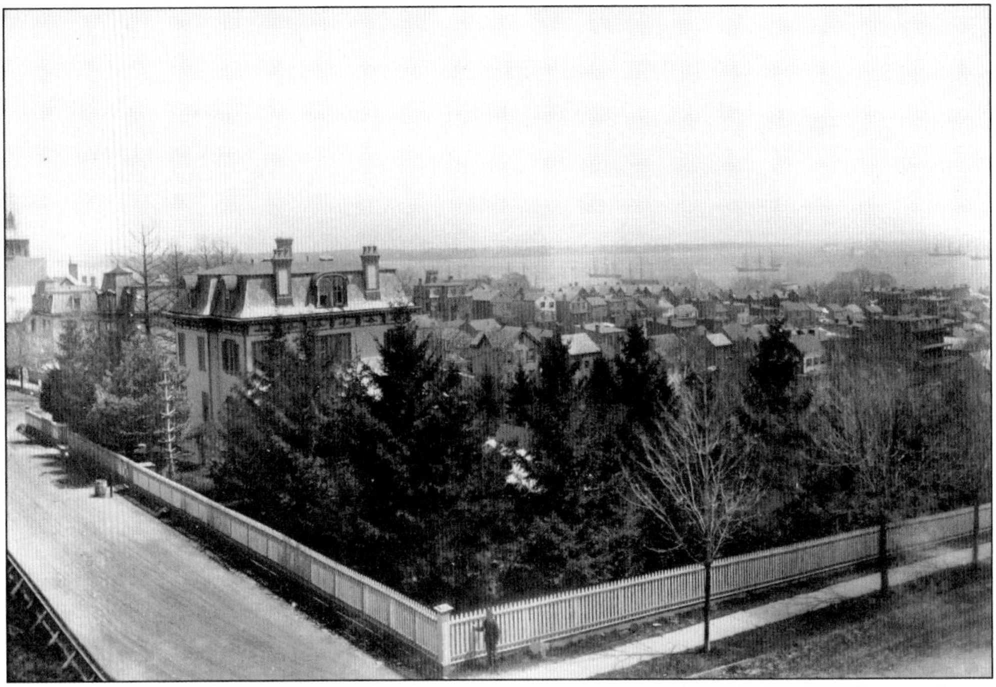

This *c.* 1885 bird's-eye view of St. George looking across New York Harbor to Manhattan shows many sailing and steam-powered craft along the Staten Island shore. Grand Second Empire homes of the mid-19th century dot the hillside, alongside smaller homes of the Greek Revival period. Brighton Heights Reformed Church can be seen at the extreme left of the photograph.

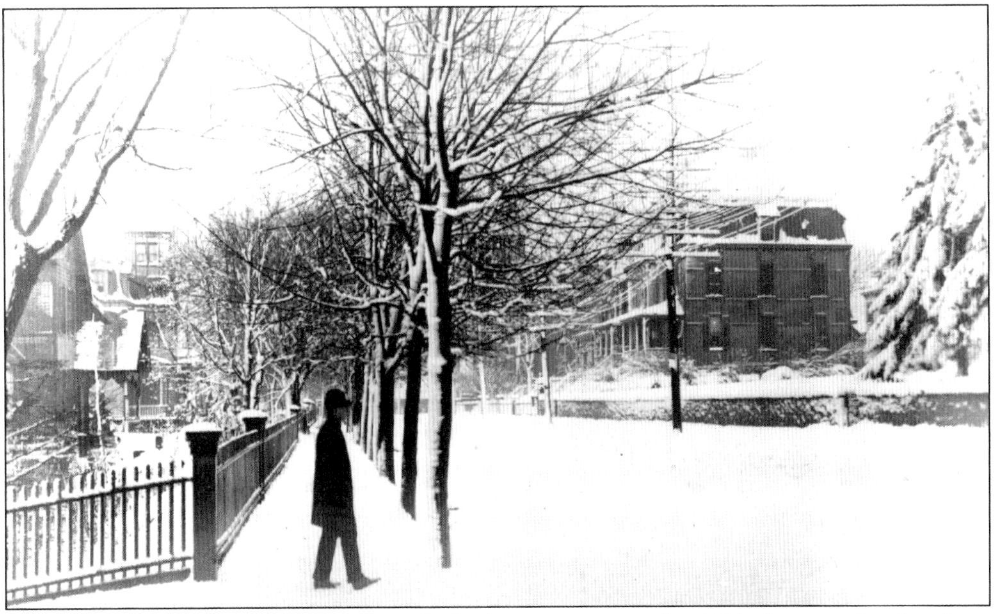

Elegant St. Mark's Place is the epitome of suburbia in winter in this 1891 photograph taken from the corner of St. Mark's Place and Westervelt Avenue.

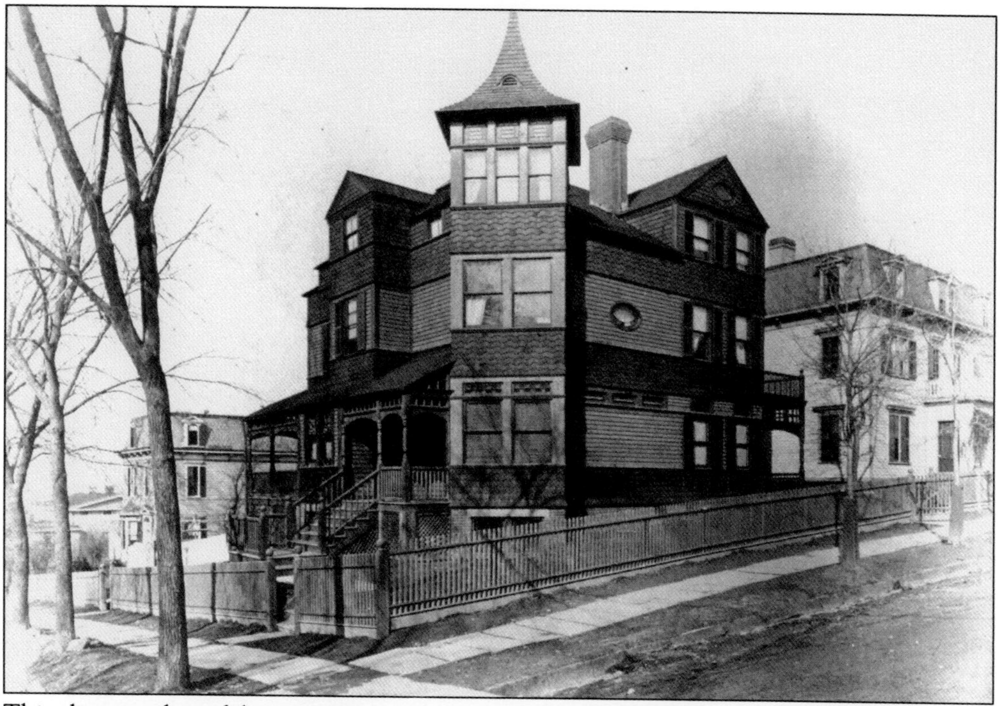

This photograph is of the same corner as the previous photograph and shows the Edward Alfred Sargent-designed home of Dr. William C. Walser, built toward the end of the 1890s.

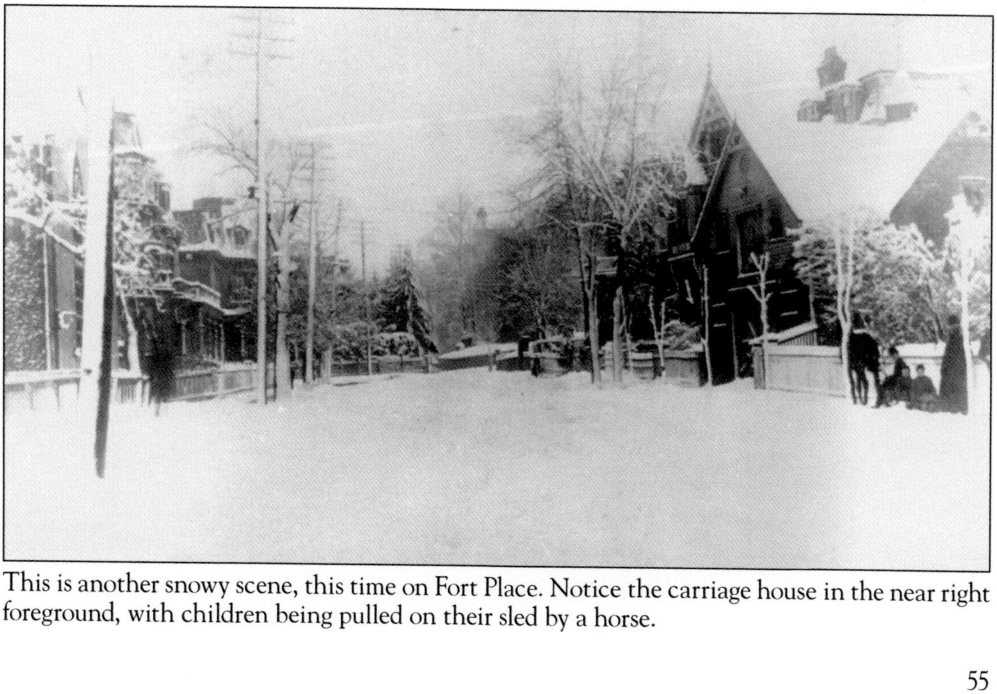

This is another snowy scene, this time on Fort Place. Notice the carriage house in the near right foreground, with children being pulled on their sled by a horse.

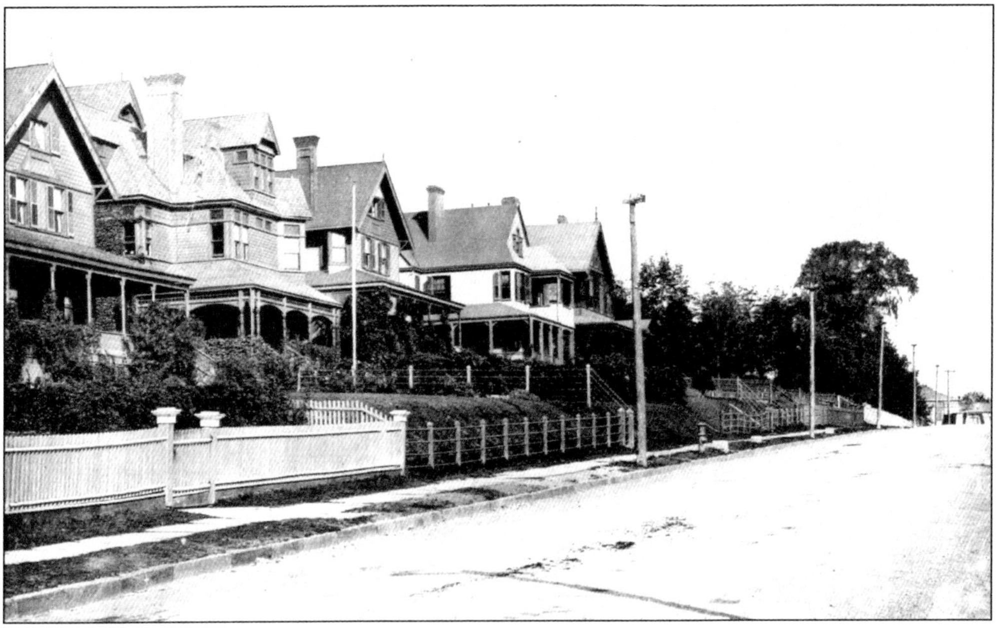

All of the homes in this *c.* 1890 photograph of Central Avenue are sadly long gone. Most of the homes are Queen Anne–style large residences that, when combined, formed a very cohesive and stylish streetscape of a late 19th century Staten Island neighborhood.

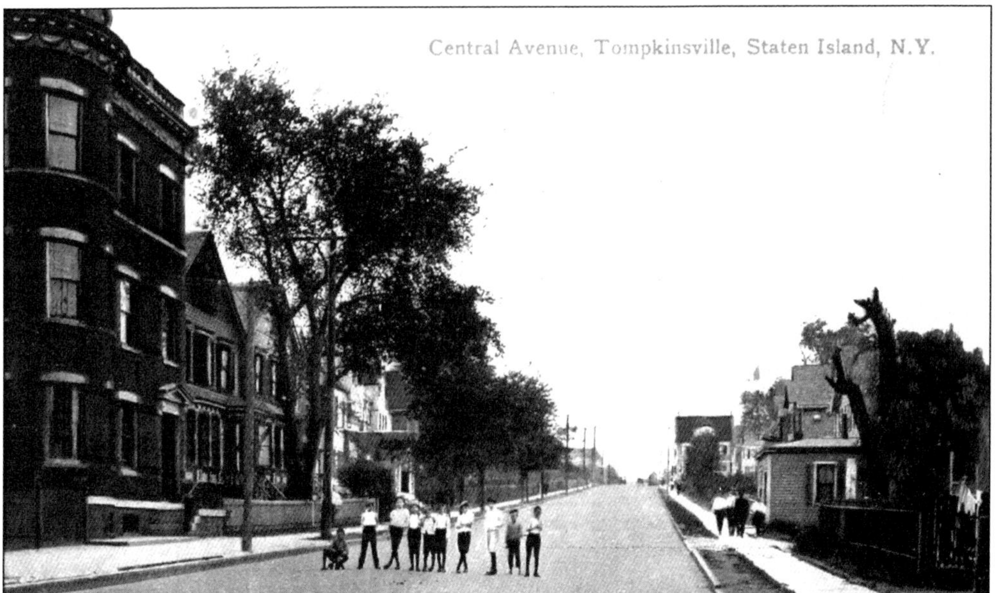

This is a postcard view of Central Avenue looking toward Slosson Terrace around 1908. (Collection of David Goldfarb.)

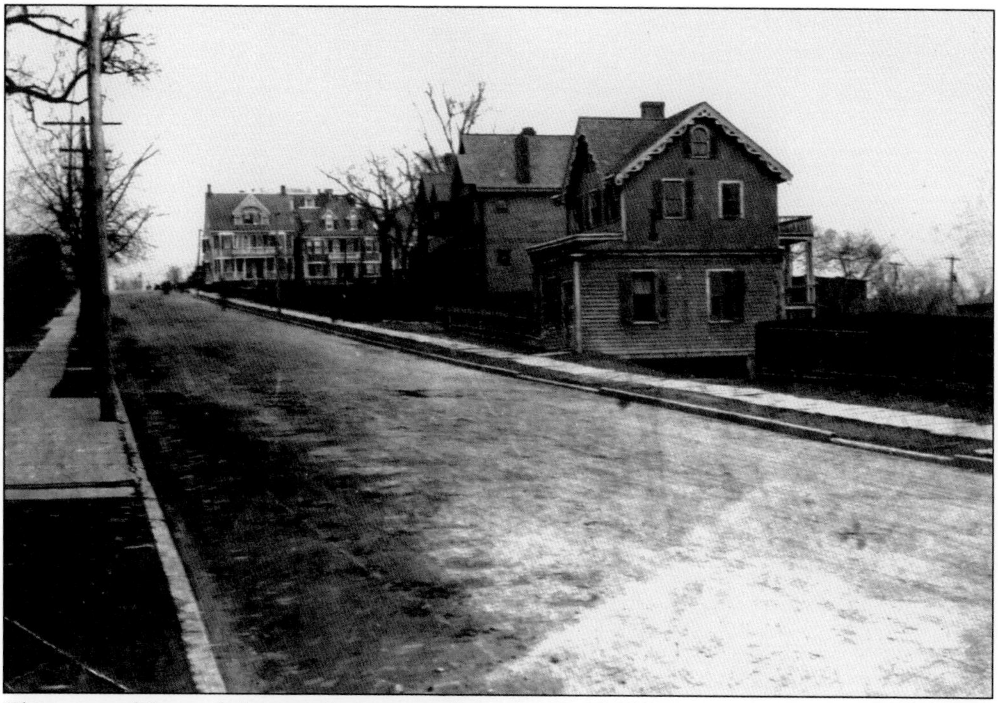

This view of Central Avenue shows a small Gothic Revival home in the foreground that was most probably built around 1845 to 1850. The large double houses in the distance appear to be the buildings that today comprise the Hotel Richmond on Slosson Terrace.

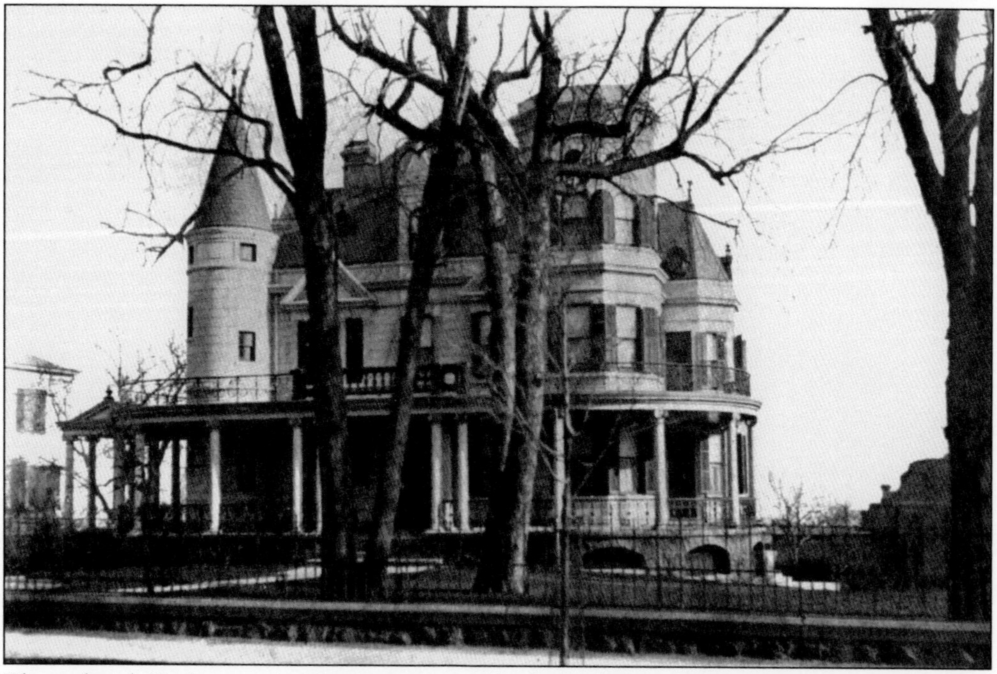

The palatial Tiedemann residence once stood where the St. George Theater stands today. The imposing home commanded harbor views in three directions from the sides and rear of the home.

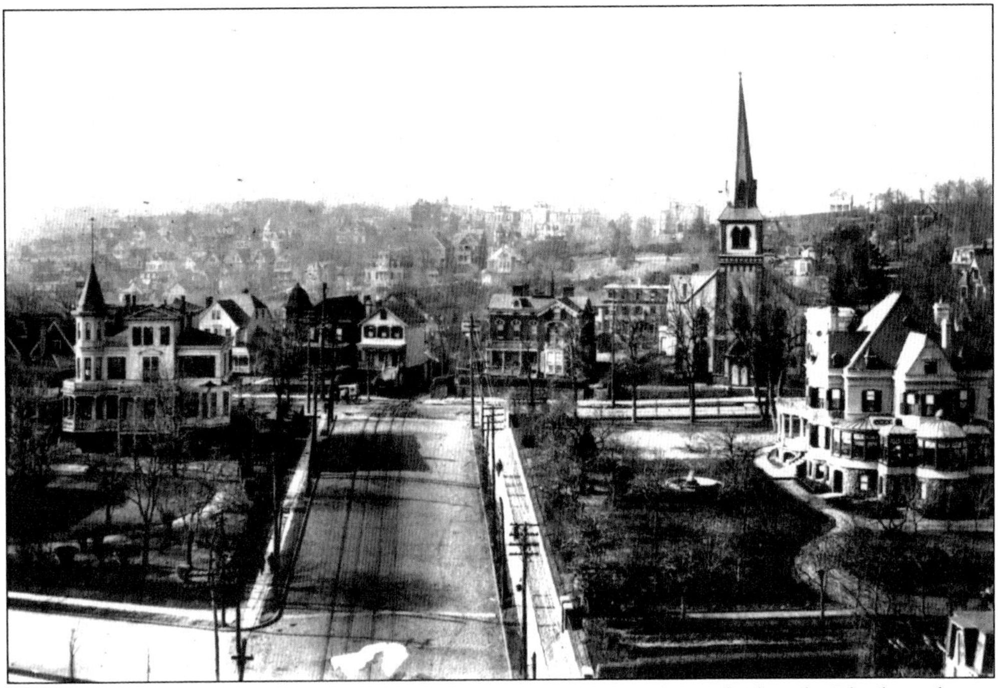

This is a view up Hyatt Street toward the Brighton Heights Reformed Church. The large home at the right is the rear of the Tiedemann House, with its spacious grounds, the site today of the St. George Theater. The homes across Hyatt Street were built on the grounds of the quarantine graveyard in the mid-to-late 19th century. These have all been demolished, and the graveyard site has been a municipal parking lot for decades.

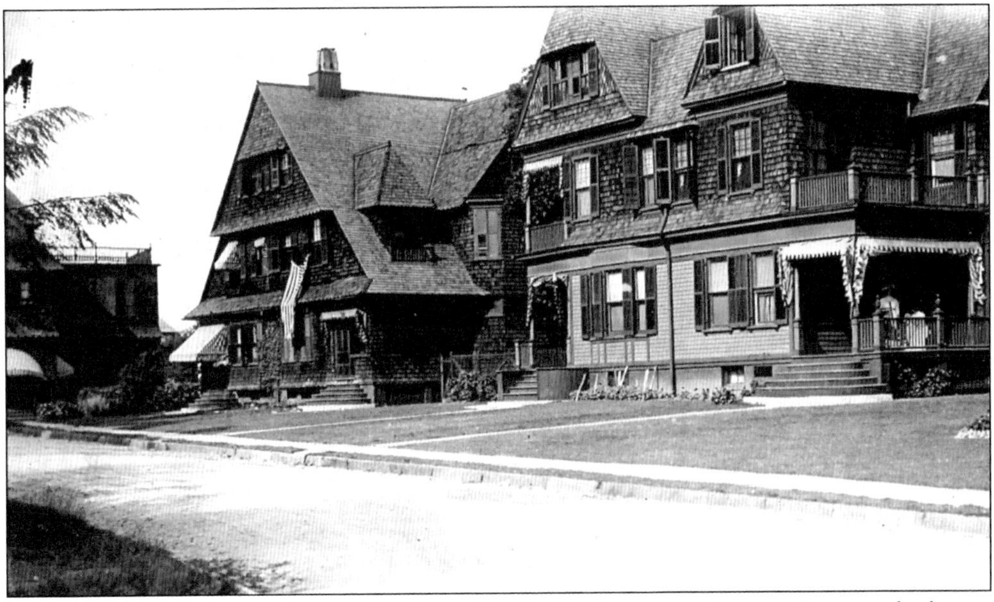

Architect Edward Alfred Sargent lived in this double house on Lennox Street, which was located near Phelps Place. Lennox Street no longer exists. On the porch are Sargent's daughter and grandchild, and the faint figure nearest the door may be Sargent himself. (Courtesy of Marjorie Johnson.)

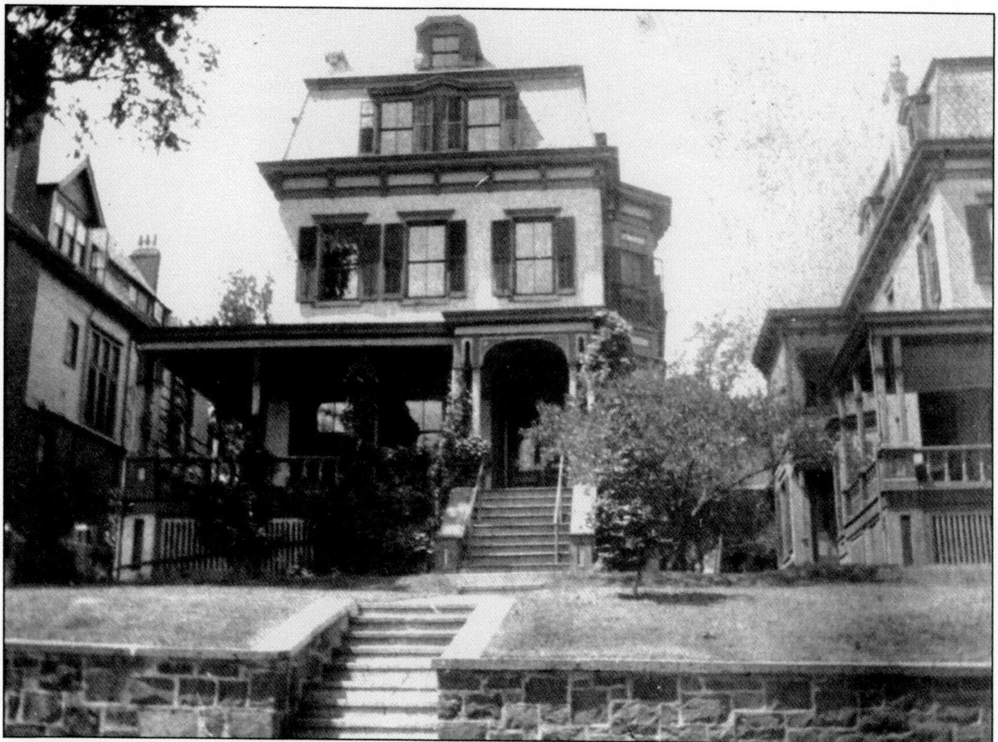

This group of Second Empire–styled homes were typical of many homes built across Staten Island in the years immediately following the Civil War, but these on Stuyvesant Place offered an amenity that homes outside of New Brighton/St. George could not—their proximity to the ferries to Manhattan.

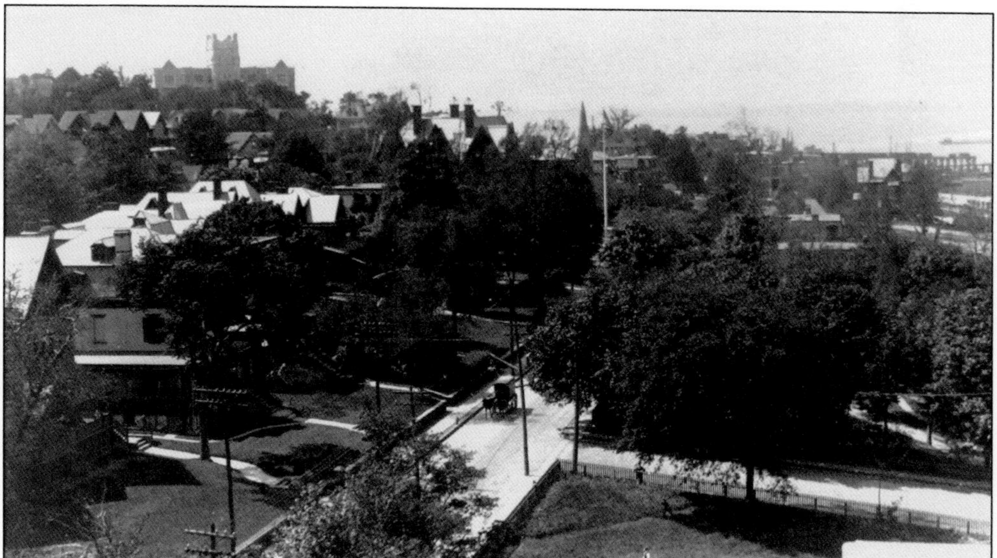

This photograph was taken around 1909 from Staten Island Borough Hall and shows Curtis High School in the distance above the rooftops of nearby the homes. Notice the lovely front yards along Stuyvesant Place in the foreground, as well as a horse-drawn carriage delivering ice or perhaps milk.

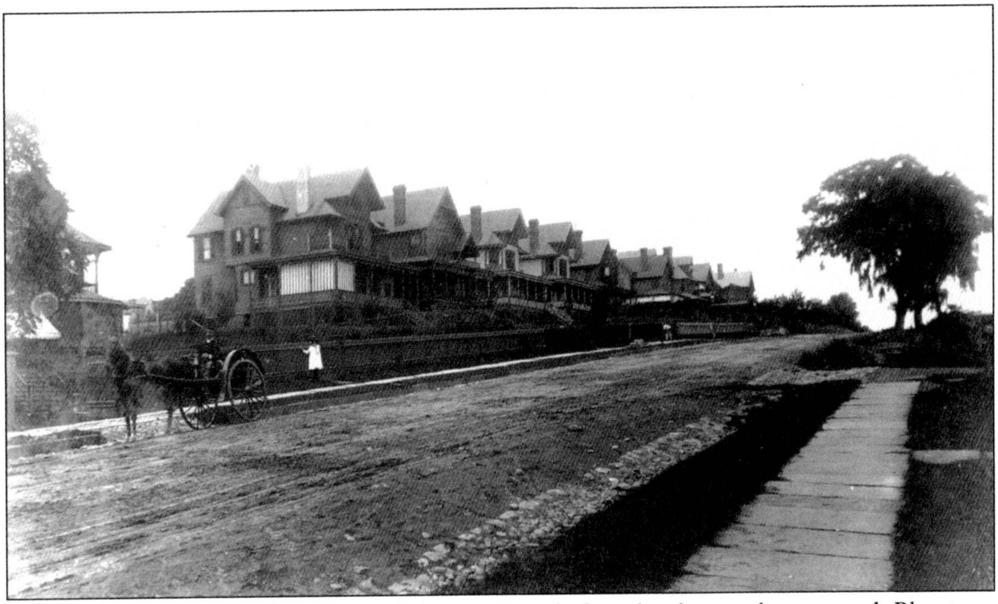

A horse-and-buggy ride along Central Avenue long before the dirt road was paved. Bluestone sidewalks in the foreground end abruptly at an undeveloped lot complete with one of the few trees visible in this early photograph.

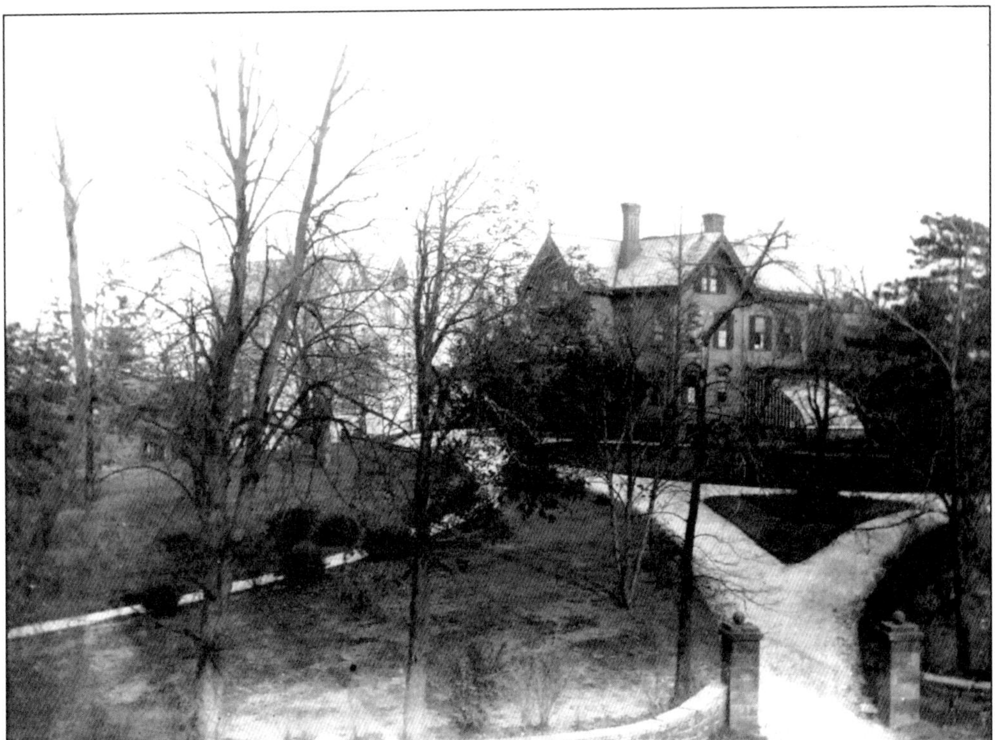

The De Escoriaza House on St. Mark's Place was one of the grand estates built prior to the Civil War.

This beautiful Mansard-roofed house was the home of renowned naturalist William Thompson Davis (1862–1945) on Stuyvesant Place. The building is no longer extant.

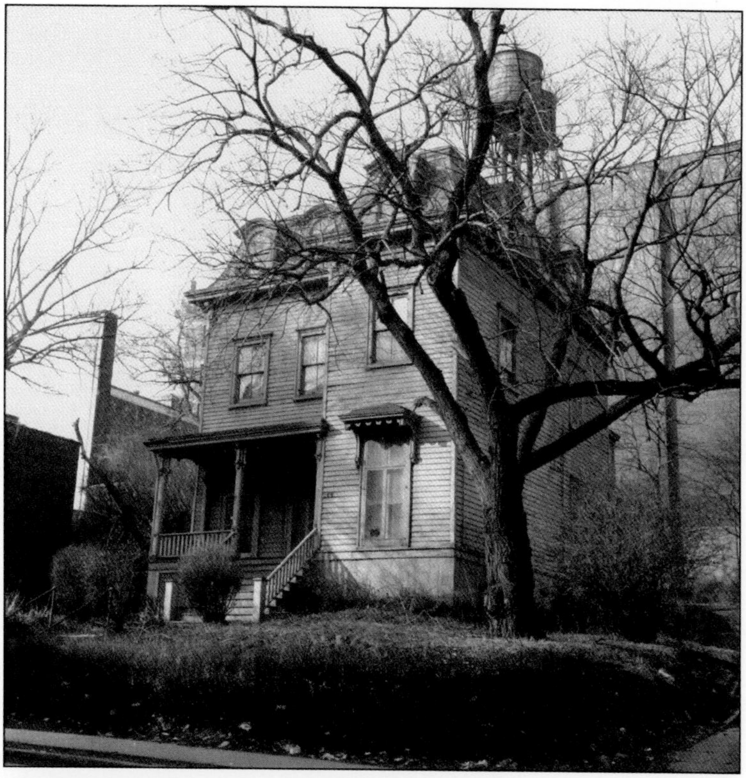

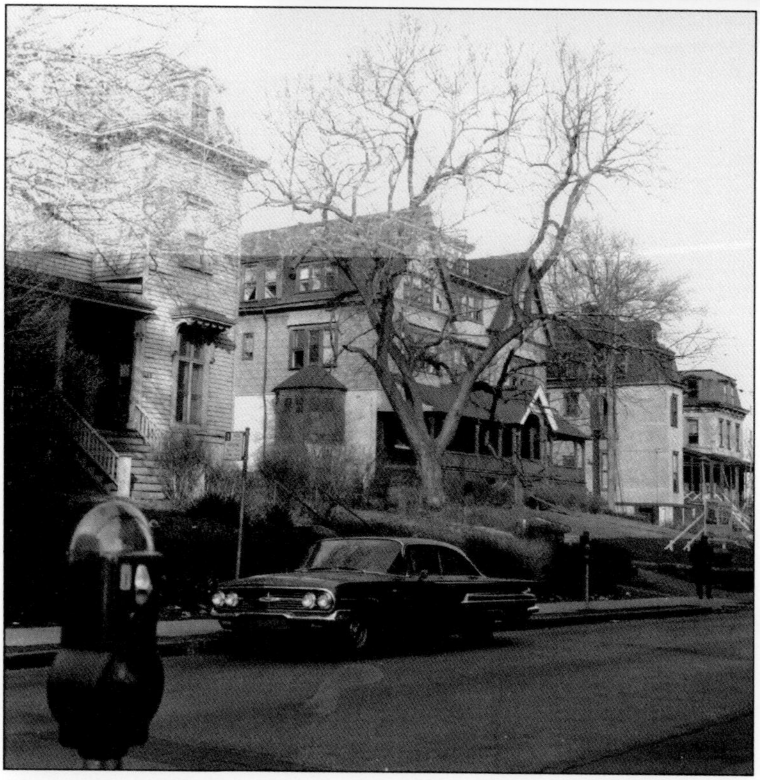

Another view of the Davis house around 1960 reveals some neglect to the home, as well as a sign on the lawn of the large building next door announcing it as the future site of the "St. George Plaza," an apartment building that was indeed built.

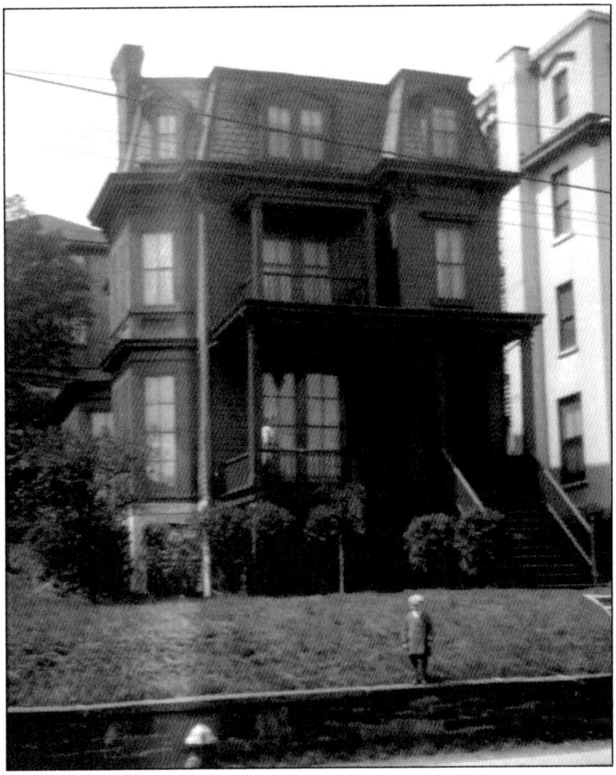

Built on the grounds of the Hotel Castleton in 1869, this stately home at 216 Richmond Terrace was one of more than a dozen elegant residences built along the shoreline in the years immediately following the Civil War. This *c.* 1925 photograph shows, as a young boy, Sherbourne Graham, who was born in the house and remained there until his death in 1997. At the right was a 22-room mansion at the corner of Nicholas Street. (Collection of James G. Ferreri.)

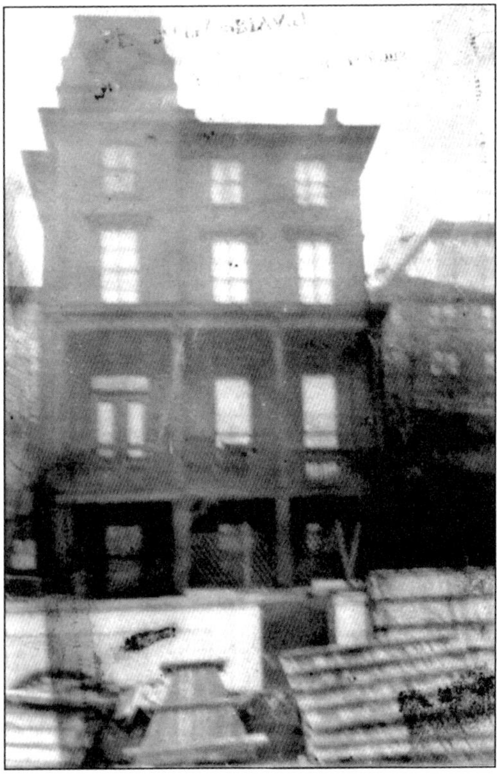

This Italianate-styled gem was located at 208 Richmond Terrace and was built in 1869. In 1929, Richmond Terrace underwent a street widening to allow for the increase in traffic. In the foreground, one can see the foundation forms for the retaining walls that were erected when the gracious homes along this strip of road lost their front lawns. (Collection of James G. Ferreri.)

This is a picture of Anna Ballback and her daughter, Mrs. Graham. Ballback purchased the Second Empire home at 216 Richmond Terrace in 1903, and her family remained in the home through 1997. In back of the two ladies is 208 Richmond Terrace. The 14 or so homes that were built on this shoreline of New York Harbor on the grounds of the St. Mark's Hotel once faced a sandy beach and were the residences of families such as the nephew of Washington Irving and the socially prominent Duers and Du Ponts. All but two of the homes have been demolished, including numbers 208 and 216, which were lost in 2007 and 2006 respectively. The postcard was written to Ballback in 1912 from a friend on the cruise ship *Kronprinz Wilhelm*. (Collection of James G. Ferreri.)

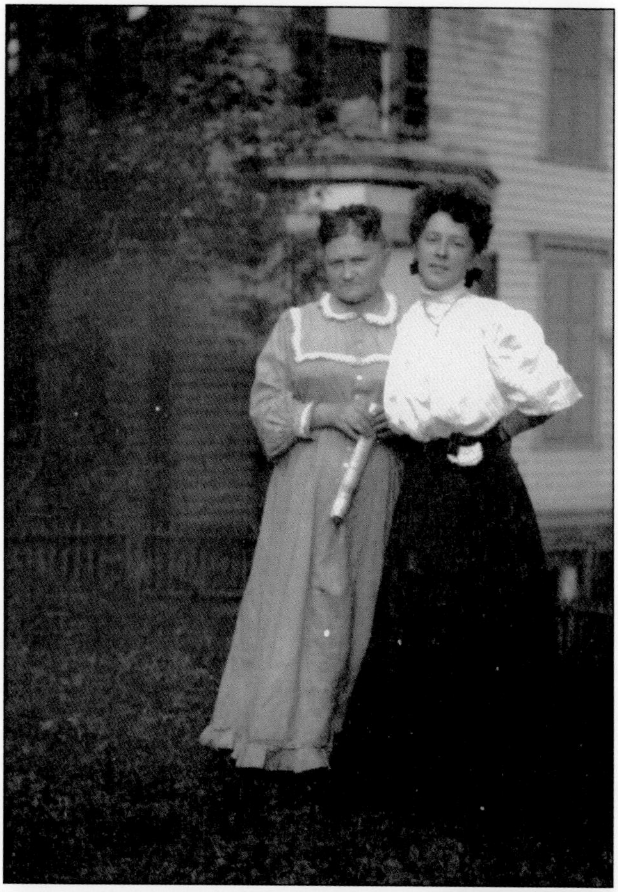

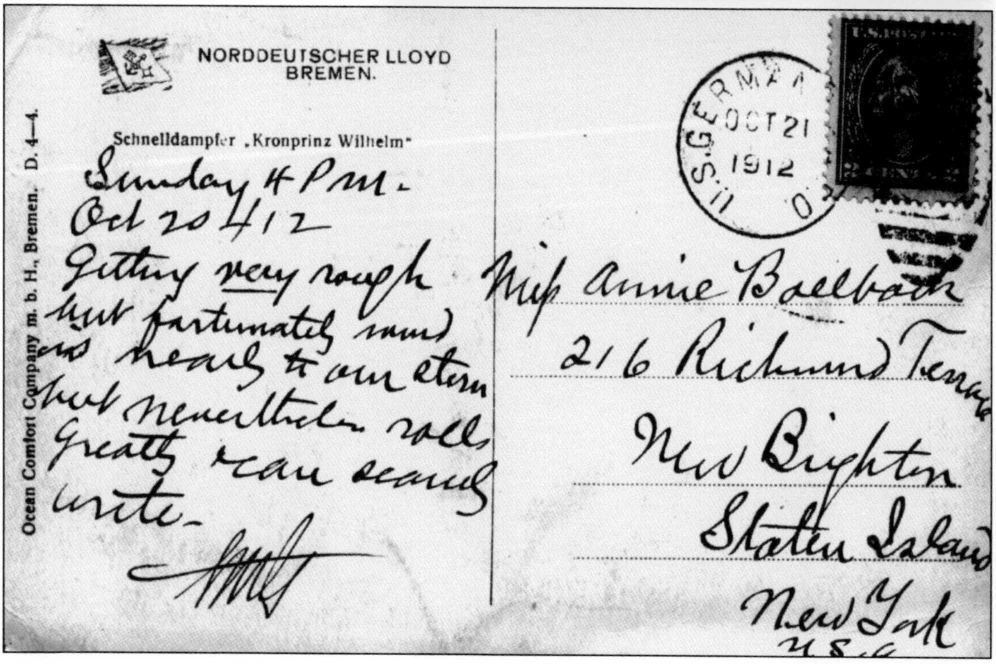

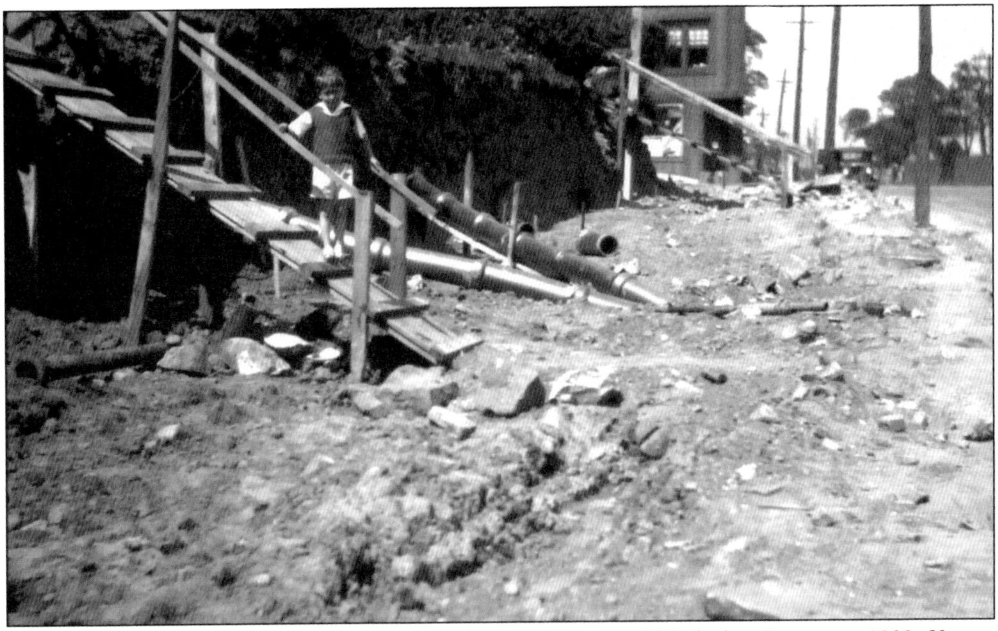

This is a picture of Richmond Terrace looking west toward Nicholas Street in 1929. Young Sherbourne (Sherbie) Graham, who was born in his grandmother's home at 216 Richmond Terrace, walks down a temporary ramp after the front yard and ancient stone walls have been excavated out of existence. Note that the sewer and water pipes coming from the homes have yet to be diverted. (Collection of James G. Ferreri.)

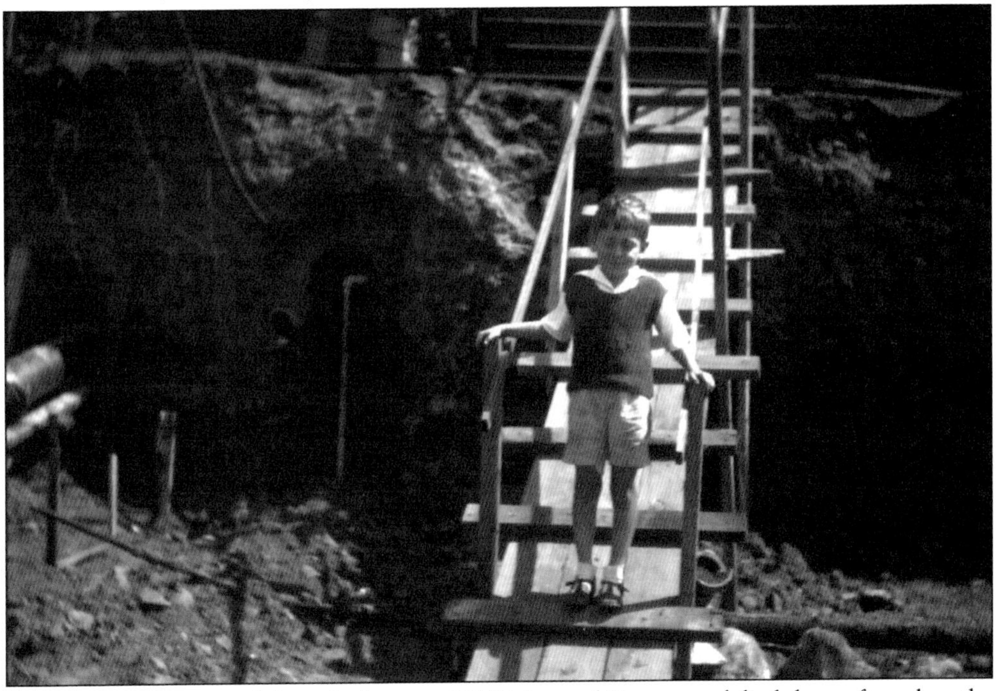

Graham lived his entire life in the home at 216 Richmond Terrace and died there after a lengthy illness in 1997, still loving the grand antique home his grandmother purchased in 1903. Here he is seen as a young boy, in front of the house. (Collection of James G. Ferreri.)

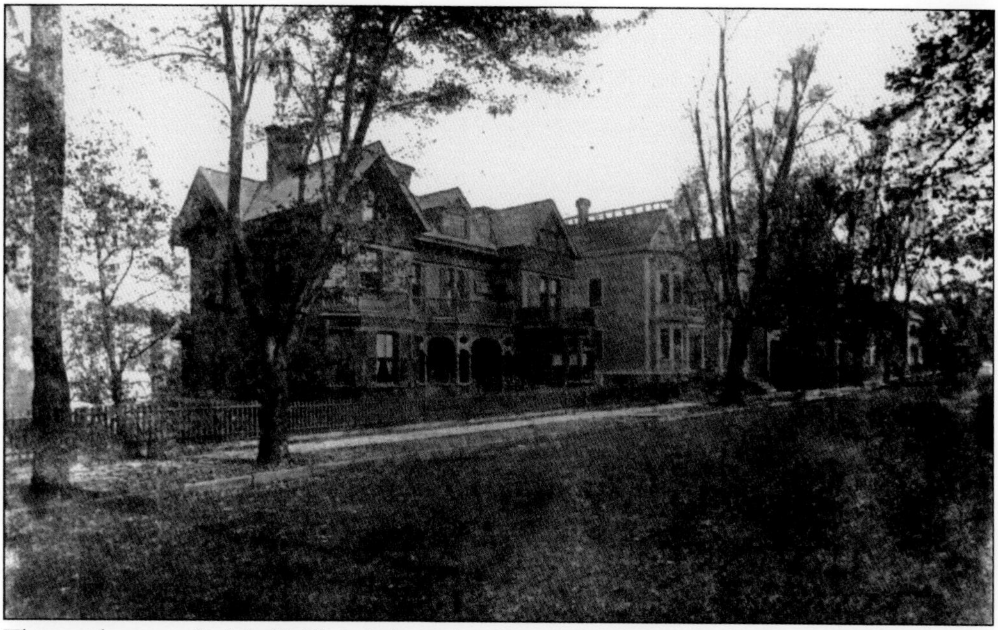

This residence on St. Mark's Place belonged to Sen. Howard R. Bayne, who was born in 1851 in Winchester, Virginia. He was a member of the New York State Senate, 23rd District, from 1909 to 1912. Bayne was a member of the Society of Colonial Wars and Sons of the Revolution. The home is part of the St. George Historic District today.

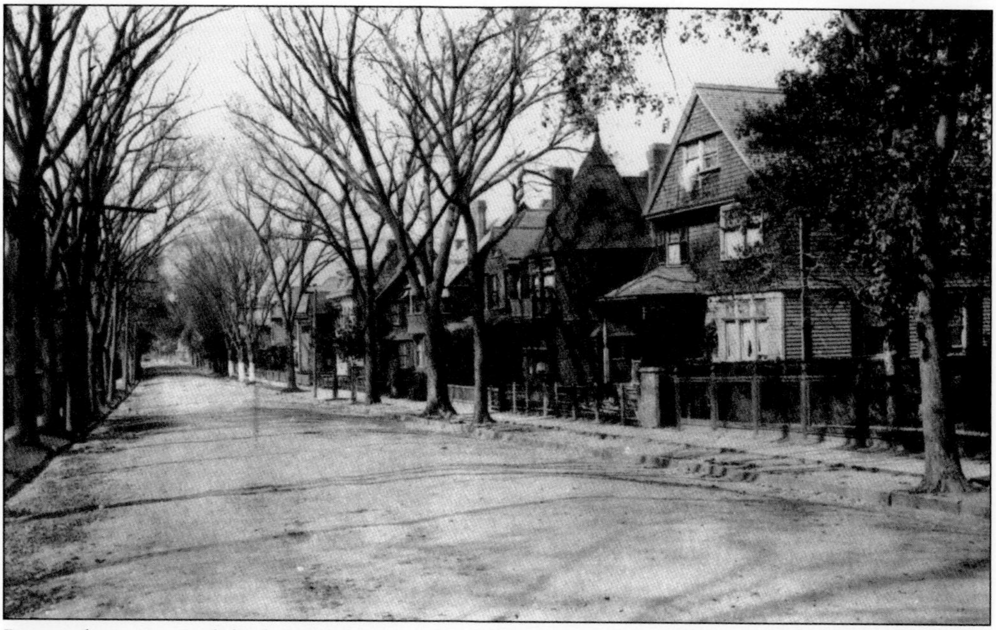

Pictured are some of the homes designed by renowned architect Edward Alfred Sargent in this view of St. Mark's Place around 1894. The home with the round conical roof was owned by silent screen star Mabel Normand, who purchased it for her parents during her years as a top comedienne. Normand was raised in New Brighton.

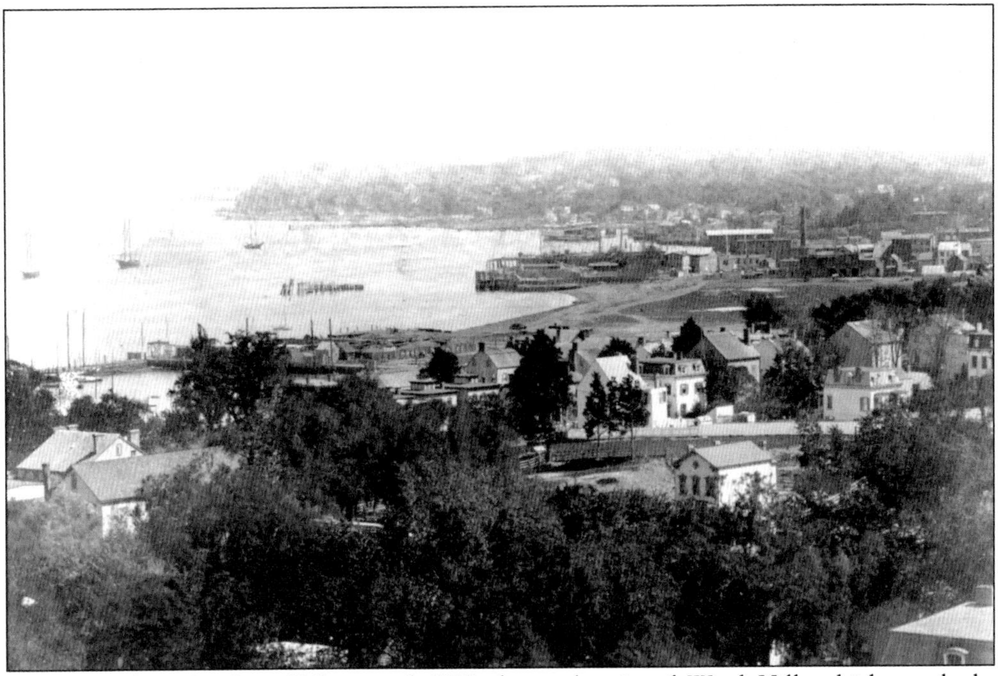

This view from Pavilion Hill around 1888 shows the tip of Ward Hill, which overlooks Tompkinsville and St. George. Ferry service at one time stopped at the end of Victory Boulevard, and guests would climb to the top of Pavilion Hill and enjoy the views and refreshments that were served. The ancient steps up from Victory Boulevard and Van Duzer Street still exist today.

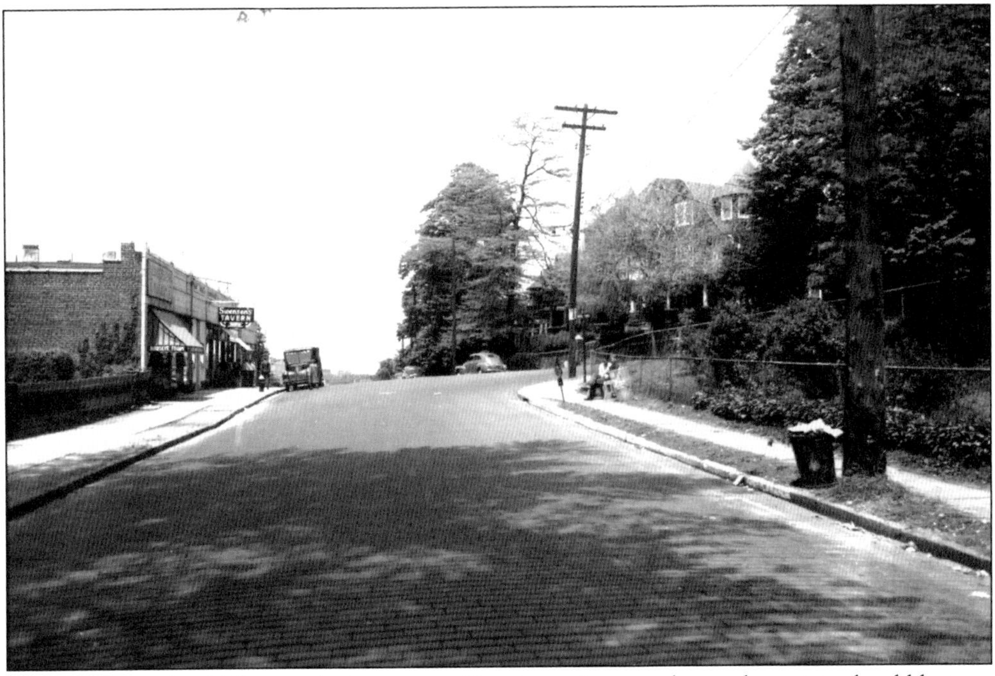

This photograph of Westervelt Avenue at Hamilton Avenue shows the original cobblestone streets. Staten Island's northeast shore is topographically interesting, mostly consisting of hills descending to the water.

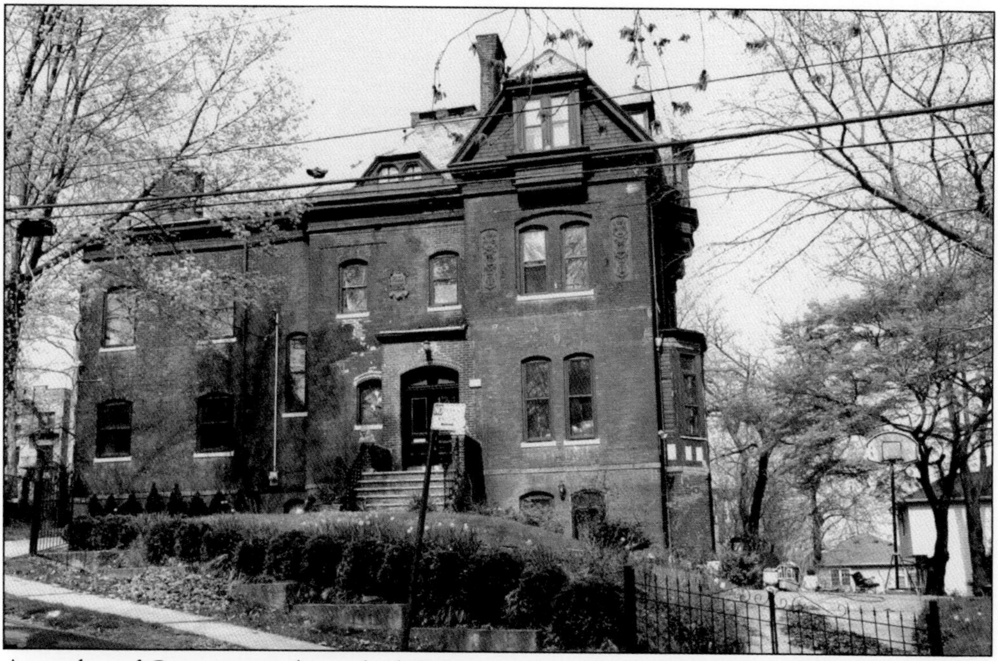

A number of German merchants built large homes in St. George in the 1880s. The Schmidt house at the corner of Fort Place and Daniel Low Terrace was built by Feodore Schmidt in 1885. (Photograph by Daniel K. Goldfarb.)

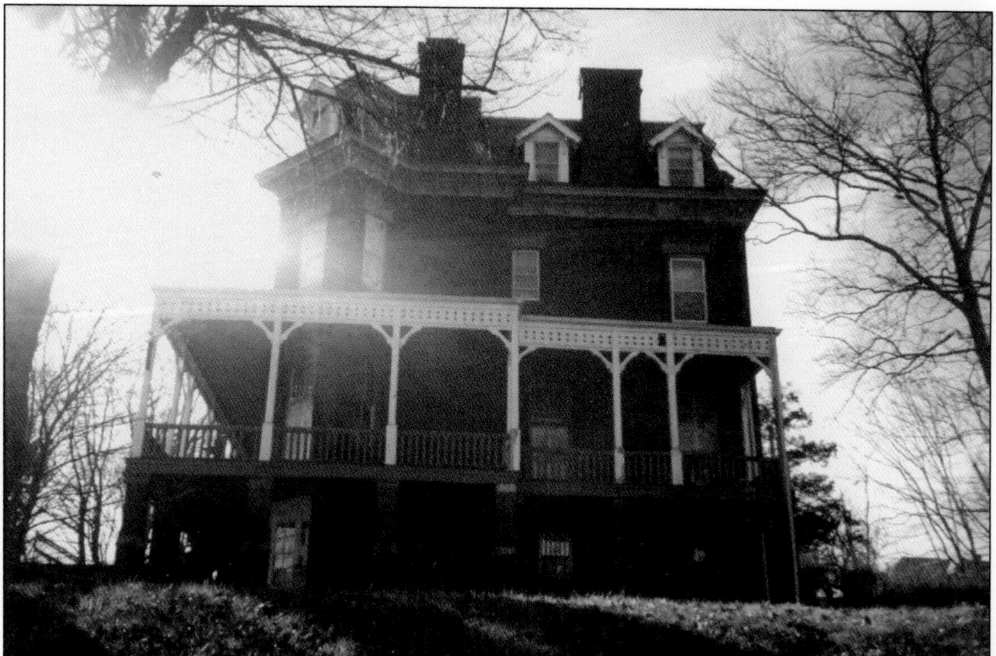

The August and Augusta Schoverling house was built by a prosperous firearms merchant between 1880 and 1882. The brick, late–Second Empire house features a deep wood porch on two sides. The Schoverling house became apartments in the 1930s. It was designated a New York City landmark in 2001. (Collection of David Goldfarb.)

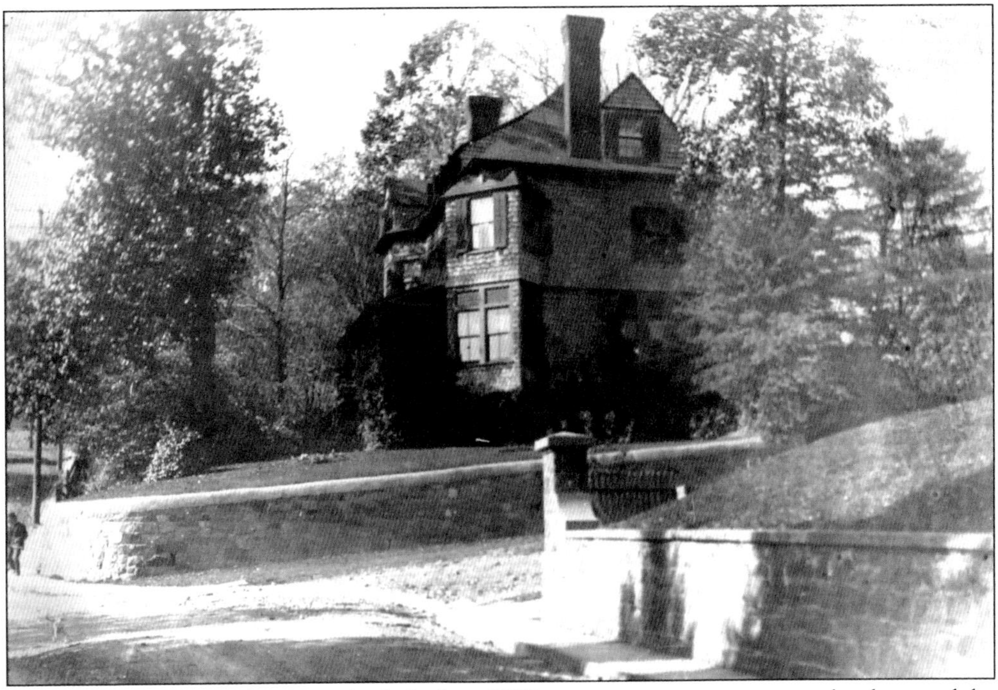

This house on Fort Place was built before 1888 as a summer cottage on land owned by Isabella M. Woodruff. It was later called the Pouch house. The Pouch family was a prominent Brooklyn family that owned businesses on Staten Island. Since 1973, it has been the home of coauthor David Goldfarb and his wife, Elizabeth.

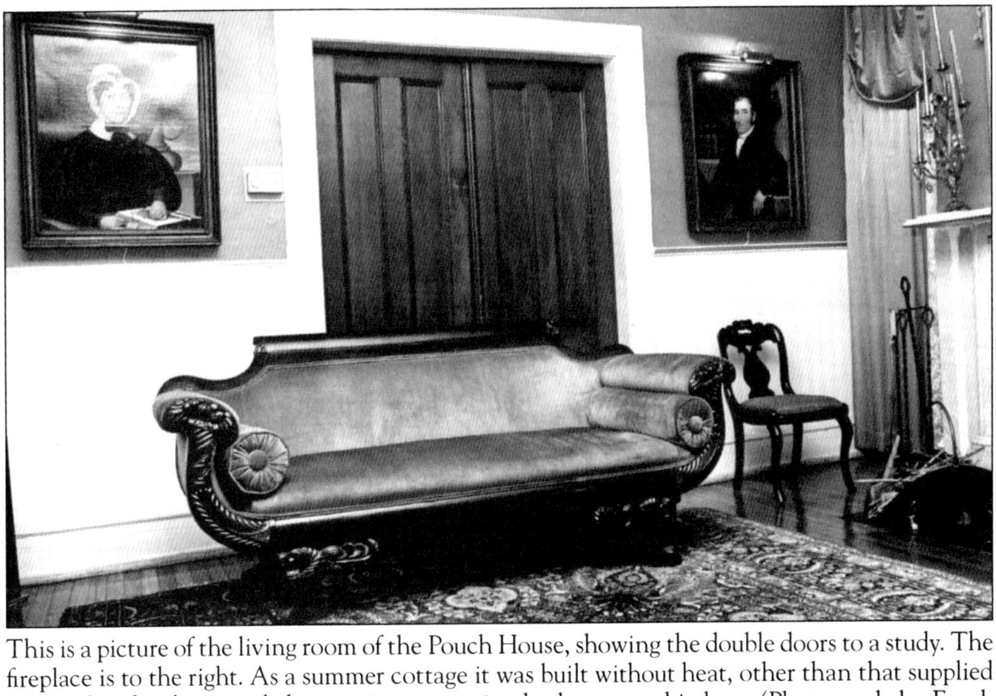

This is a picture of the living room of the Pouch House, showing the double doors to a study. The fireplace is to the right. As a summer cottage it was built without heat, other than that supplied by the five fireplaces and the cast-iron stove in the basement kitchen. (Photograph by Frank Johns; courtesy of the Staten Island Advance.)

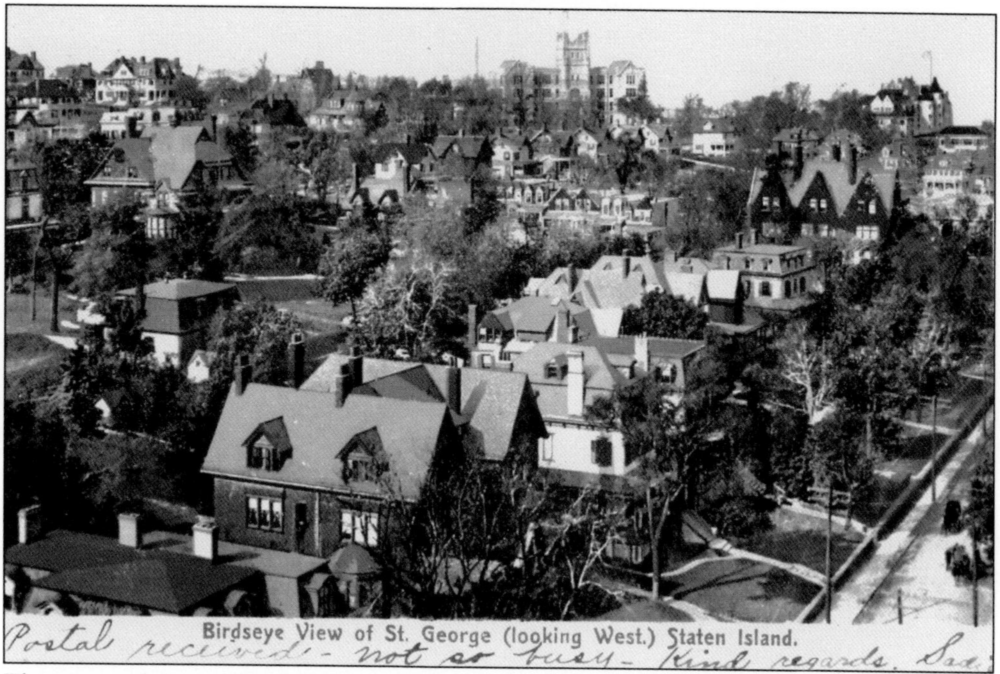

This postcard shows a bird's-eye view of St. George, looking toward Curtis High School in the distance. (Collection of David Goldfarb.)

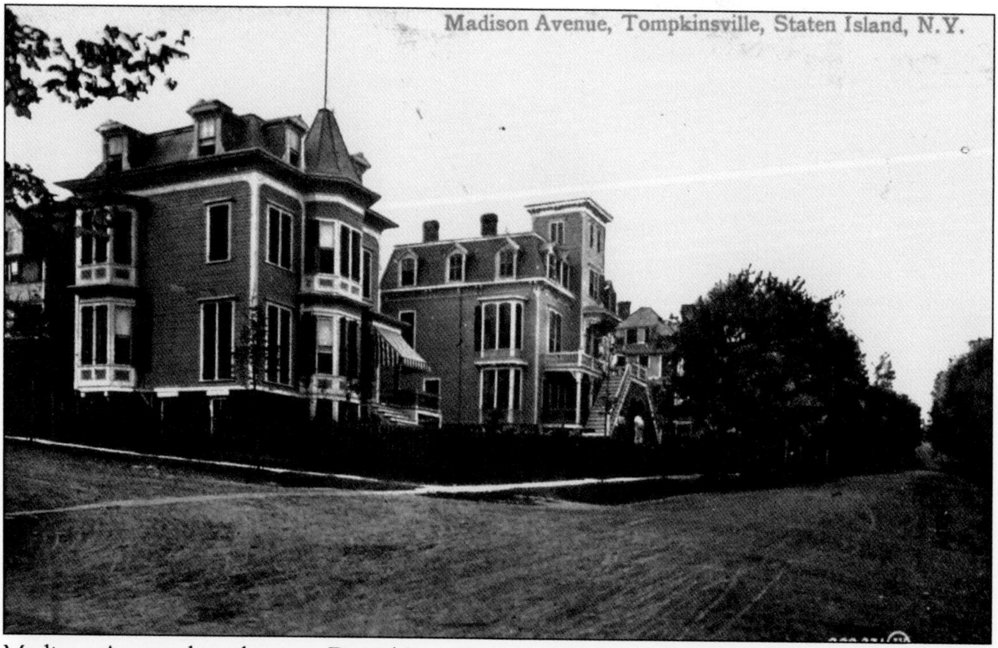

Madison Avenue later became Daniel Low Terrace. These houses are at the corner of Benziger Avenue. (Collection of David Goldfarb.)

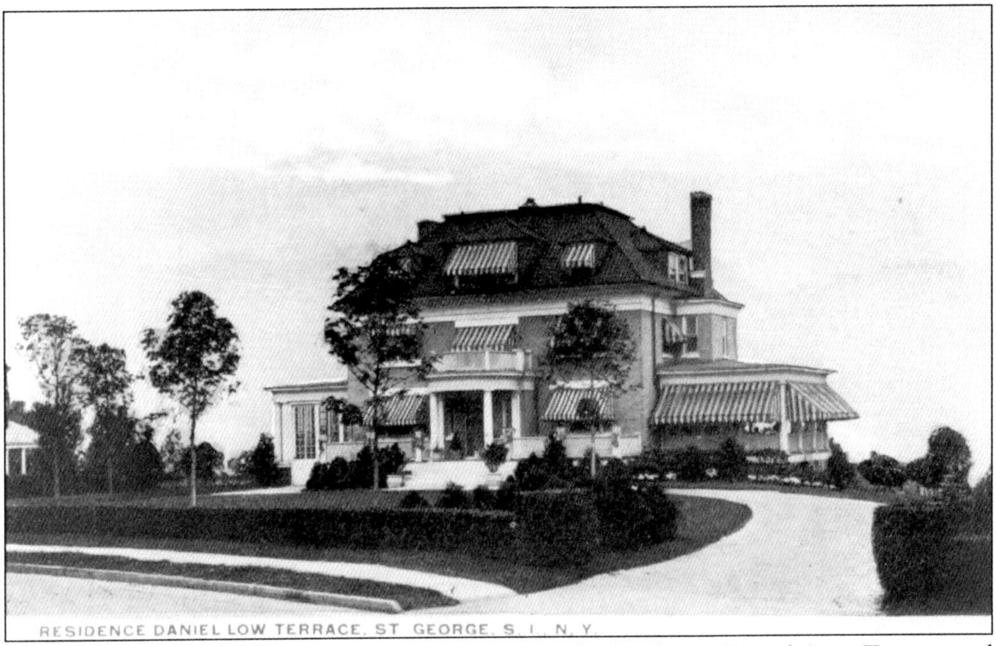

This pre–World War I house was built by the Pouch family on Daniel Low Terrace and Vine Street.

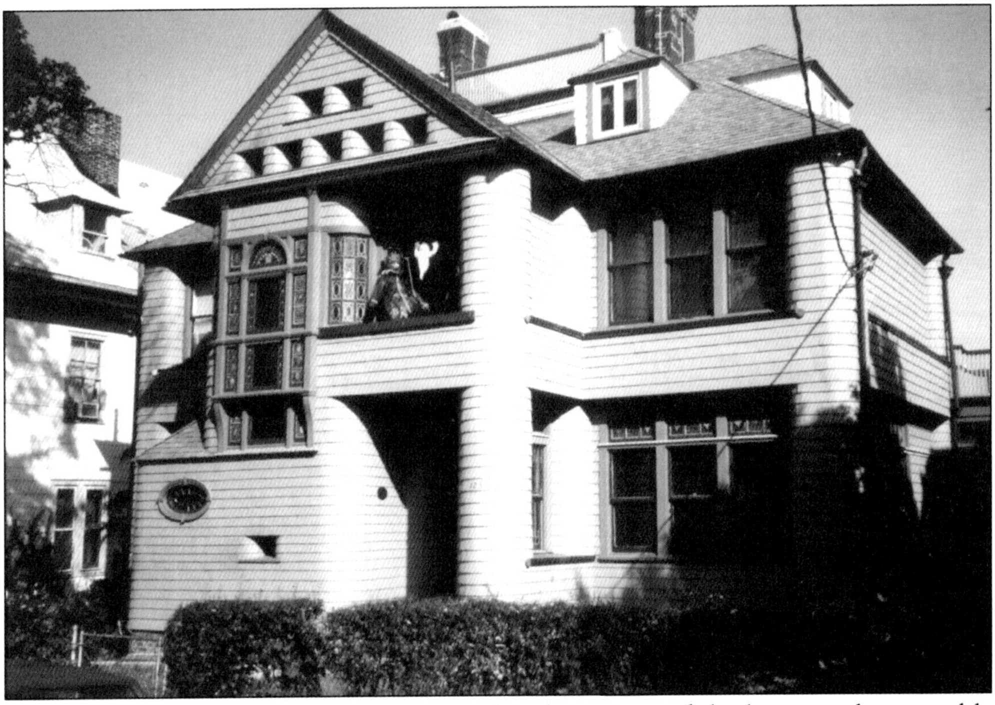

The Frederick L. Rodewald house on St. Mark's Place is one of the largest and most richly detailed houses in the current St. George Historic District. It was designed by architect Edward A. Sargeant for Rodewald around 1890 in the Colonial Revival–shingle style. It was converted to a rooming house in the 1930s, then to a two-family home, and eventually a single-family home. (Collection of David Goldfarb.)

The Henry R. Cammann House on St. Mark's Place is another Sargeant-designed house from 1892. It is distinguished by a large two-story tower with a conical roof pierced by eyebrow dormers. It appears to have been influenced by architectural firm McKim, Mead and White's small houses with towers built in Newport Rhode Island, in the 1880s. (Collection of David Goldfarb.)

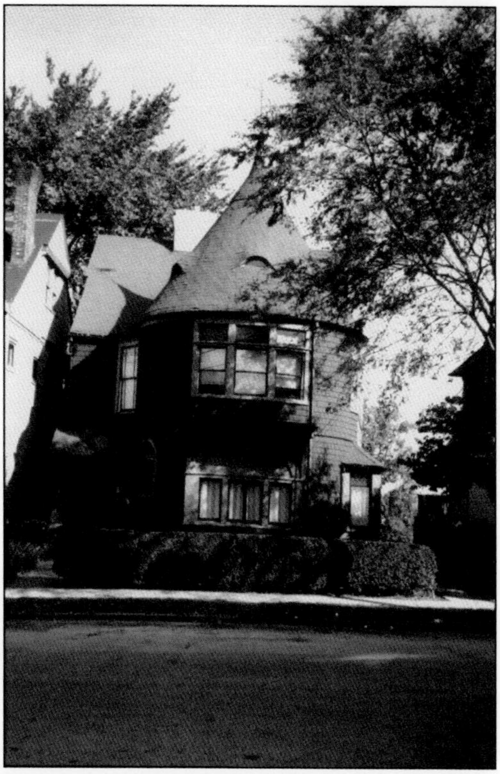

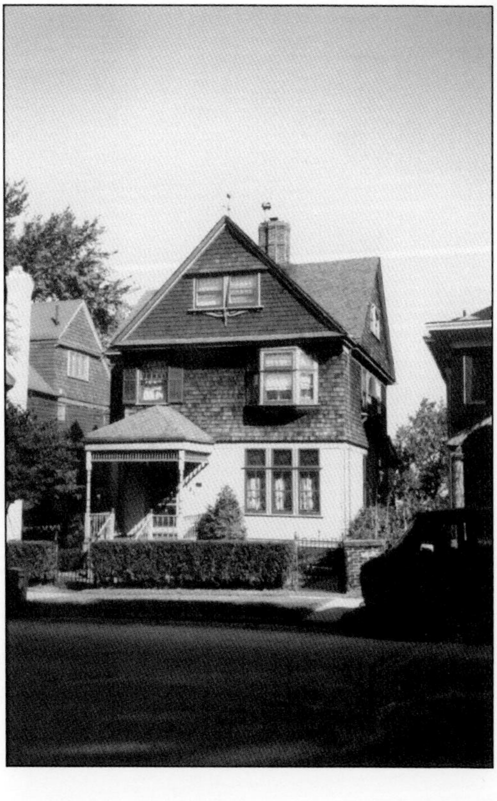

The William and Sarah Rogers House on St. Mark's Place was built for noted cartoonist William A. Rogers (who drew for *Harper's Magazine*) in 1886. It was later occupied by author, art critic, and painter Samuel G. W. Benjamin, who described it as "a pleasant and artistic house." (Collection of David Goldfarb.)

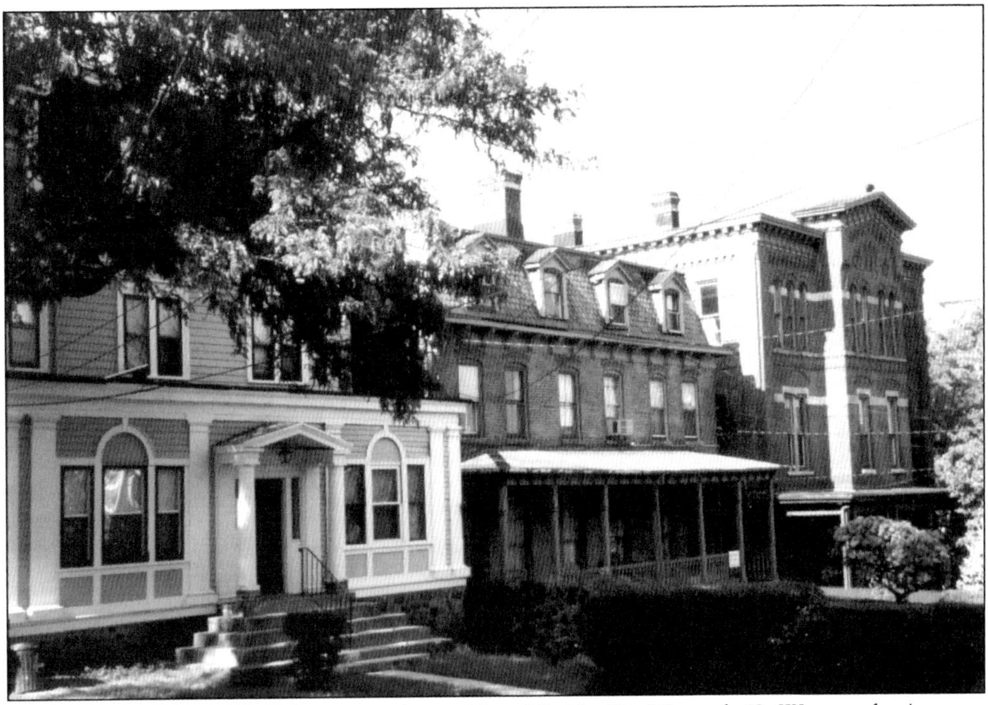

Starting from the right, this view shows Nos. 30–32, 36–38, and 42 Westervelt Avenue. No. 30–32 is a Romanesque Revival home built by Joseph Wilkes. The two other houses are of Second Empire style, built respectively by Beatrice and Clement Newton and Jane and William Elliott. The Second Empire houses date from the 1860s and 1870s and the Romanesque Revival from 1878 to 1882. (Collection of David Goldfarb.)

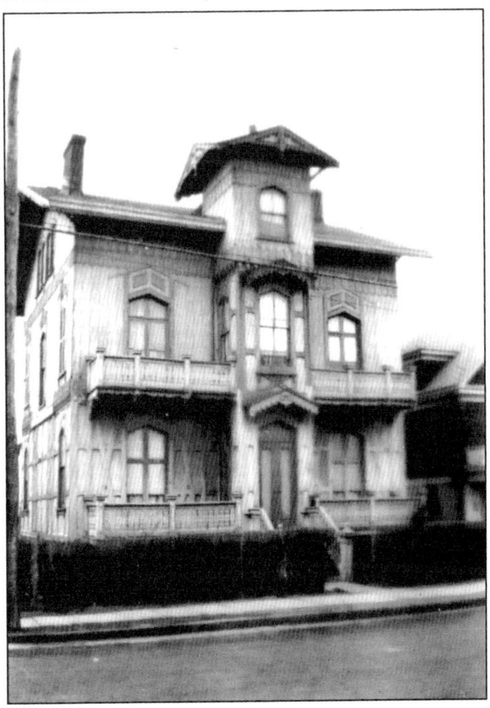

The Copp House on Benziger Avenue is an example of the ornate homes built above Westervelt Avenue. The street was named for the Benziger family that was part of the "German society" on Staten Island. The Benzigers were Swiss immigrants who controlled a well-known publishing house called Benziger Brothers. Bertha Benziger, the wife of Aldrich Benziger, was from an Austrian baronial family. Their daughter Falicitas married Baron Maximilllian von Schnehen on Staten Island in 1898.

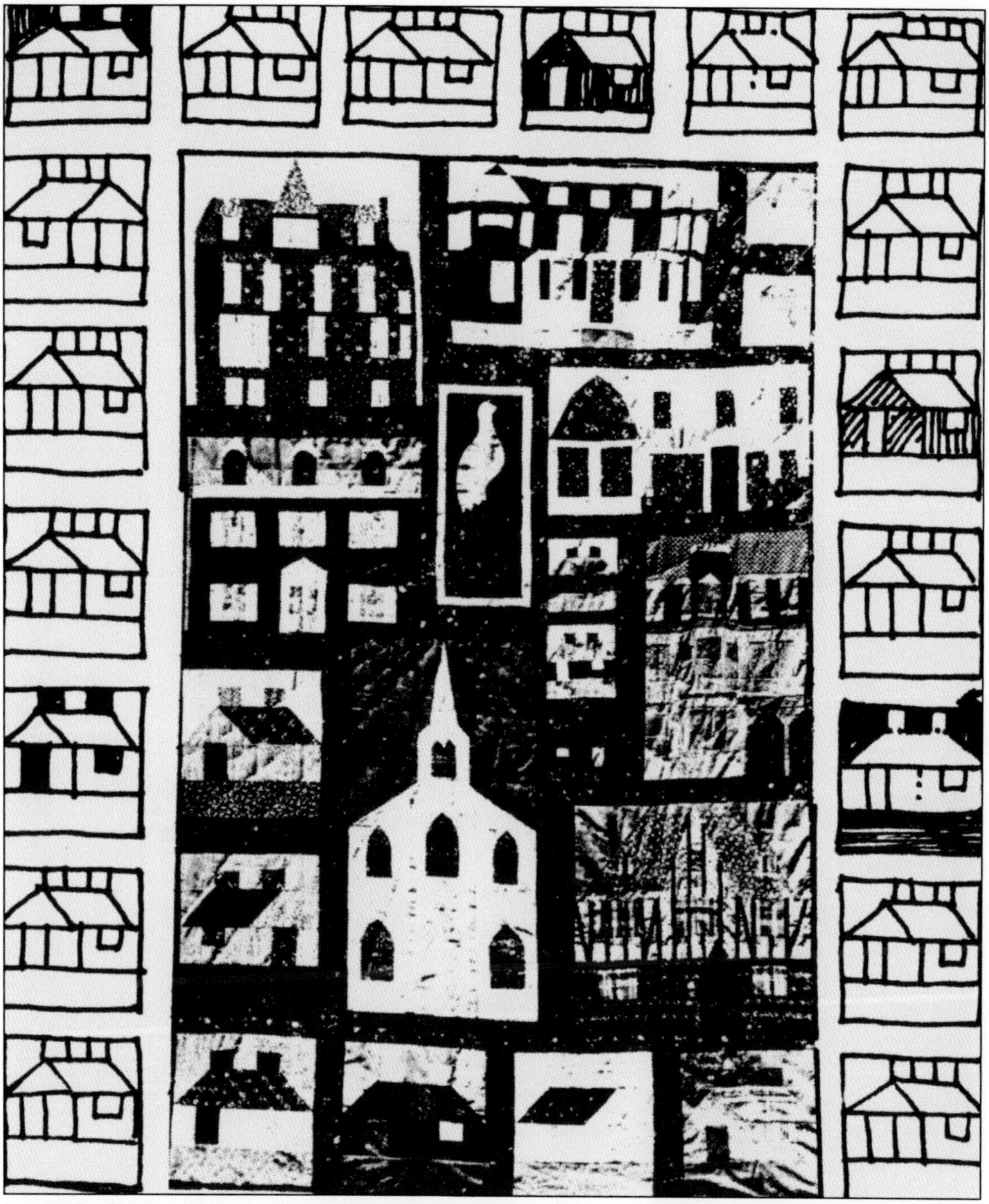

In 1983, the St. George Civic Association began efforts to create a historic district within the St. George area. This picture of a quilt, made by St. George quilters, was raffled at the 1983 house tour as part of an effort to rally support for the proposed district. (Collection of David Goldfarb.)

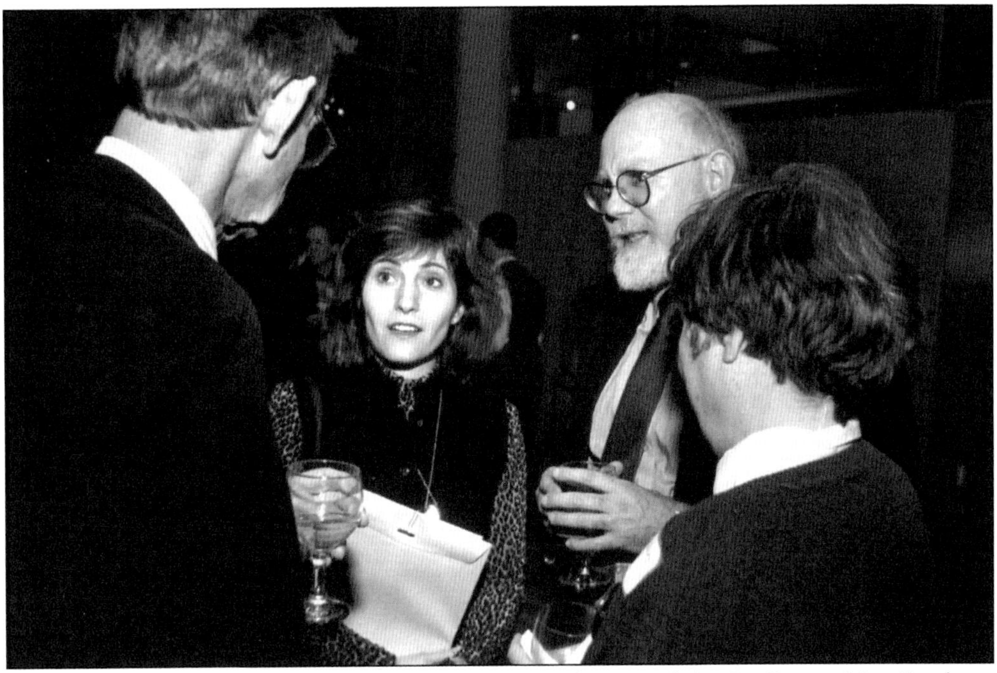

In 1994, the New York City Landmarks Commission designated the St. George-New Brighton Historic District. Laurie Beckelman was landmarks commission chair at the time of the designation. Jennifer Raab became chair when the district was before the city council for approval. The picture shows landmarks commission chair Raab meeting with local residents. From left to right are Channel Graham, president of the Preservation League of Staten Island; Raab; David Goldfarb, president of the St. George Civic Association; and Linda Jones, past president of the Preservation League. (Photograph by Steven Tucker, collection of David Goldfarb.)

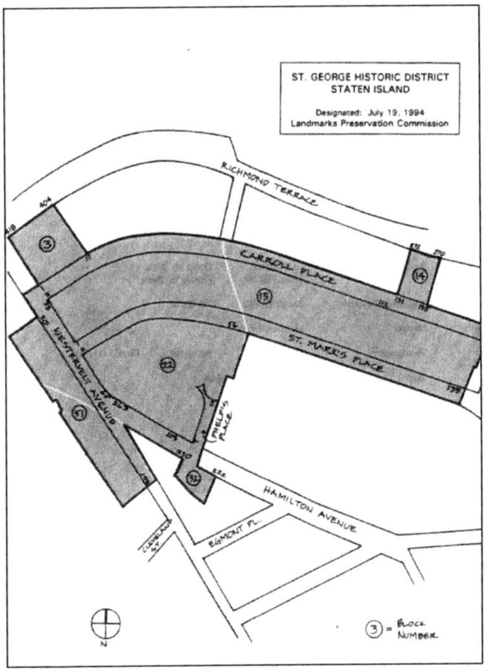

The map shows the boundaries of the historic district. The designation report states "The majority of houses in the proposed district were constructed in the 1880s and 1890s and reflect a combination of the decorative Queen Anne style and aspects of the Colonial Revival and Shingle styles; it is these houses which give the proposed district its predominant architectural character." (Courtesy of New York City Landmarks Preservation Commission.)

Five

The Civic Center

With the consolidation of Greater New York in 1898, Staten Island was subsumed along with Brooklyn, Queens, and the Bronx into the new New York City. For more than a century and a half, Richmond Town had been the center of government for Staten Island. The island's first borough president, George Cromwell, instigated the move of the governmental center from Richmond Town to the north shore, and St. George as a civic center began to take shape.

During this transition, a master plan was conceived that included buildings such as a borough hall, the county courthouse, and the public library to be built among public parkland facing Manhattan. Carrere and Hastings' beautiful Staten Island Borough Hall and the firm's Richmond County Courthouse were built in 1906 and 1919, respectively. In 1907, Carrere and Hastings' St. George Library was completed.

As the area grew into the civic and commercial center of the island, a main branch of the United States Post Office was erected, as well as the island's first high school built after consolidation, the C. B. J. Snyder–designed Curtis High School.

Large estates, as well as more modest Victorian-era homes, began to disappear under the weight of the transition from a mostly residential to a commercial neighborhood. During the 1920s, Richmond Terrace was widened in order to handle the increase in traffic to the area, and office buildings began to sprout up along most of St. George's main streets. By 1929, the large edifice designed by Eugene De Rosa on Hyatt Street at St. Mark's Place was constructed to house stores, offices as well as the grandest theater on Staten Island, the St. George.

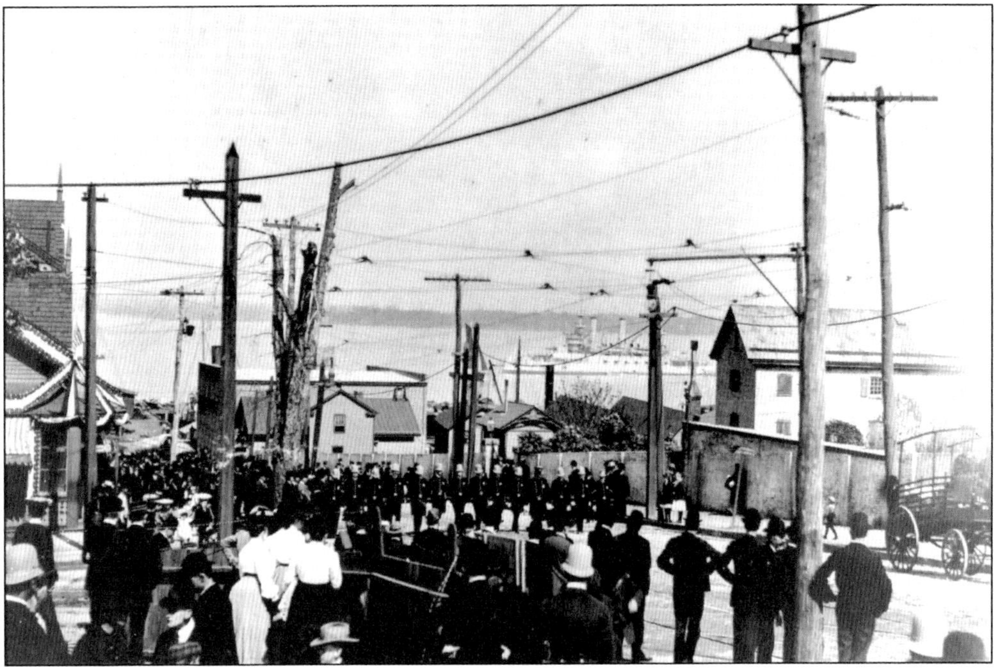

In 1904, this crowd gathered at the site of the future Staten Island Borough Hall for a ceremonial laying of the cornerstone. The view, looking toward New York Harbor, shows the surrounding neighborhood still retains its mostly residential character. Note the large vessel off the St. George shoreline.

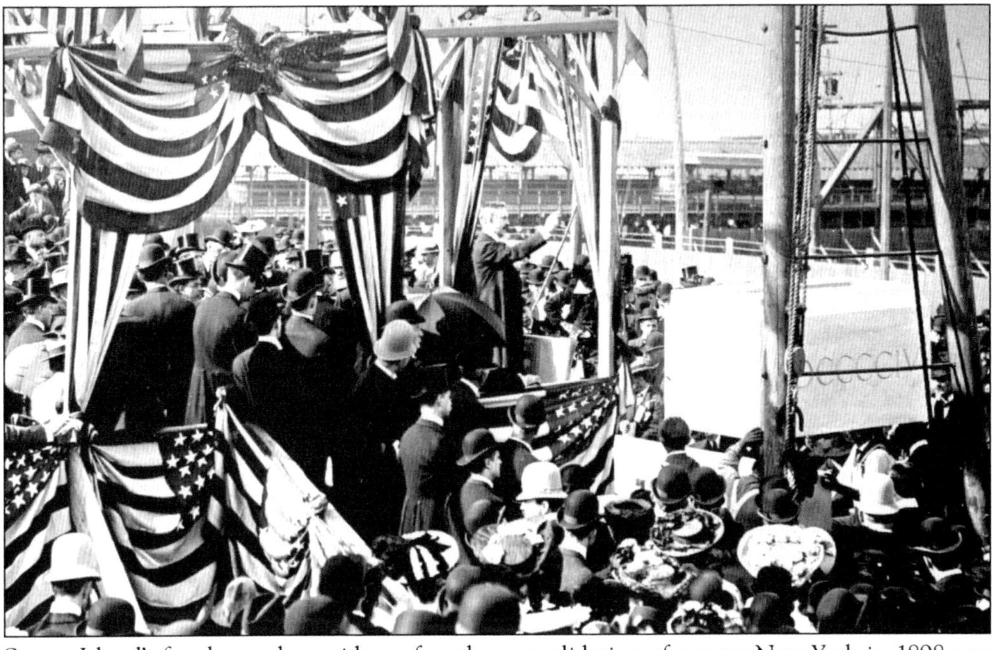

Staten Island's first borough president after the consolidation of greater New York in 1898 was George Cromwell. In this photograph dated May 21, 1904, Cromwell, at the podium in the center of the photograph, speaks at the dedication ceremony of Staten Island's borough hall. Note the cornerstone with the carved Roman numerals.

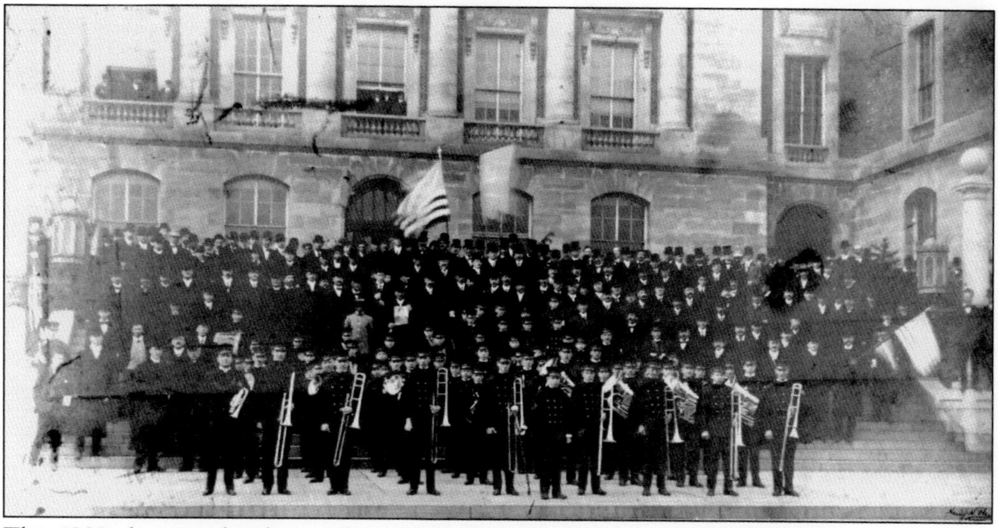

This 1909 photograph taken in front of the Bay Street facade of borough hall is annotated on its reverse that Borough President Cromwell is at the center. Perhaps he is the man holding a photograph?

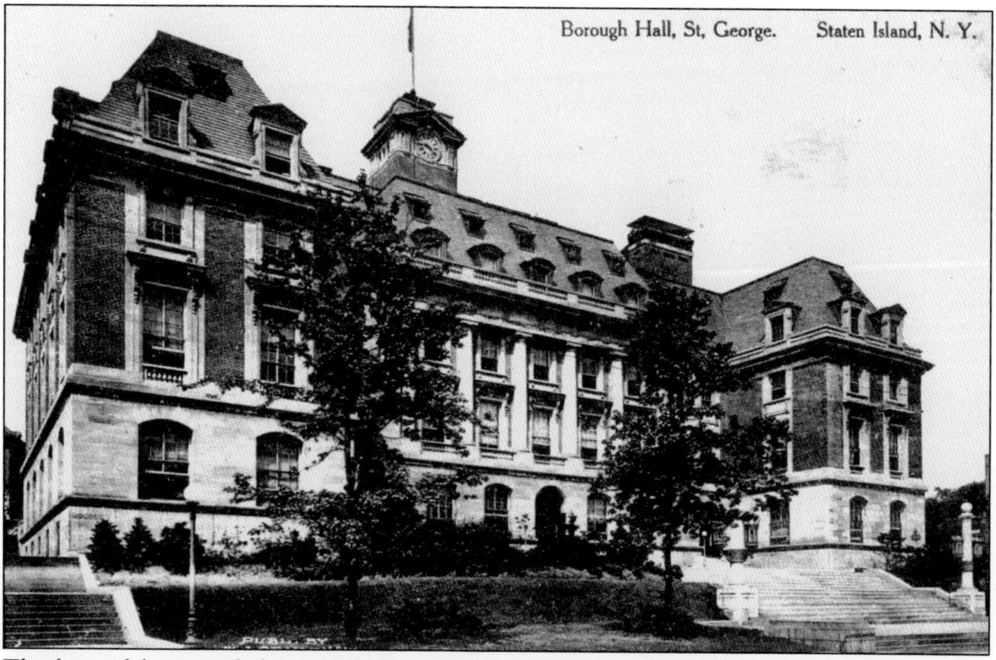

This beautiful postcard photograph shows Staten Island's borough hall designed by John Carrere and Thomas Hastings. The idea to consolidate all of Staten Island's governmental structures in St. George belonged to Cromwell. During his five terms as borough president, from 1898 to 1913, he oversaw the move of the civic center from Richmond Town to St. George. The building's plan consists of a center section and two pavilions. (Collection of David Goldfarb.)

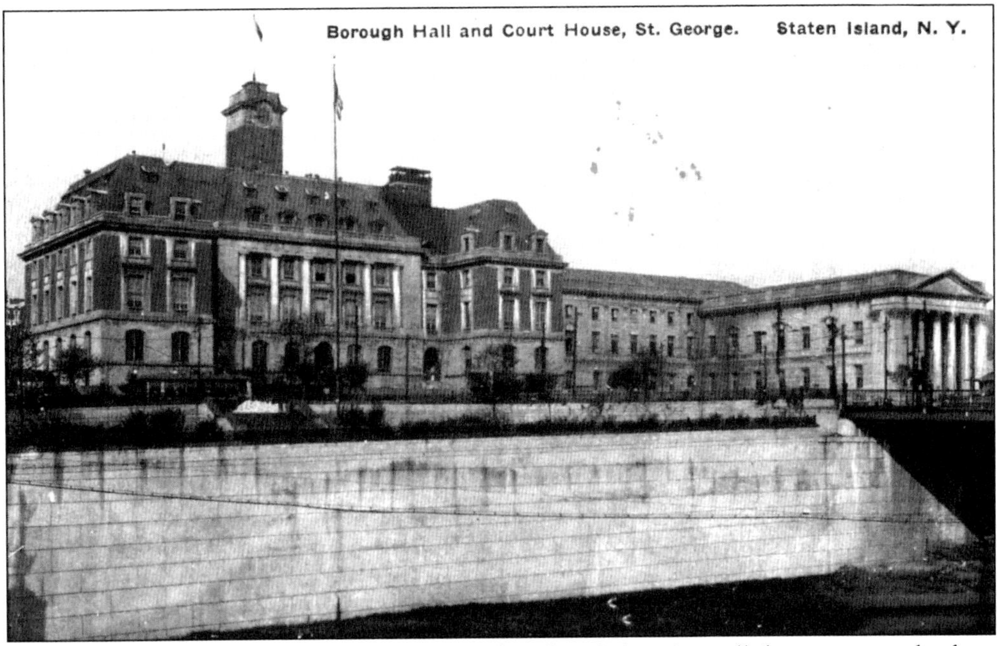

This view of Staten Island Borough Hall was taken from below the wall that separates the ferry terminal property from Bay Street proper. The French Renaissance–style brick borough hall building is three stories high with a massive two-story mansard roof. The clock tower in the center can be seen from the harbor. This facade faces Richmond Terrace and overlooks New York Harbor. Note the courthouse building to the right. (Collection of David Goldfarb.)

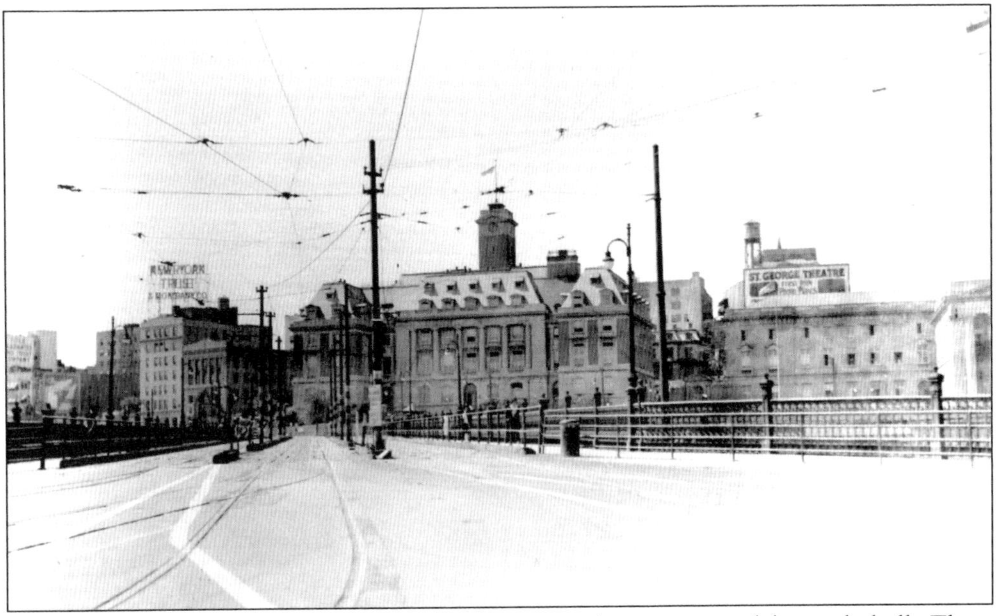

This is a view from the Staten Island Ferry Terminal ramps toward borough hall. These ramps were destroyed along with the ferry terminal in a spectacular fire on June 25, 1946, in which three died, and 280 were injured. Note that to the right of borough hall, the side of the St. George Theater building on Hyatt Street is visible, with a large sign proclaiming, "St. George Theater, First Run Photo Plays."

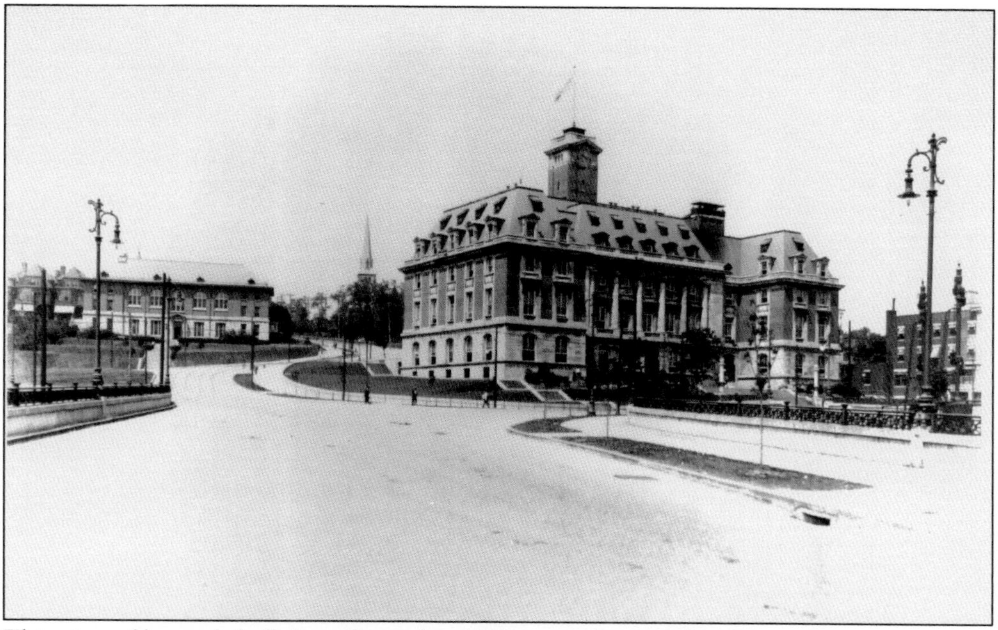

This view of borough hall dates from after 1907, since the completed St. George Library is to the left. The initial intention of a beautiful civic center is clearly evident in this photograph. However, commercial buildings along Bay Street and Hyatt Street today obscure the library, and the surrounding vistas have been lost. Note that the courthouse to the right of borough hall has yet to be built, so this photograph can be dated between 1907 and 1913.

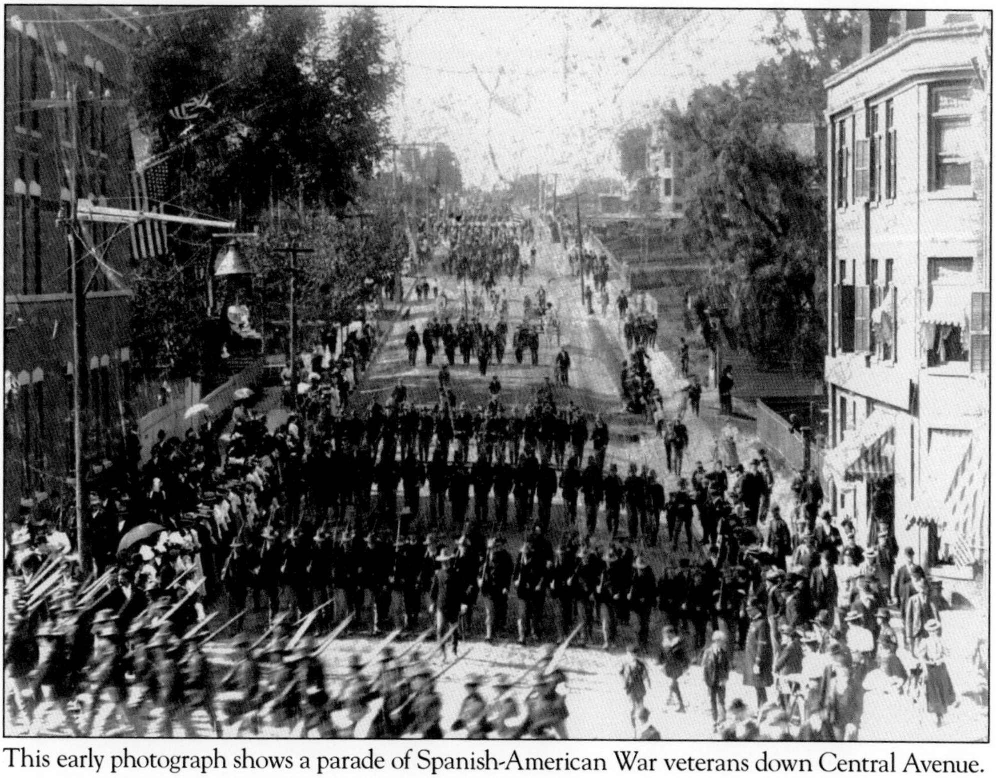

This early photograph shows a parade of Spanish-American War veterans down Central Avenue.

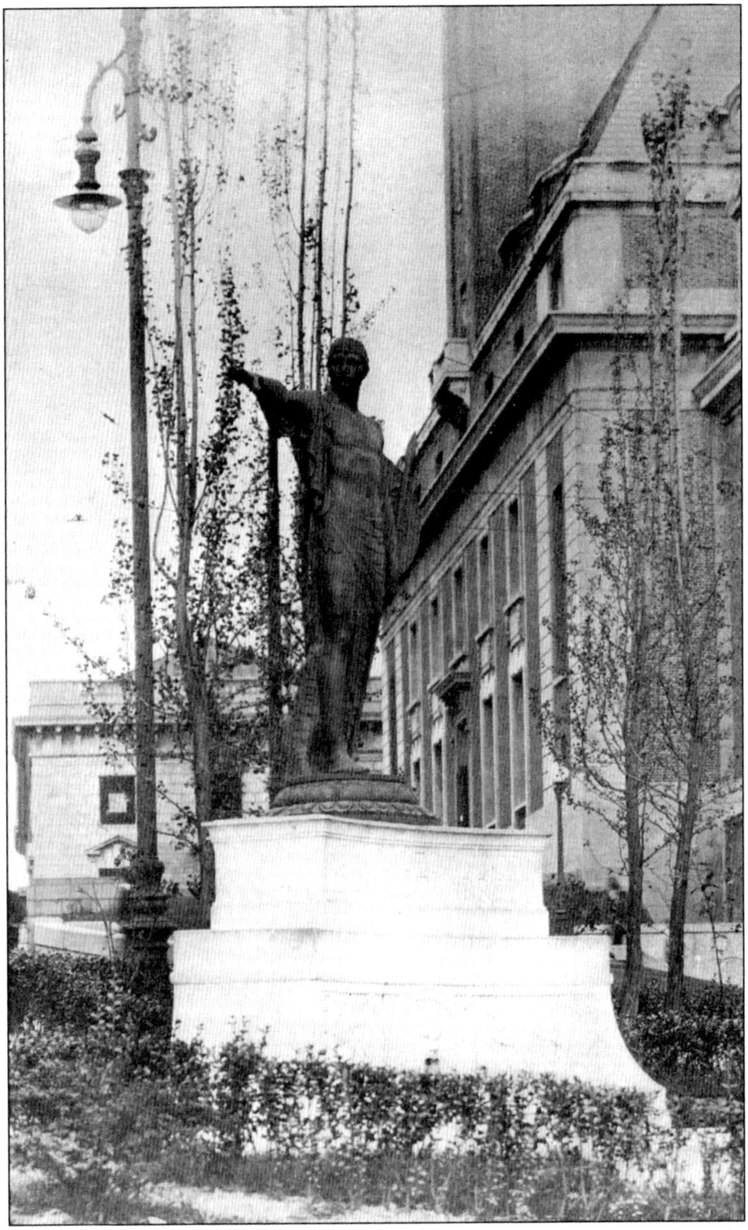

Unveiled on November 11, 1915, the Barrett Memorial stands near Staten Island Borough Hall. The bronze heroic statue by sculptor Sherry Edmundson Fry is mounted on a base of pink Tennessee marble. Maj. Clarence Tynan Barrett (1840–1906) distinguished himself through careers in landscape architecture, sanitation engineering, and the military. Barrett was involved in the battle at Richmond, Virginia, near the end of the Civil War in 1865, after which he returned to Staten Island, establishing himself as an expert in his chosen fields, landscape architecture, and sanitation engineering. He also was acting police commissioner and as superintendent of the poor. The statue was given to the city by Barrett's widow. The triangular base is inscribed with the words "Loyal, Honest, Brave and True," which are carved with relief figures in a Grecian-style processional. In 1945, the monument was moved to its present site at Major Barrett Triangle, near the bus shelter on Bay Street.

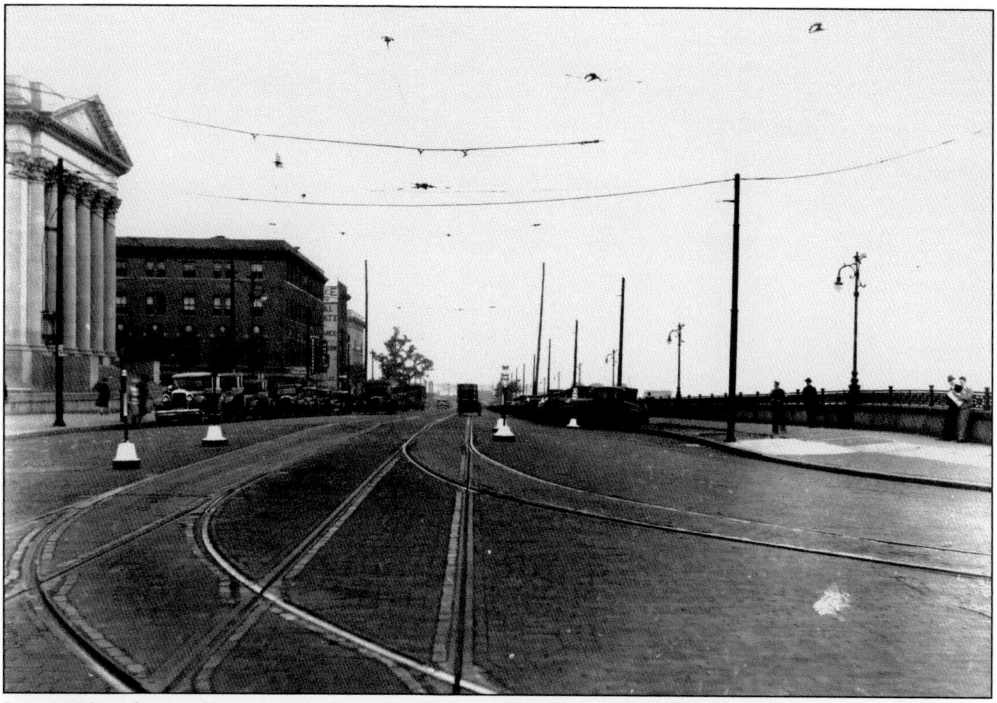

It is 1935 in front of borough hall on Richmond Terrace, and the cobblestone streets are pierced with trolley tracks curving their way up the ramps to the Staten Island Ferry.

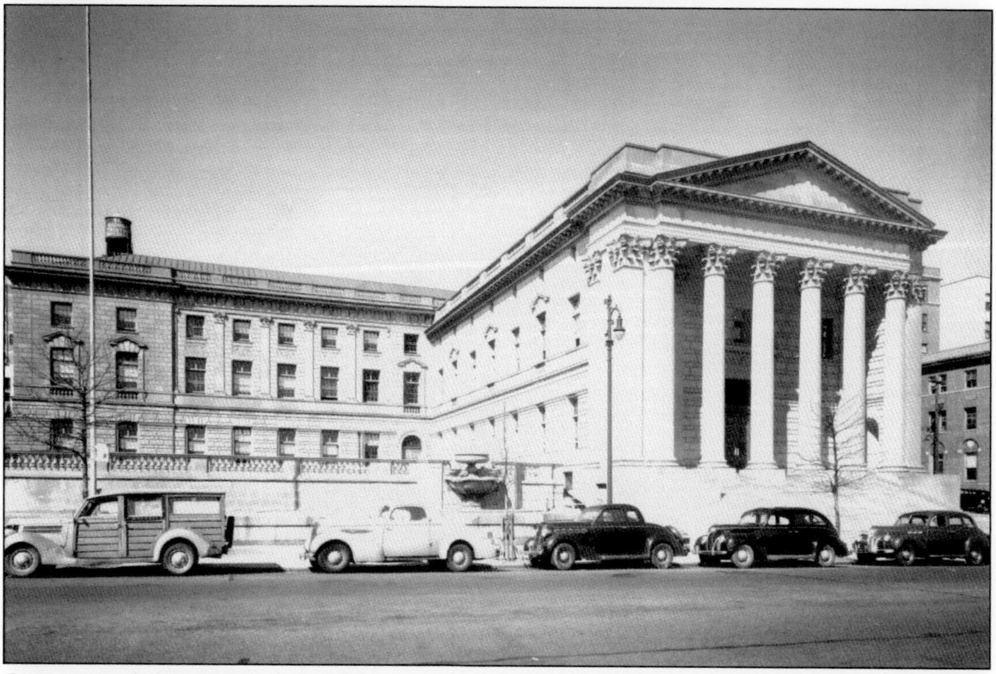

Carrere and Hastings's beautiful neoclassical Richmond County Courthouse was built 1913–1919. This photograph was taken around 1935, and there is a wonderful old "Woody" station wagon at the head of the line of cars parked along Richmond Terrace. Today the courthouse is home to the supreme court, surrogate court, and various other municipal offices.

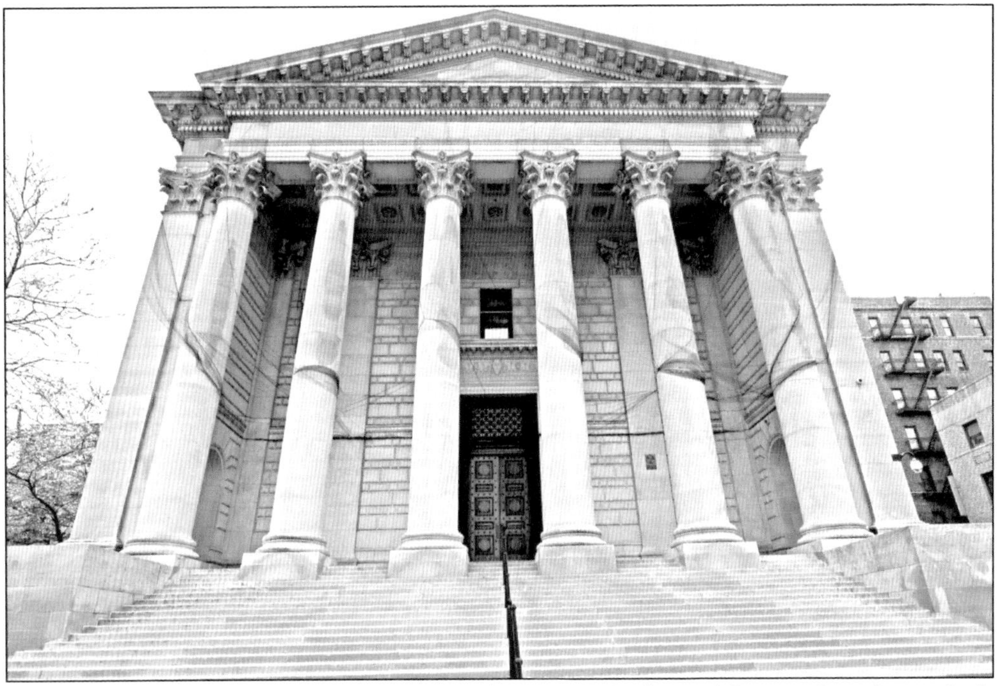

This is another more recent view of Carrere and Hastings's Richmond County Courthouse, built from 1913 to 1919. (Photograph by Daniel Goldfarb.)

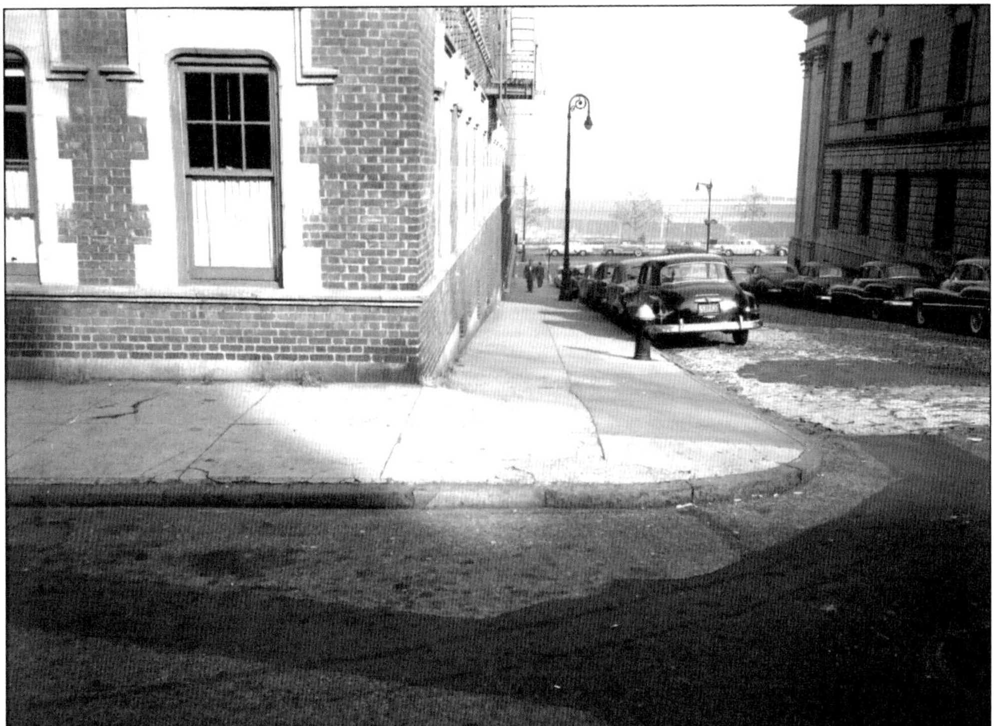

A c. 1953 view looking down Schuyler Place from Stuyvesant Place shows the county courthouse to the right and the Staten Island Ferry ramps across Richmond Terrace in the distance.

This picture shows the inside of the courtroom in the surrogate's court in the county courthouse. (Collection of David Goldfarb.)

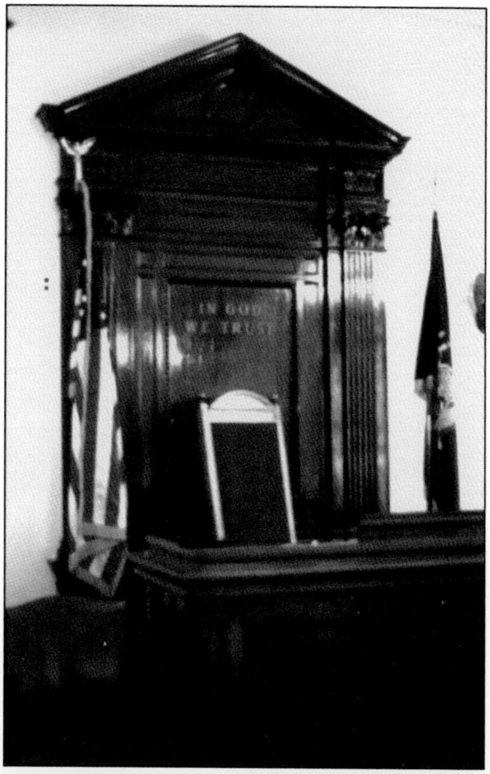

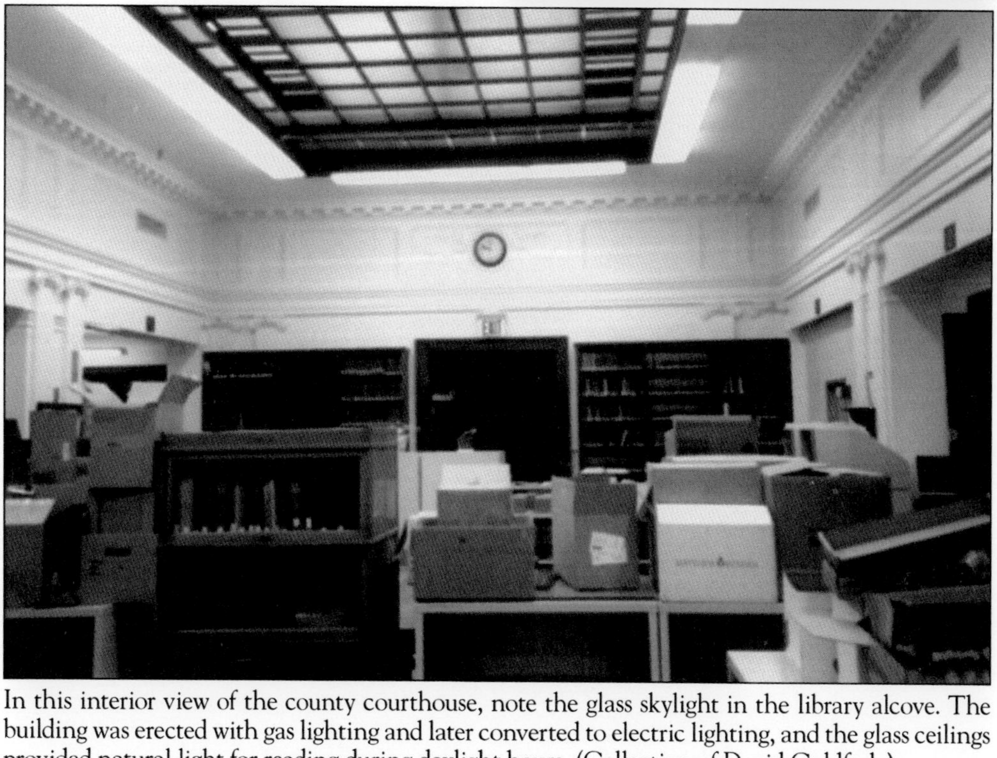

In this interior view of the county courthouse, note the glass skylight in the library alcove. The building was erected with gas lighting and later converted to electric lighting, and the glass ceilings provided natural light for reading during daylight hours. (Collection of David Goldfarb.)

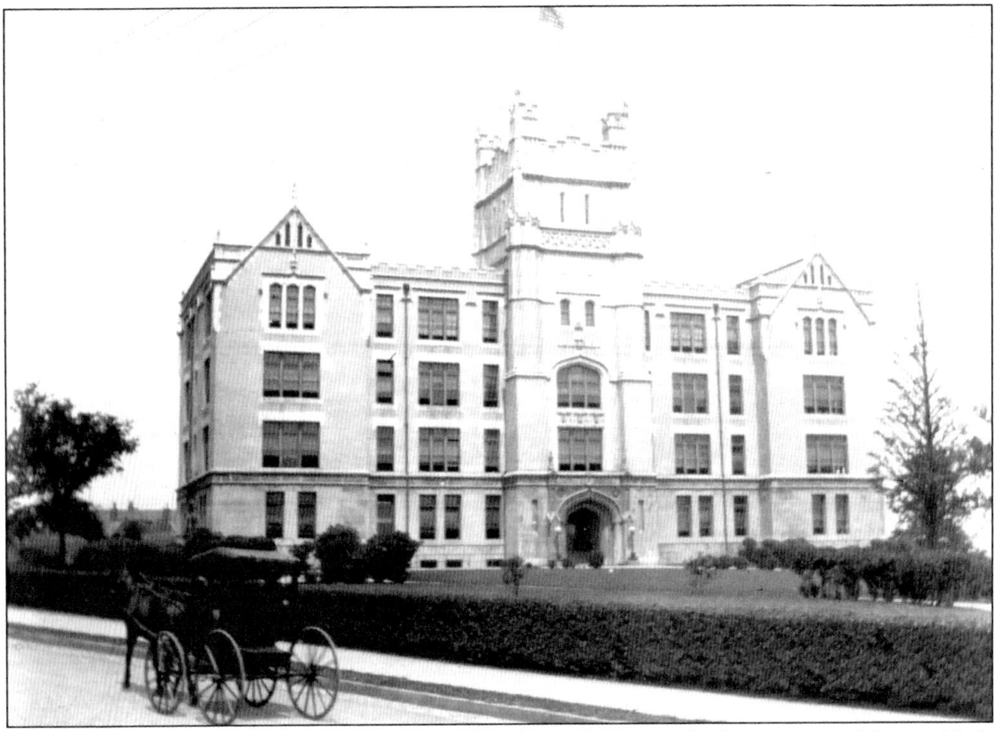

Developer Cornelius G. Kolff is credited with taking this *c.* 1905 photograph of Curtis High School. The school was the first public building built following the consolidation of greater New York. It was part of a plan to erect a major high school in each of the outlying boroughs. Note the horse and carriage.

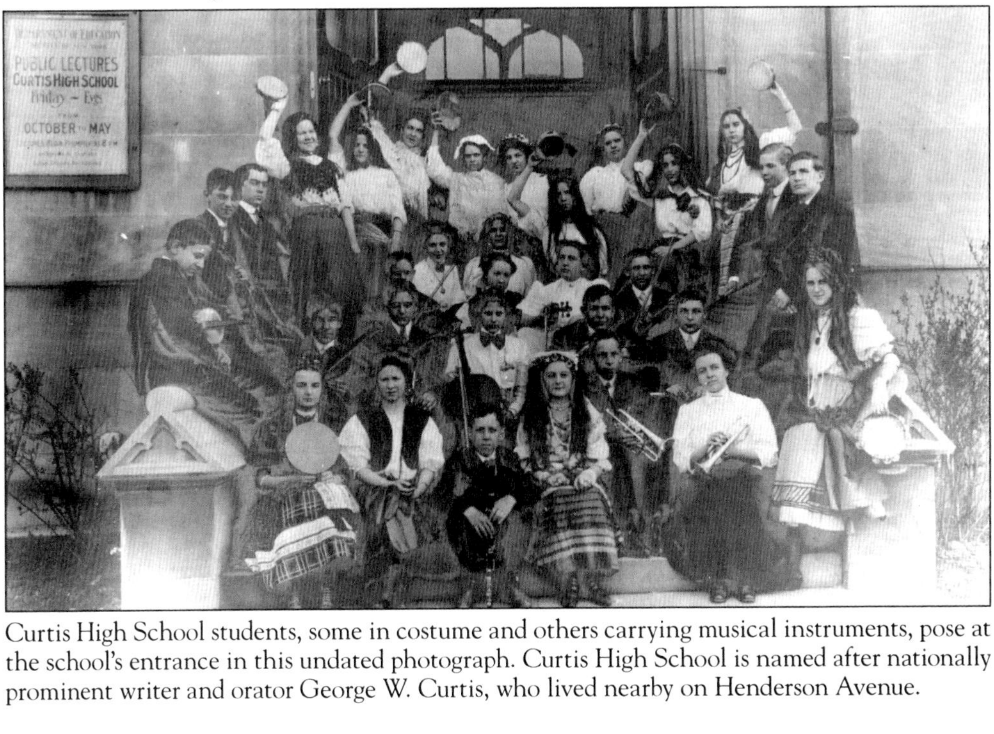

Curtis High School students, some in costume and others carrying musical instruments, pose at the school's entrance in this undated photograph. Curtis High School is named after nationally prominent writer and orator George W. Curtis, who lived nearby on Henderson Avenue.

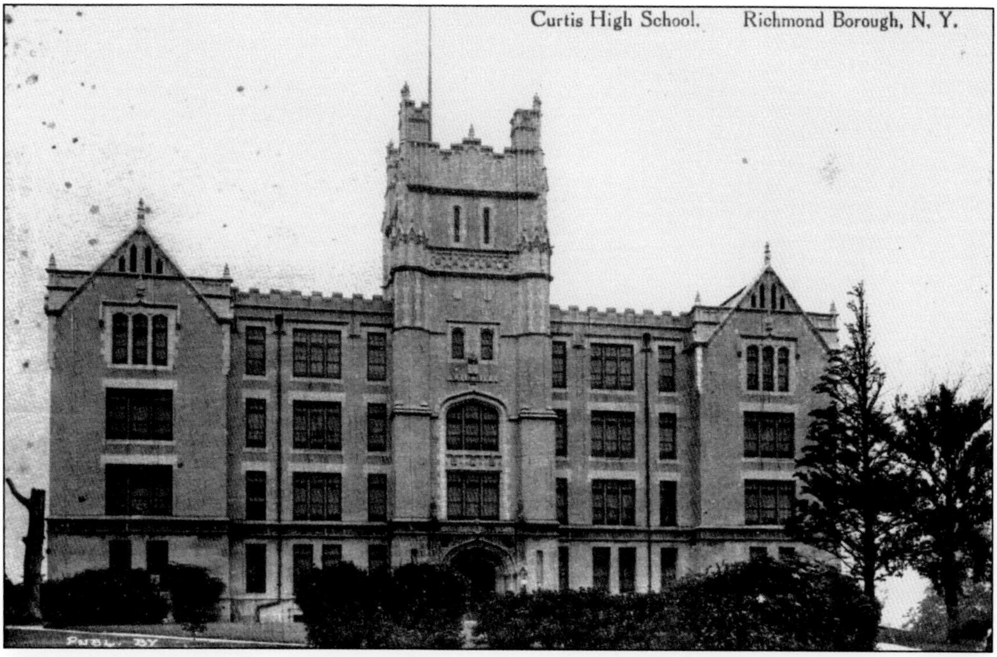

A postcard postmarked 1915 reveals the beauty of Curtis High School's architecture. Curtis High School was designed by the architect C. B. J. Snyder and built between 1902 and 1904. The school was designated a New York City landmark on October 12, 1982. (Collection of David Goldfarb.)

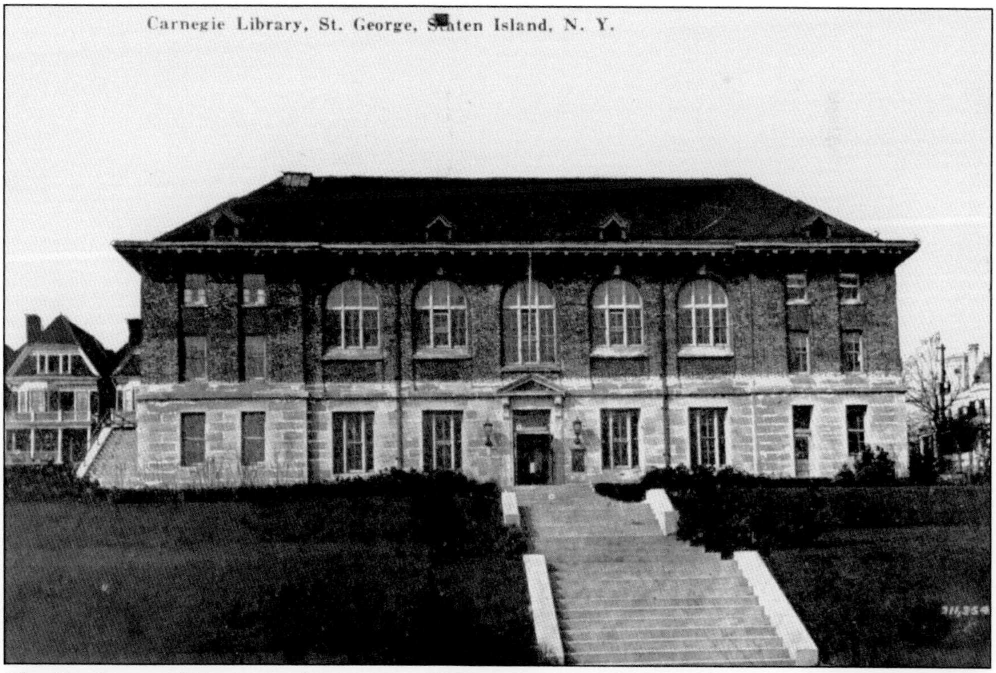

The St. George Library at the corner of Hyatt Street and Central Avenue, the main library branch on Staten Island, is part of the New York Public Library and is one the Carnegie Libraries built with funds donated by Andrew Carnegie.

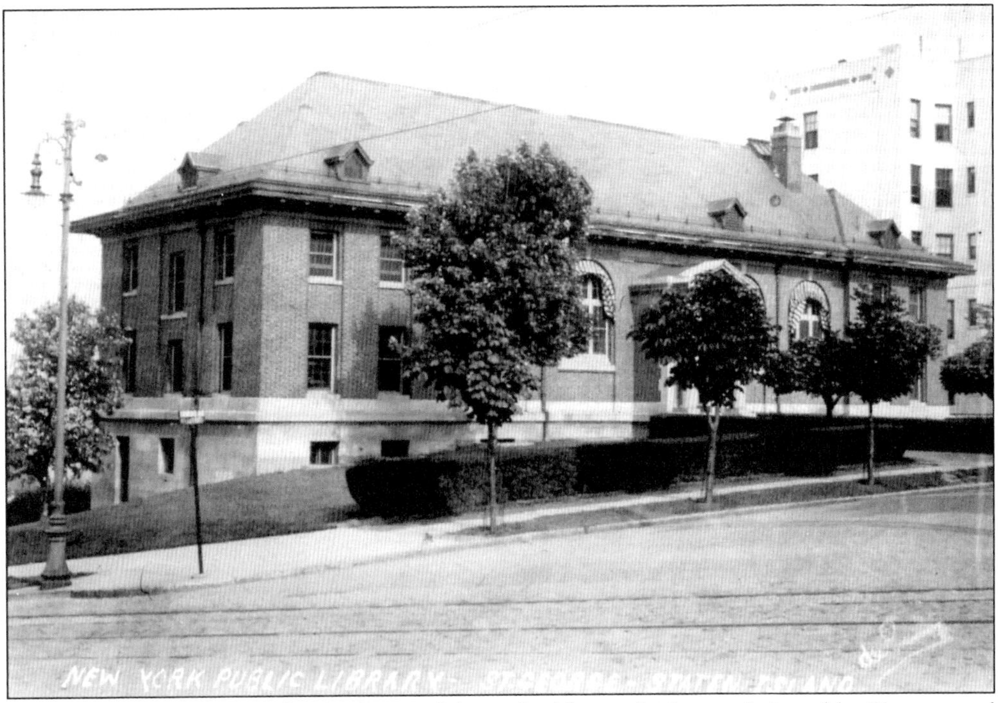

The postcard view shows the St. George Library building, which was designed by Carrere and Hastings and opened on June 26, 1907. (Collection of Daniel Kursrow.)

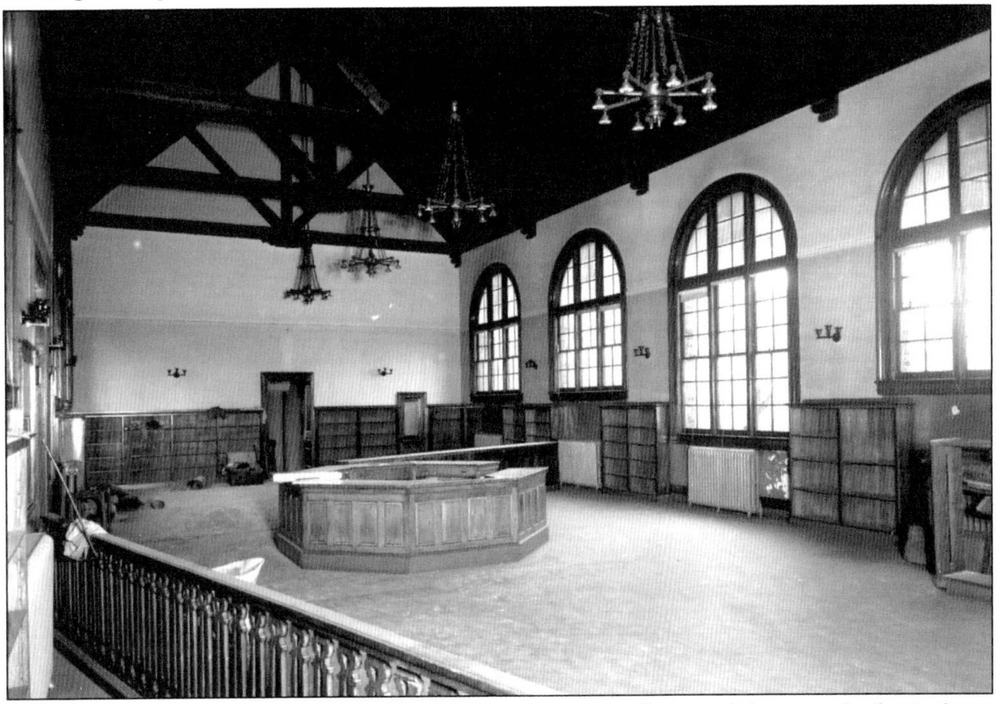

The interior of the St. George Library has a soaring ceiling and large arched windows. The books have yet to be "reinstalled" after this early 1950s restoration of the then nearly 50-year-old building.

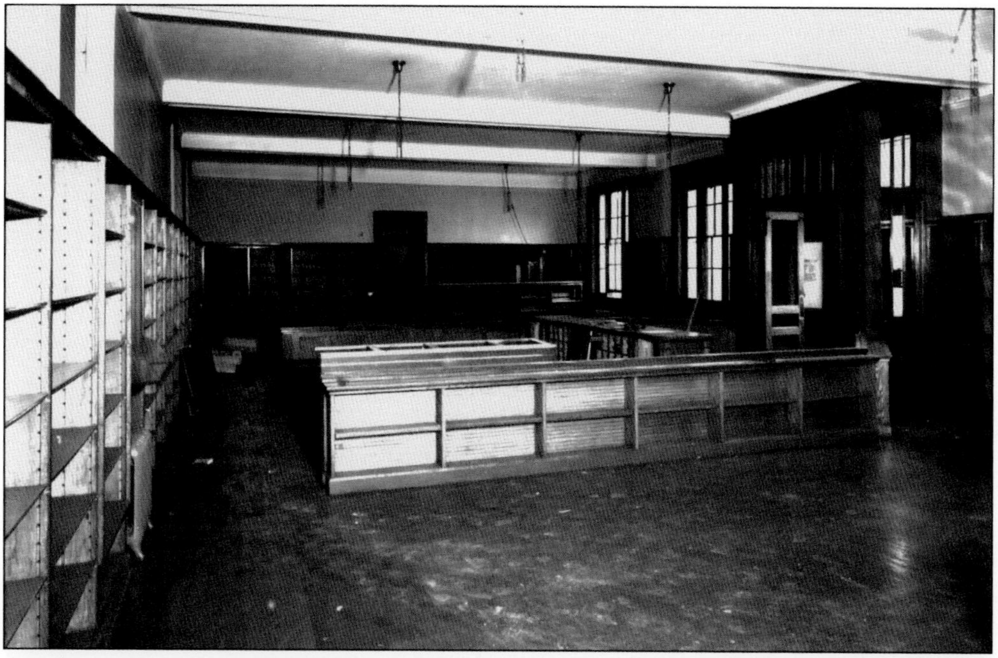

Another reading room at the St. George Library is under construction. The new lighting fixtures have yet to be installed during the 1950s restoration.

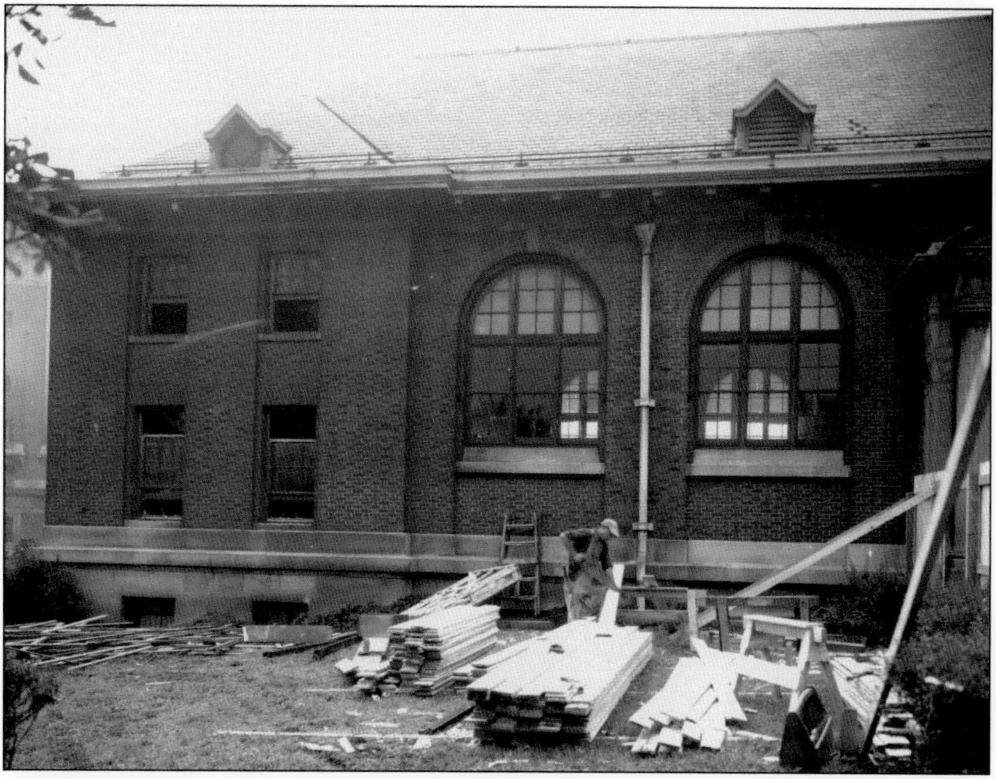

A carpenter works outside of the St. George Library using a hand saw. The photograph is dated September 14, 1950, as the library was undergoing a complete update and restoration.

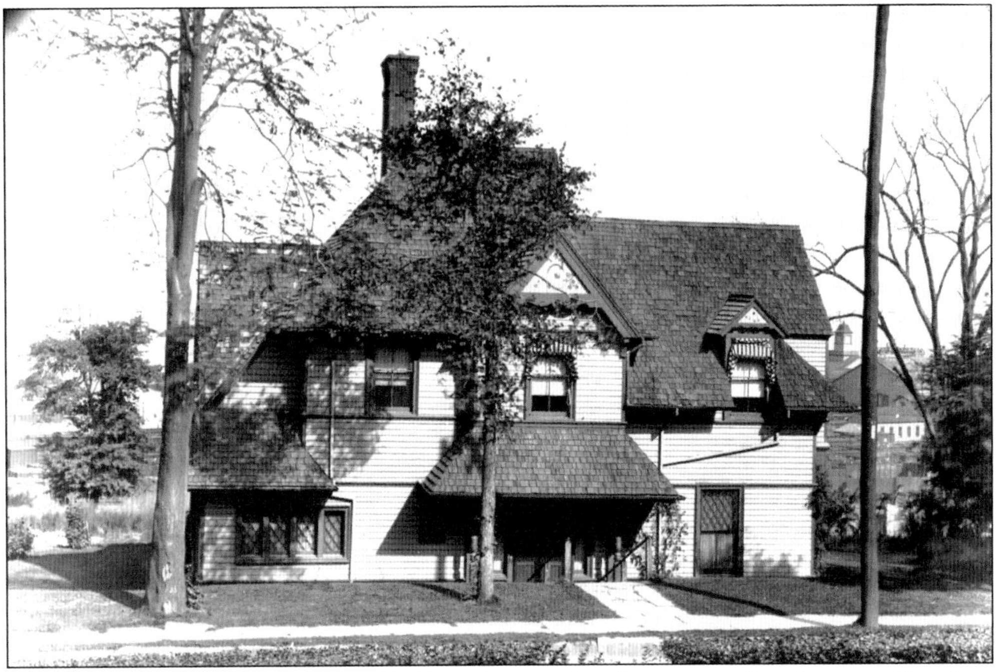

The American Legion headquarters building that stood on Stuyvesant Place between Hamilton Avenue and West Street is the epitome of small-town America with its wood shingled roof and striped awnings. The block today is filled with low-rise buildings housing small businesses.

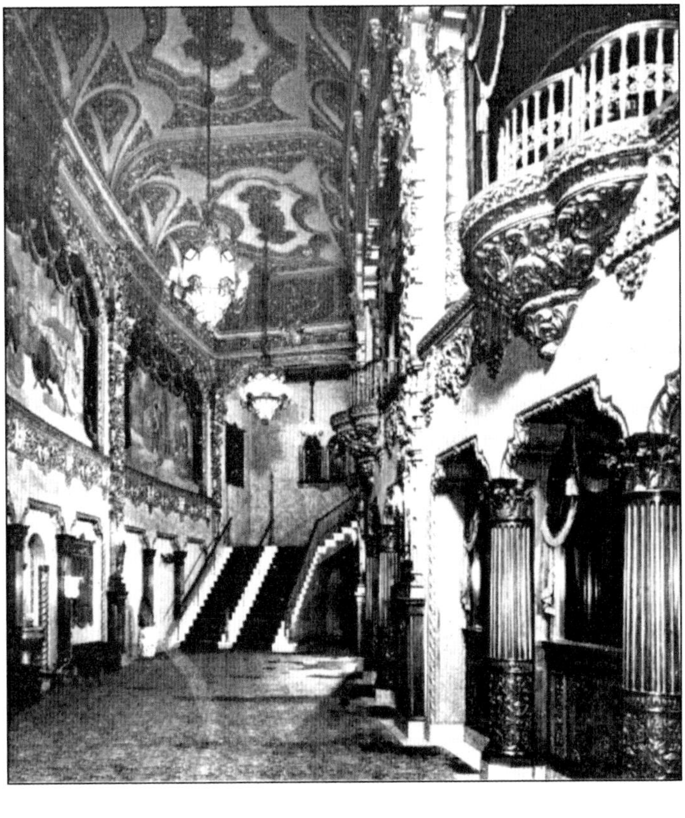

This picture shows the exuberant interior decoration of the St. George Theater lobby, the last great movie "palace" on Staten Island. The theater was built by Solomon Brill and opened on December 4, 1929. It originally sat 2,800 and was considered the most magnificent of the island's many theaters. The interior is of the Spanish and Italian Baroque styles and was designed by Eugene DeRosa, who was assisted by Staten Island architect James Whitford.

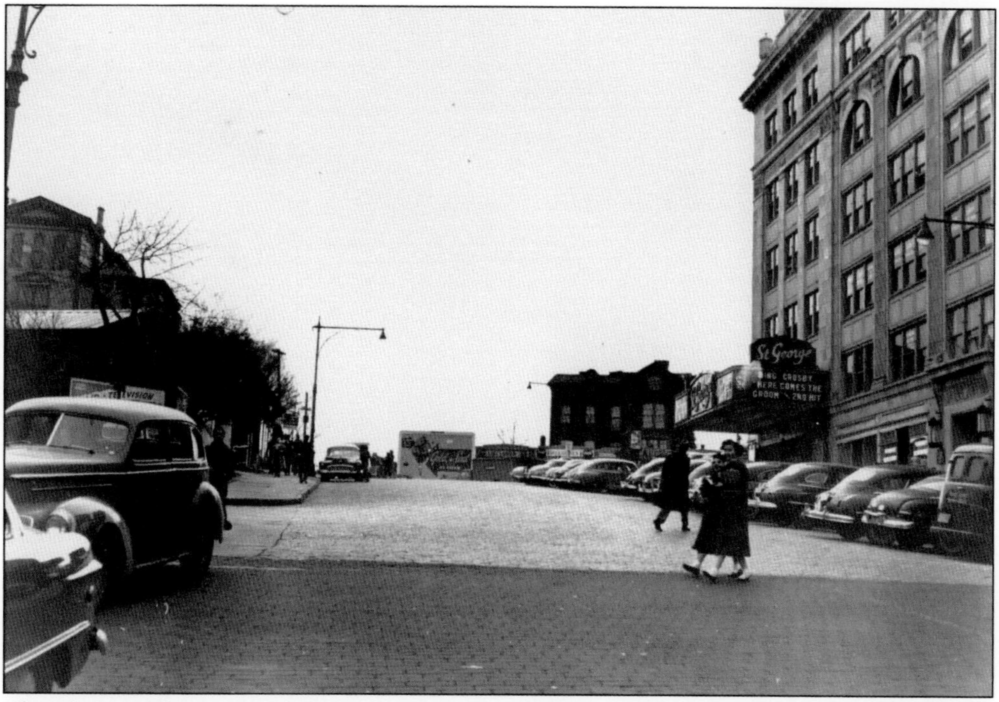

This photograph is a time capsule of information. The St. George Theater marquee heralds the 1951 movie *Here Comes the Groom*, starring Bing Crosby; in the distance is the empty lot of the demolished minister's residence of the Brighton Heights Reformed Church; and to its left is empty land where once stood large Victorian-era homes that have been demolished for the 350 St. Mark's Place office building. Across Hyatt Street stands a mansion built on the quarantine burial grounds, later razed to make way for the municipal parking lot.

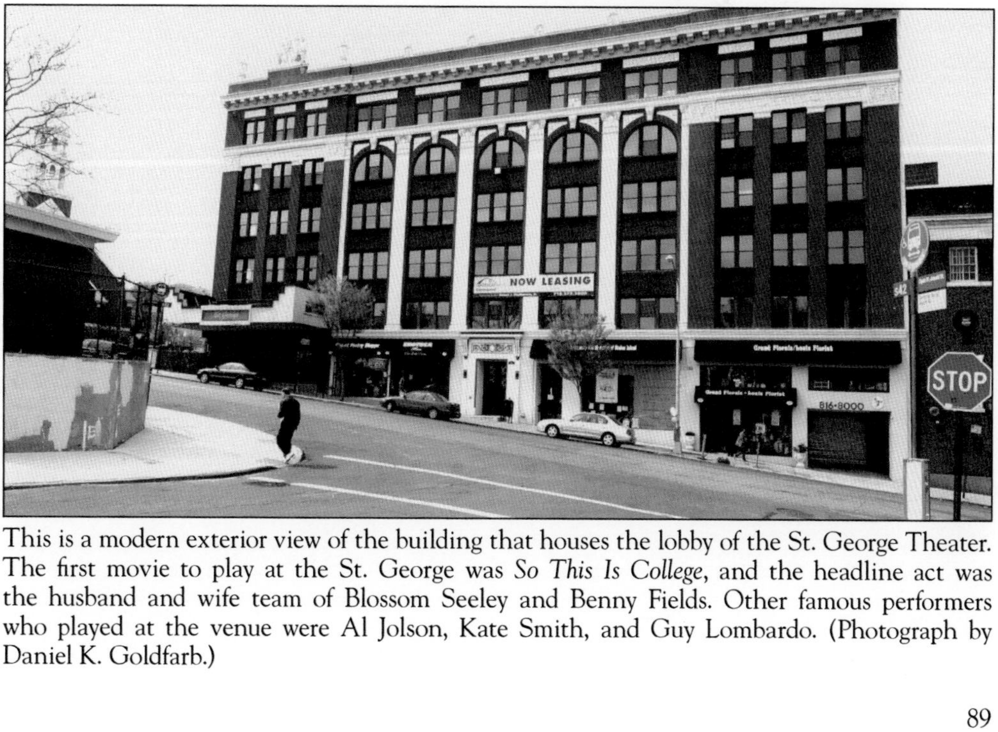

This is a modern exterior view of the building that houses the lobby of the St. George Theater. The first movie to play at the St. George was *So This Is College*, and the headline act was the husband and wife team of Blossom Seeley and Benny Fields. Other famous performers who played at the venue were Al Jolson, Kate Smith, and Guy Lombardo. (Photograph by Daniel K. Goldfarb.)

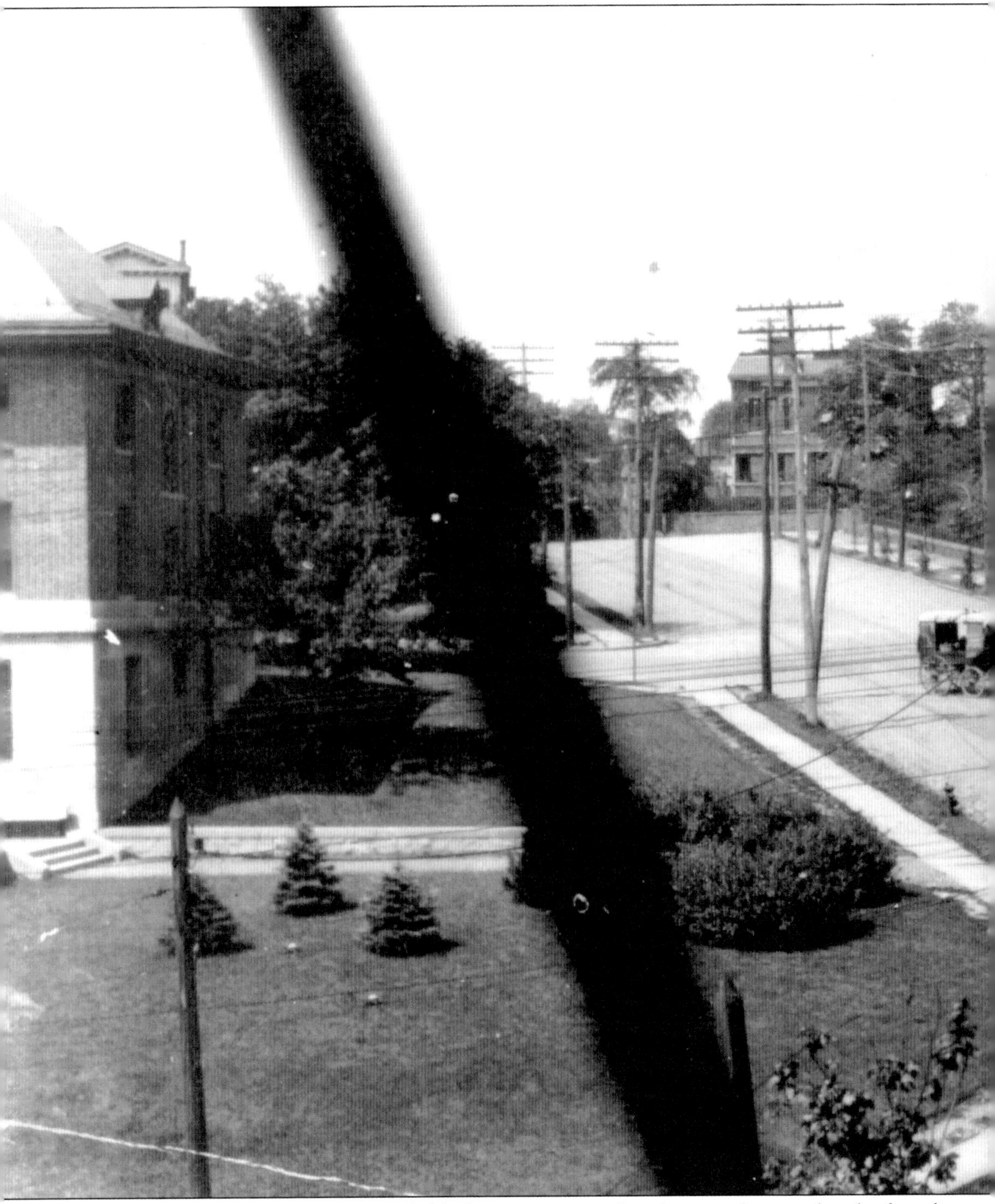

This view up Hyatt Street is remarkable for two reasons; the photograph was taken by famed Staten Island architect Edward Alfred Sargent, and it shows that there was trolley service up the steep incline at one time. Anyone who has walked up the hill knows that it is a trip that would

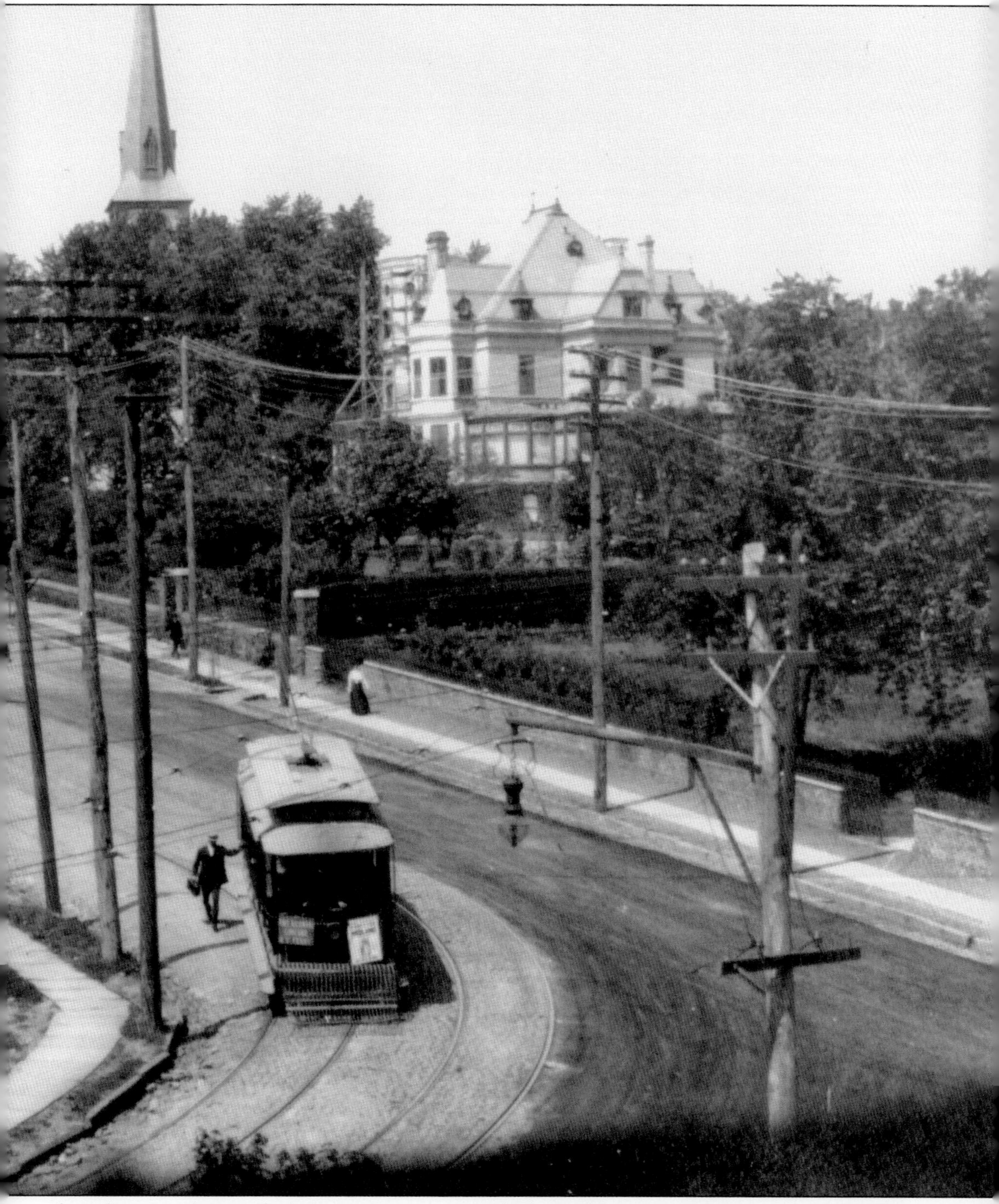

have been much easier by hopping on a moving vehicle, as the man carrying a briefcase is doing. Note the St. George Library has been completed and landscaped, but the fabulous Tiedeman mansion still stands to the right where the St. George Theater was later built.

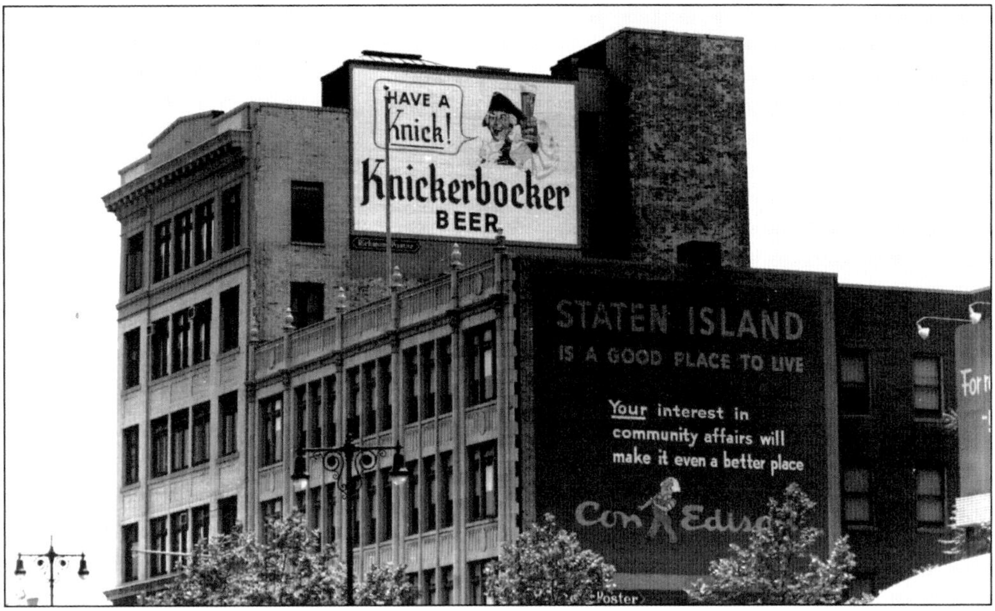

These are some of the first "skyscrapers" built along Bay Street. The building to the right housed the offices of Con Edison at 50 Bay Street.

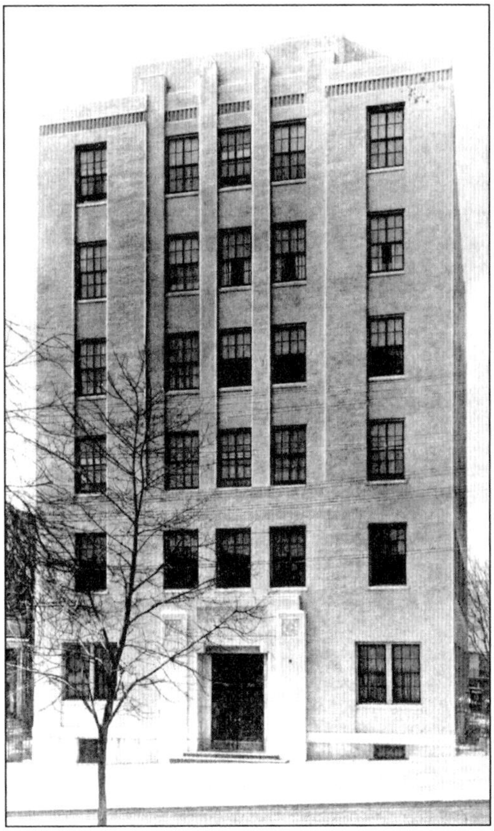

The medical arts building at 100 Central Avenue in all its art deco–glamour is today part of the Project Hospitality shelters for the homeless.

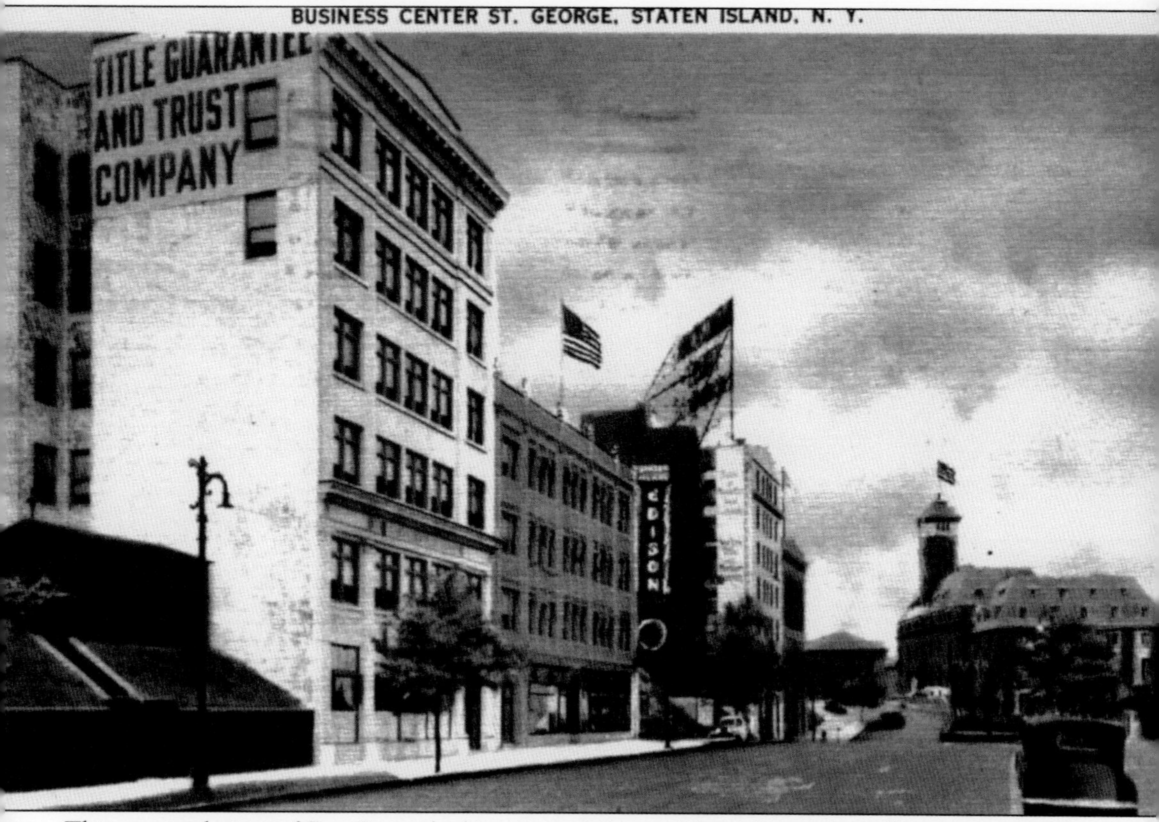

This postcard view of Bay Street looking toward Staten Island Borough Hall is postmarked January 21, 1941, and shows the business center that St. George had become. Note the small carriage house and retaining wall to the extreme left of the postcard. Obviously one of the original homes that had Bay Street or Central Avenue addresses still stood in 1941. Today there is a large office building on that property. (Collection of David Goldfarb.)

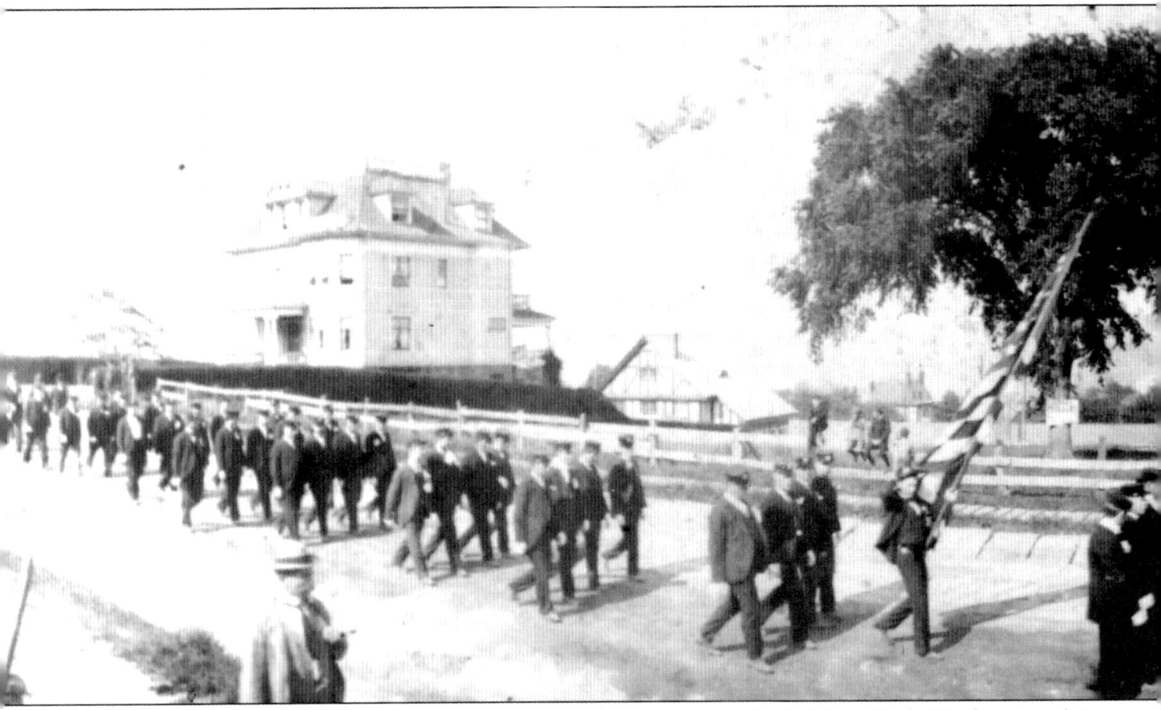

Wonderful Victorian-era homes along Central Avenue overlook New York Harbor in this undated photograph of a parade. The men at the right are in civilian dress, while the group

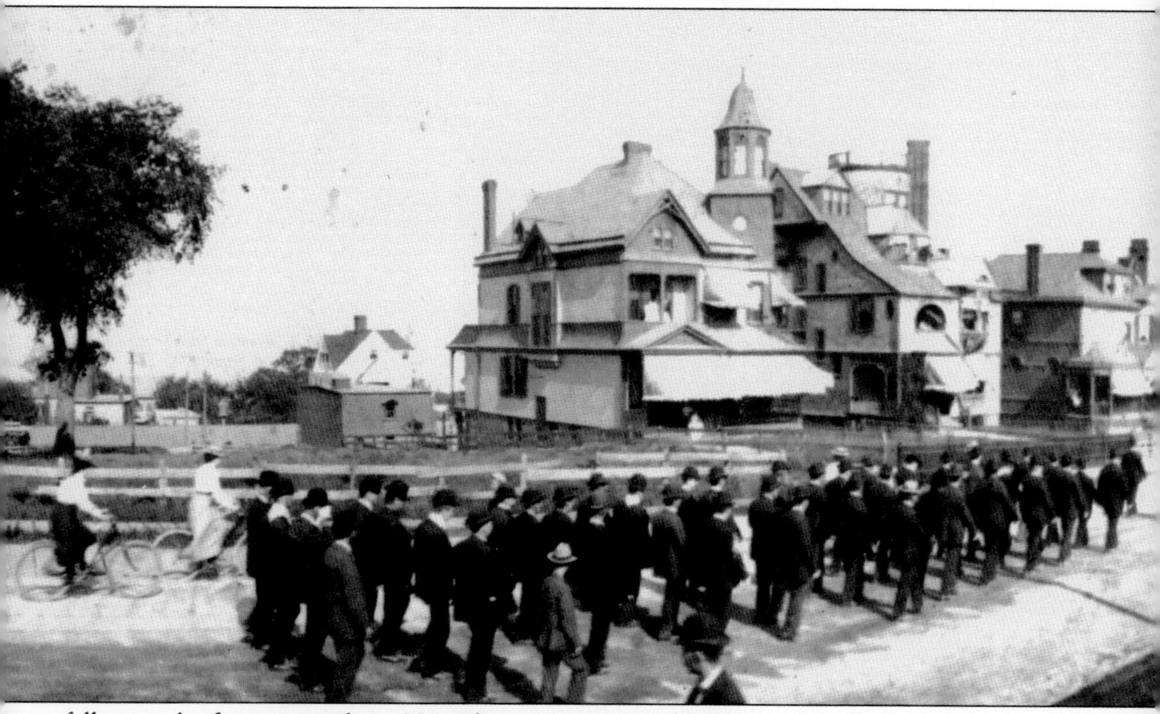

following the flag is in uniform. Note the two women on bicycles, a sport that was considered genteel enough for the "modern" woman.

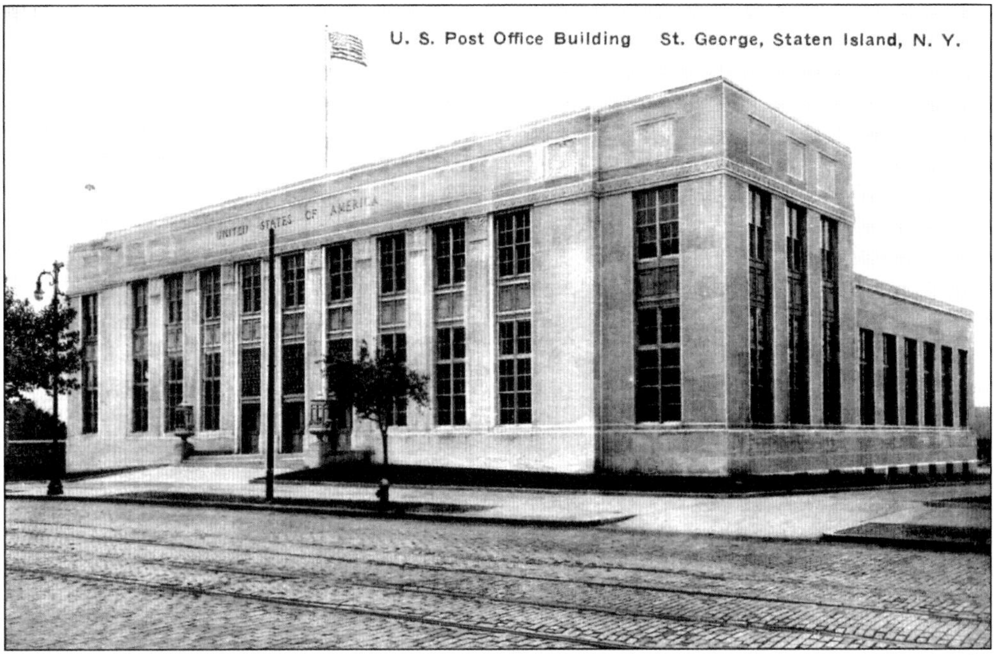

These are two views of the St. George Post Office on Bay Street. Today the post office serves the 10301 zip code. (Collection of David Goldfarb.)

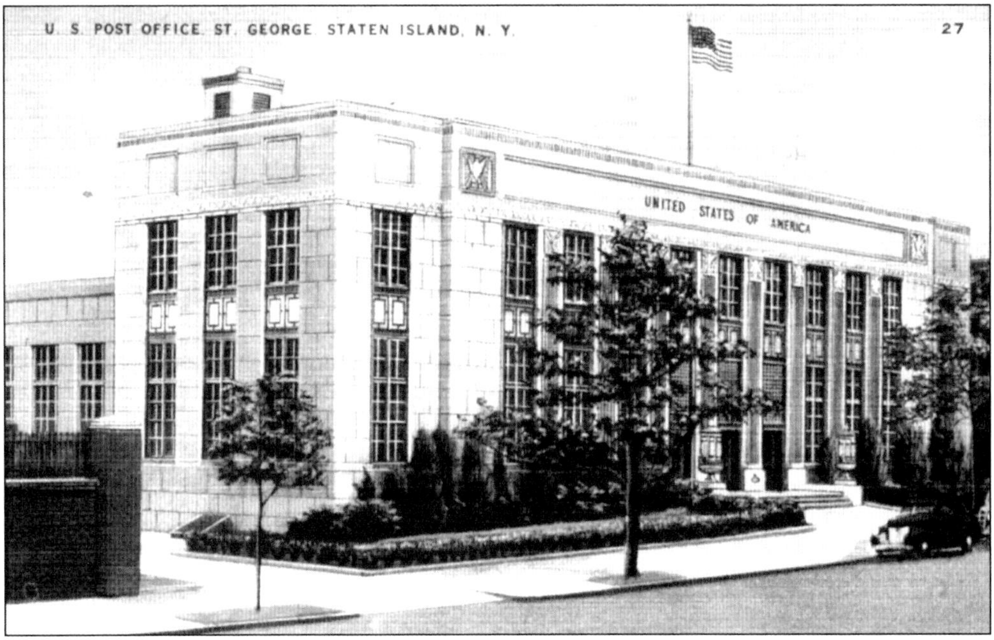

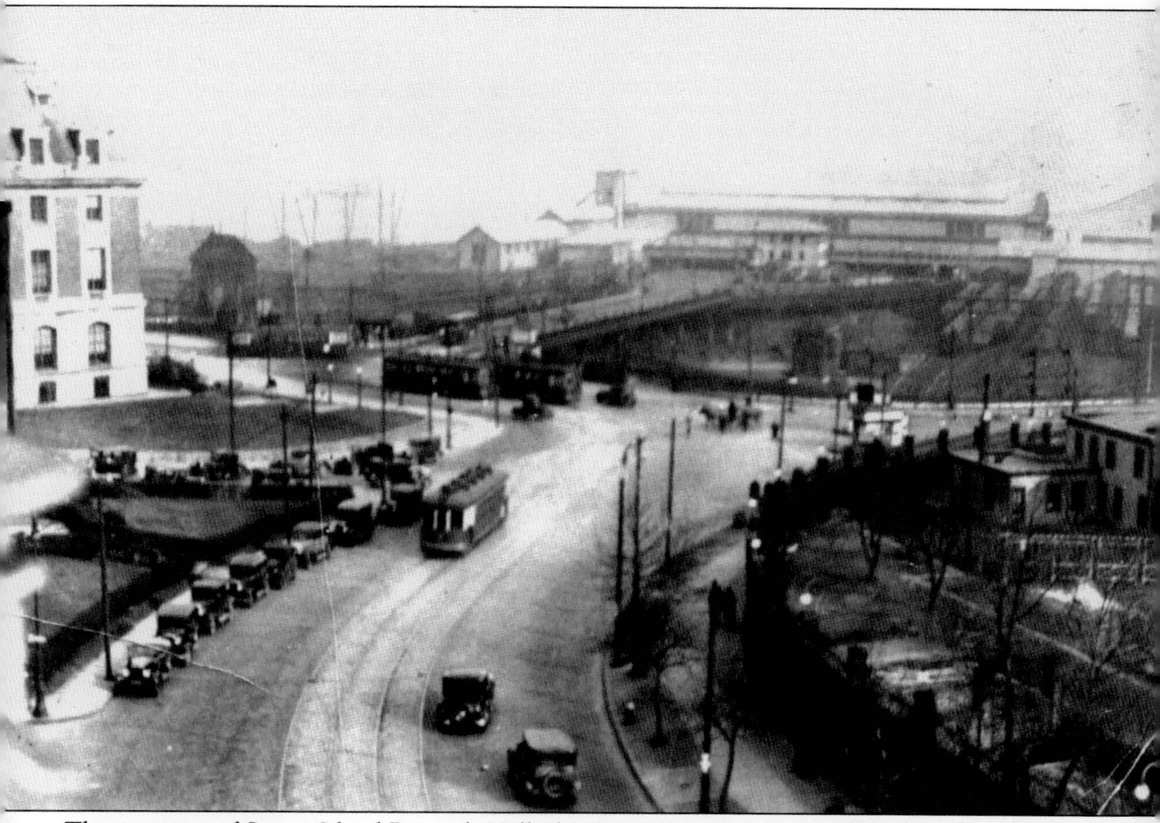

This is a view of Staten Island Borough Hall, the Coast Guard station, and the ferry terminal. Note the brick wall around the Coast Guard station that, except for a recent opening for a driveway, still stands today.

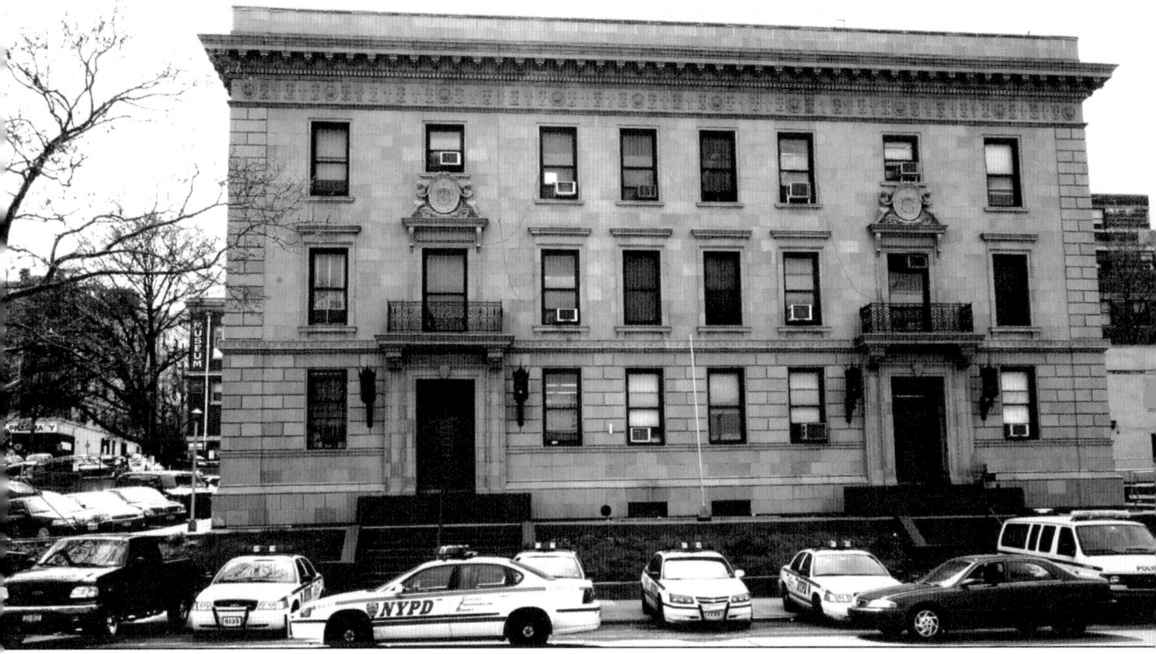

The 120th Police Precinct Station House (former 66th Police Precinct Station House and Headquarters) was designed by James Whitford Sr. and built in 1920–1923. Whitford was called the "dean of Staten Island architects." The building was designated a New York City landmark in 2000. (Photograph by Daniel K. Goldfarb.)

Six

The Staten Island Ferry and Transportation Hub

The concept of ferry service from Staten Island to New York began almost as soon as early Dutch settlers inhabited the island. Cornelius Vanderbilt saw the potential in carrying people and supplies across the bay early in his life and became quite successful running his own small boat, but it was not until Gov. Daniel D. Tompkins's arrival on Staten Island in 1814 that a plan for transportation both to and across Staten Island was created.

In 1816, Tompkins incorporated his Richmond Turnpike Company to create a toll road from the Watering Place, where the ferry service from New York terminated. Passengers disembarked to a waiting coach to ride the turnpike to another ferry at Blazing Star (Travis) for the trip to New Jersey, and then by coach to Philadelphia. In 1817, the Richmond Turnpike Company ran the first motorized ferry between New York and Staten Island.

By 1838, the ferry service had been purchased by Vanderbilt, who in turn sold it during the Civil War to the Staten Island Railway. There were other ferries in operation at the time, and by 1884, all competing ferry service had been sold to the Baltimore and Ohio Railroad and operated by the Staten Island Rapid Transit Railroad, a plan implemented by Erastus Wiman, along with his partners William Pendleton and Robert Garrett. Pendleton managed the North Shore Ferry, while Garrett was president of the railroad. Wiman's plan included connecting the ferries with the rail lines and moving the ferry terminal to St. George.

Ferry service between the Whitehall Terminal in Manhattan and the St. George terminal on Staten Island was transferred to the New York City Department of Docks and Ferries on October 25, 1905, and a new terminal was dedicated. This building was destroyed by fire in 1947, and a new terminal building opened in 1949. The current ferry terminals in Manhattan and Staten Island are wonderfully contemporary in style and house the thousands of commuters and tourists who crowd them daily to await the free ferry ride across the harbor that offers some of the most breathtaking views of the Manhattan skyline available.

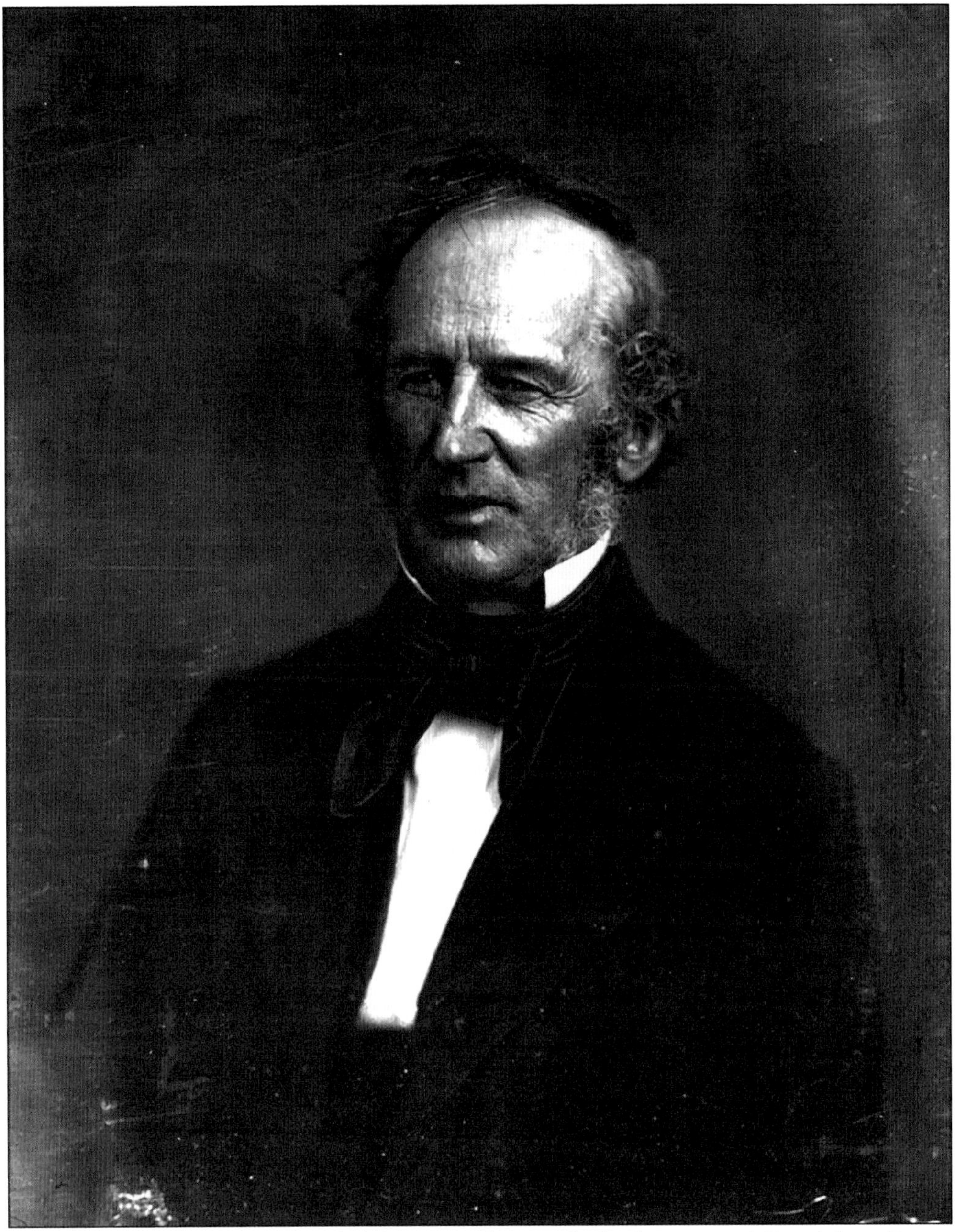

Eighteen-year-old Cornelius Vanderbilt operated a speedy flat boat named *Dread* from Staten Island to New York City by 1812. These "periaguas," as they were known, were propelled by oars and a square sail, and often carried animals as well as passengers across the bay. Born on Staten Island, by 1817, Vanderbilt was running a steam ferry service between New York City and New Brunswick, New Jersey, where he lived until 1829, returning to Staten Island that same year. Vanderbilt was Staten Island's first millionaire. This daguerreotype attributed to Matthew Brady shows "the Commodore" later in his life. (Courtesy of Library of Congress.)

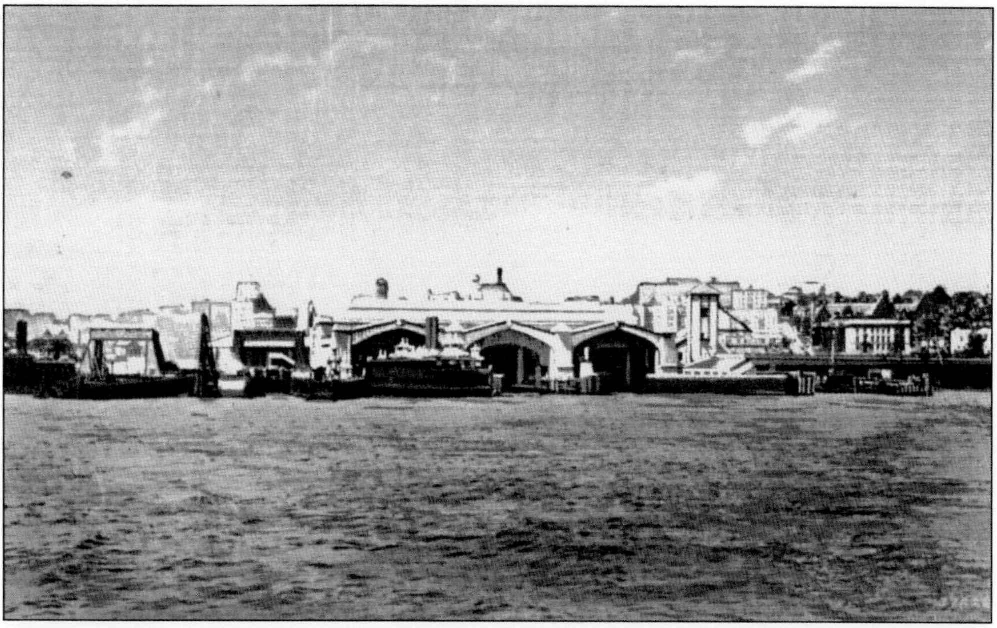

"St. George Ferry Terminal, Staten Island" is the title of this postcard, showing a ferryboat in its slip and a very low-rise landscape along the St. George shoreline. (Collection of David Goldfarb.)

On July 30, 1871, the boiler exploded on the ferryboat *Westfield*, while it was in its slip at South Ferry in Manhattan, causing one of the worst ferry disasters in history. Some 85 persons were killed and hundreds injured. Jacob Vanderbilt, president of the Staten Island Railway, was arrested for murder but was not convicted. The engraving by W. Long Palen is from the August 12, 1871, edition of *Harper's Weekly*. (Collection of David Goldfarb.)

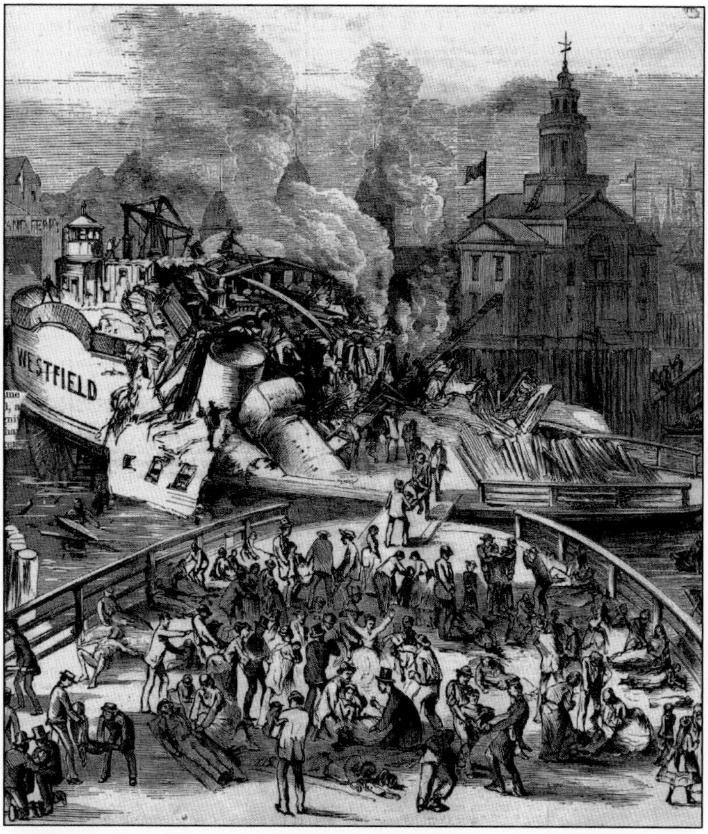

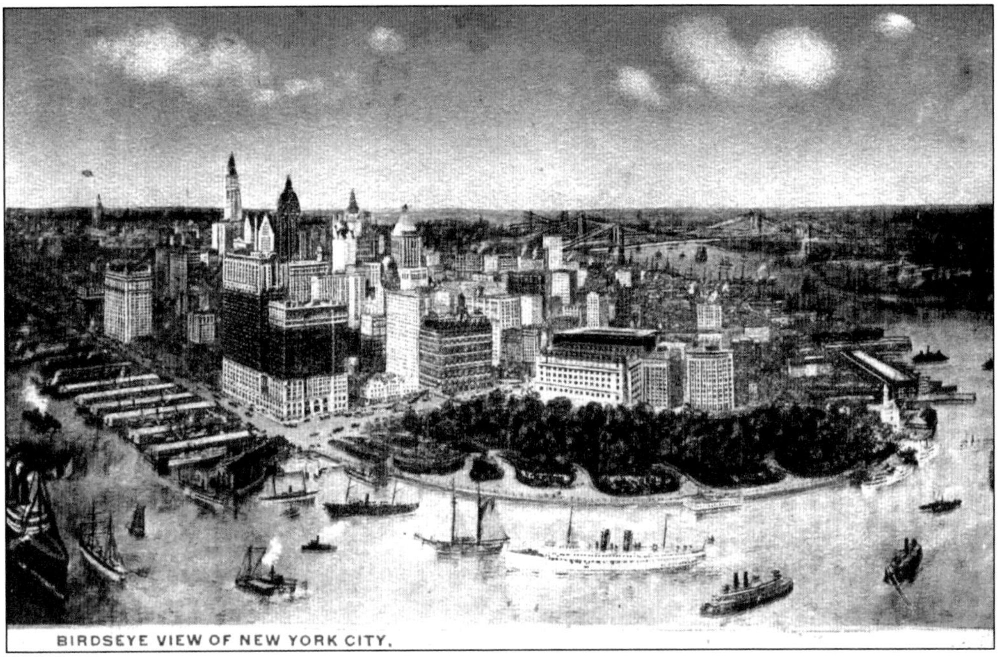

This postcard view shows the ferryboat nearing the slips at lower Manhattan. The ferry terminal is on the right hand side of the picture. (Collection of James G. Ferreri.)

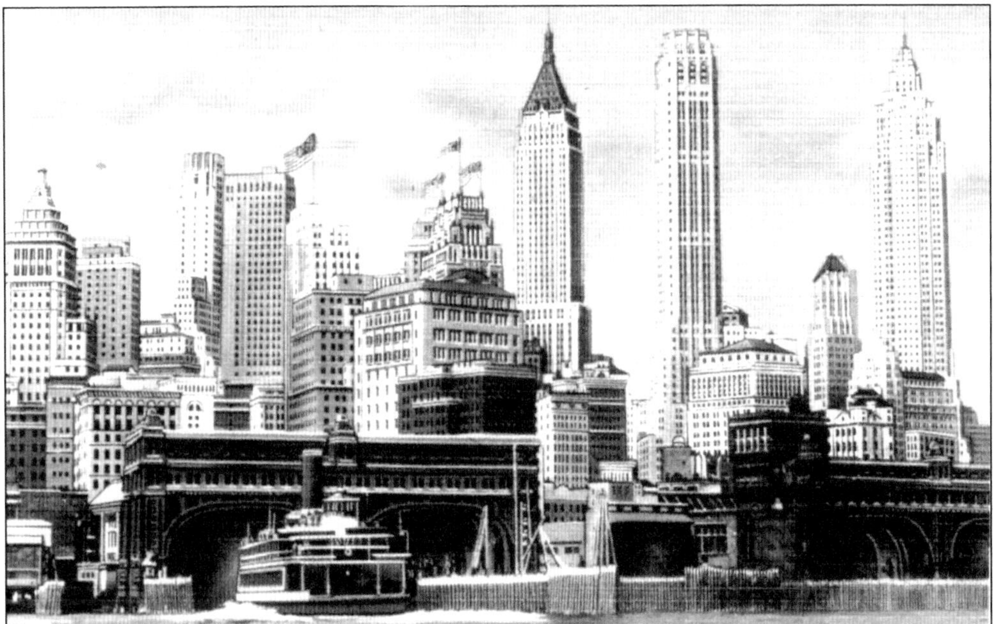

This later postcard titled "Downtown Skyline from Staten Island Ferry" shows a boat entering a ferry slip with a view of New York City's world famous skyline behind it. (Collection of David Goldfarb.)

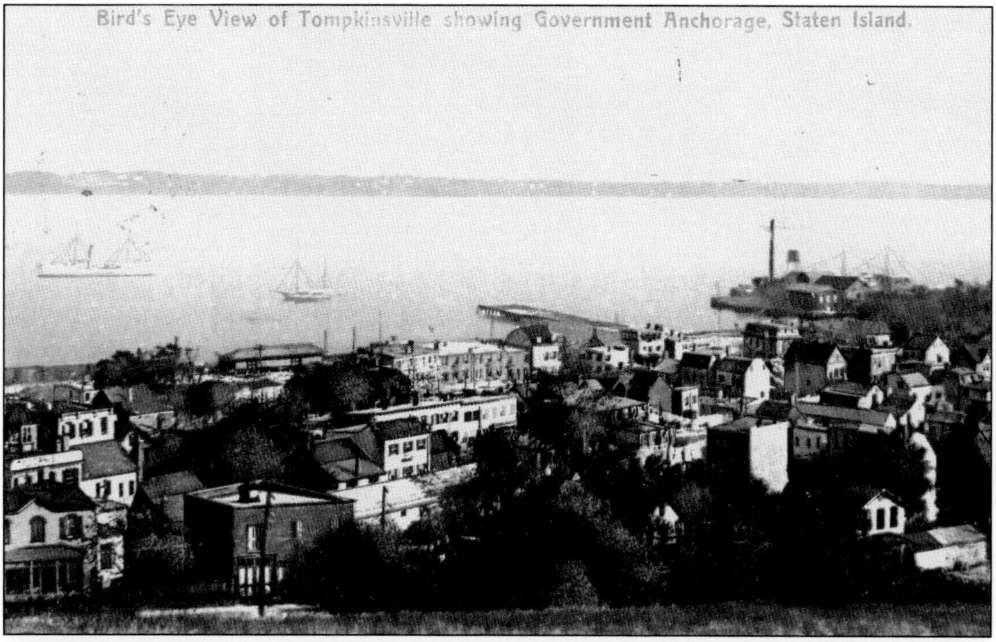

Another postcard view of early-20th-century Staten Island's shore shows a bird's-eye view of government anchorage, near Tompkinsville, showing tall sailing ships in the harbor. (Collection of David Goldfarb.)

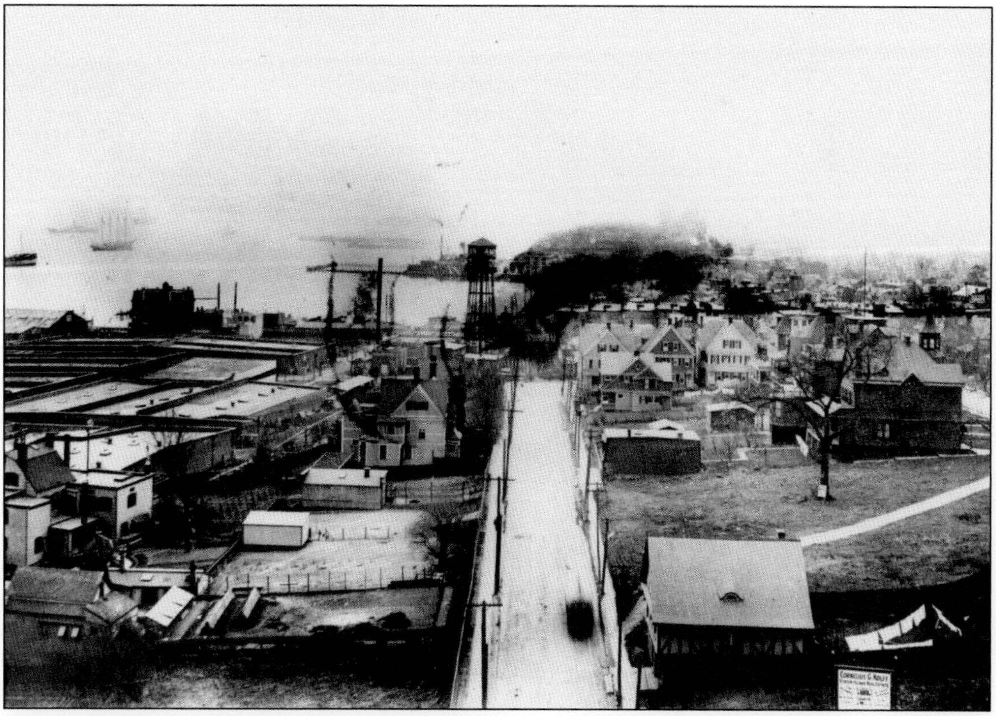

This early photograph taken from Staten Island Borough Hall shows Bay Street looking south, past the former quarantine station on the left. Note the tall sailing ships off shore.

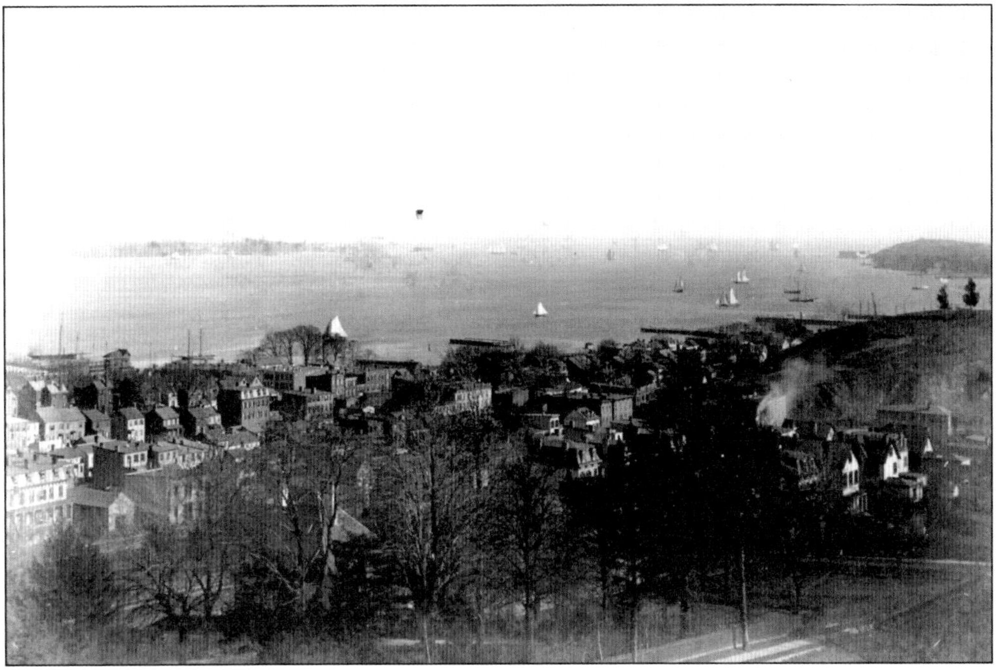

This view taken from Brighton Heights shows a shoreline and harbor bustling with maritime activity. The undeveloped hill at the right is "Pavilion Hill," today known as Ward Hill.

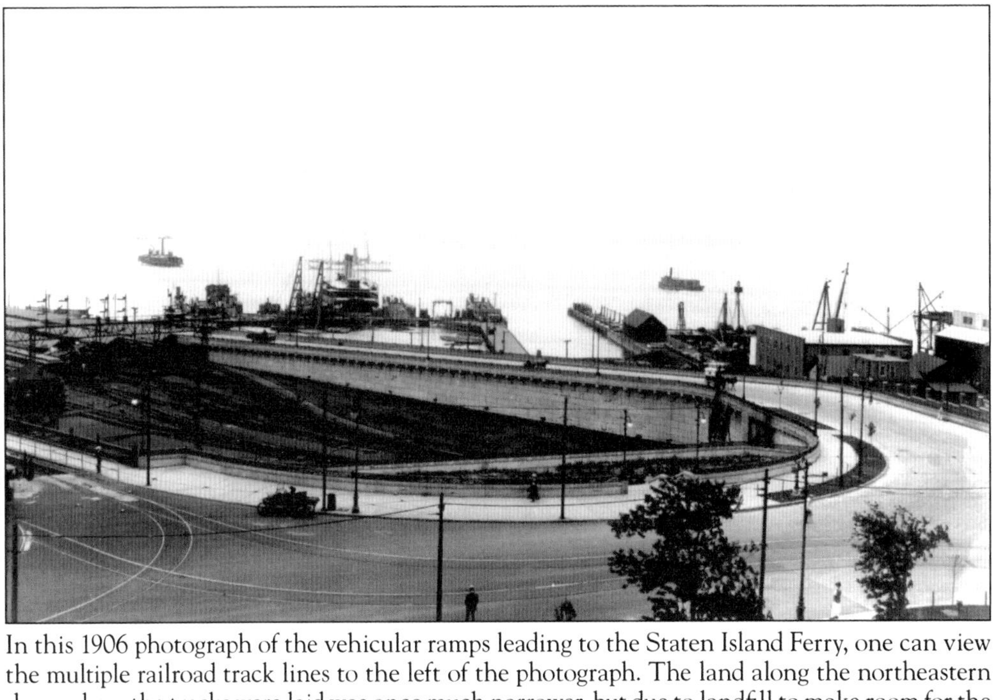

In this 1906 photograph of the vehicular ramps leading to the Staten Island Ferry, one can view the multiple railroad track lines to the left of the photograph. The land along the northeastern shore where the tracks were laid was once much narrower, but due to landfill to make room for the expanding railroad hub what was once beach-front property became much more utilitarian.

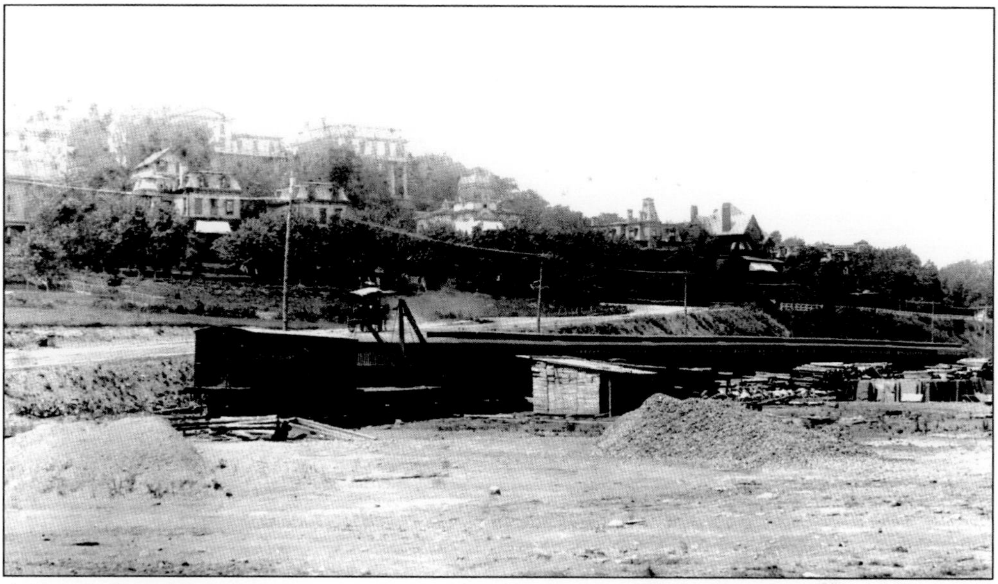

A Staten Island rapid transit train arrives in St. George. This photograph was taken years before the immense retaining wall was built that today separates the former rail property from Richmond Terrace. In this photograph, it is quite easy to see that the large homes along the shore at one time had access to the beach and shore. Many of these homes had riparian rights written into their deeds as well.

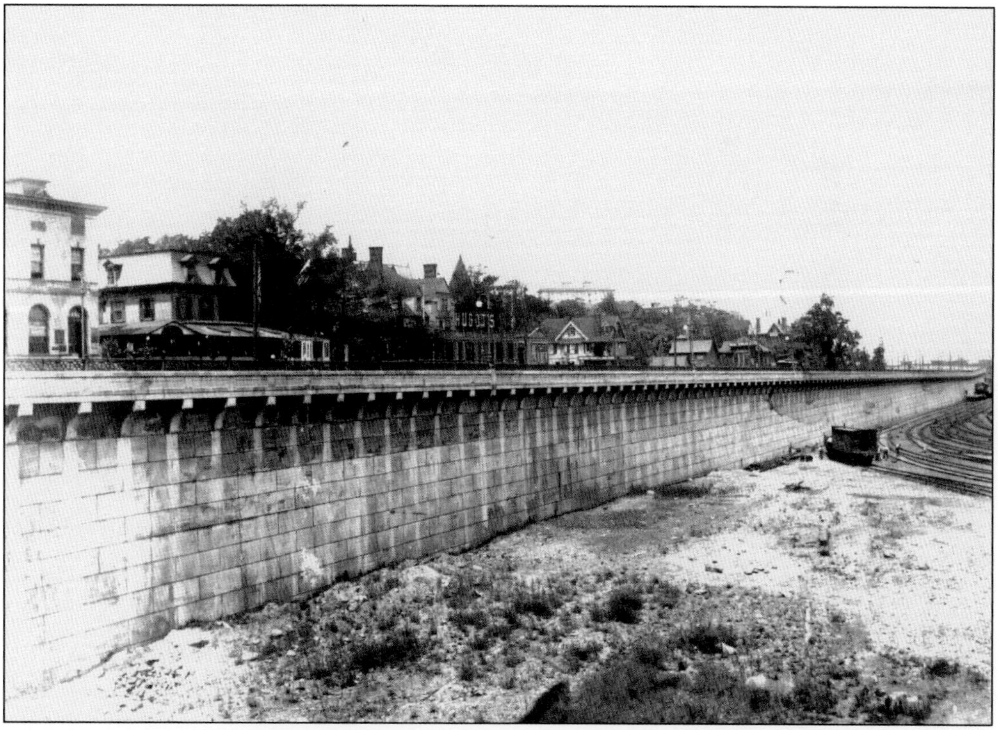

This view of the railroad property at the St. George Ferry shows the newly constructed retaining wall that, in its day, was billed as the "million dollar wall." It was quite a feat of engineering for its time, and today it still separates the ferry parking lots from Richmond Terrace.

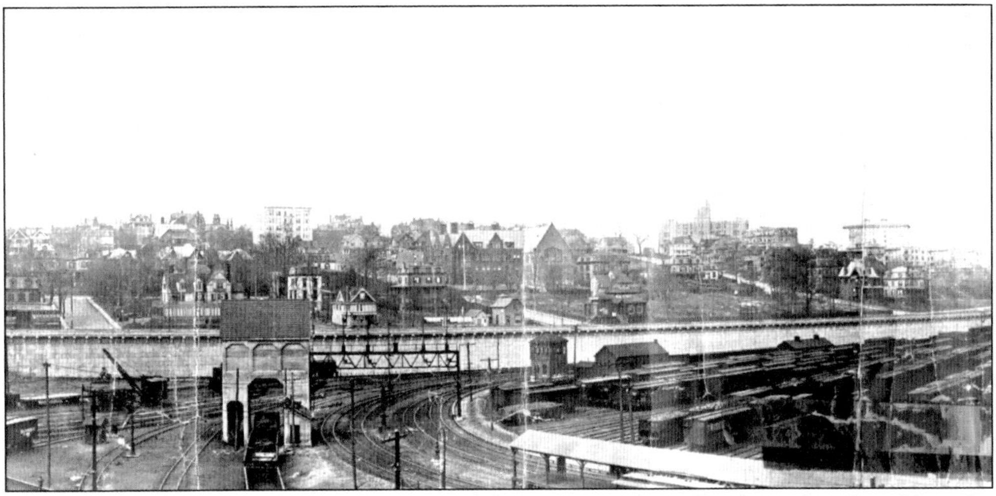

This photograph is a portion of a panorama of the St. George/New Brighton shoreline. Note the many landmarks visible on the hillside, such as Curtis High School to the right and the railroad tracks in the foreground. The large building at the center with the many pointed gables was the original home of the Staten Island Academy. (Collection of James G. Ferreri.)

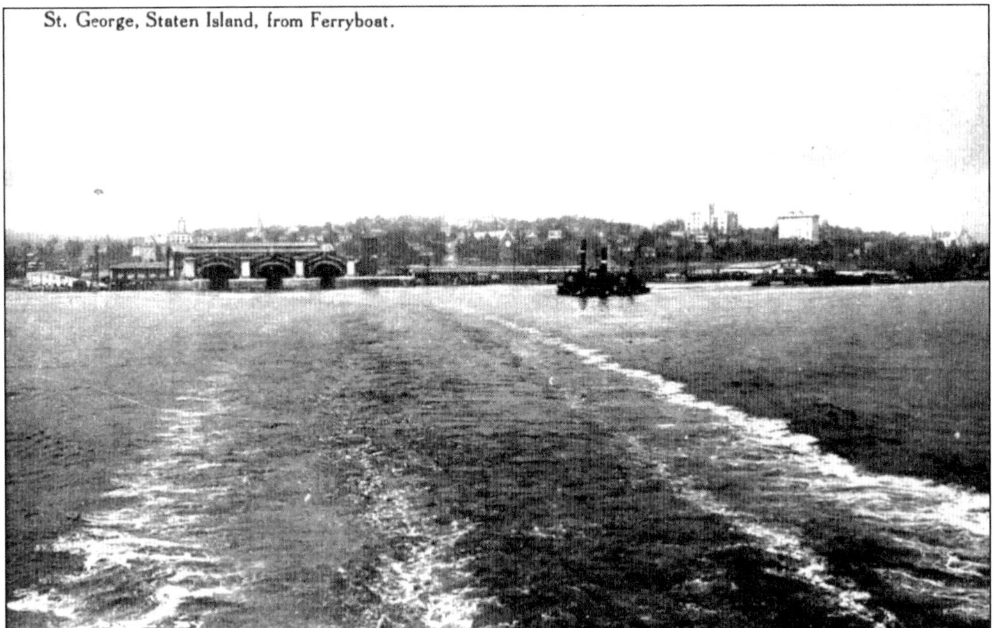

This is a postcard view of St. George and the ferry terminal from a ferryboat. (Collection of David Goldfarb.)

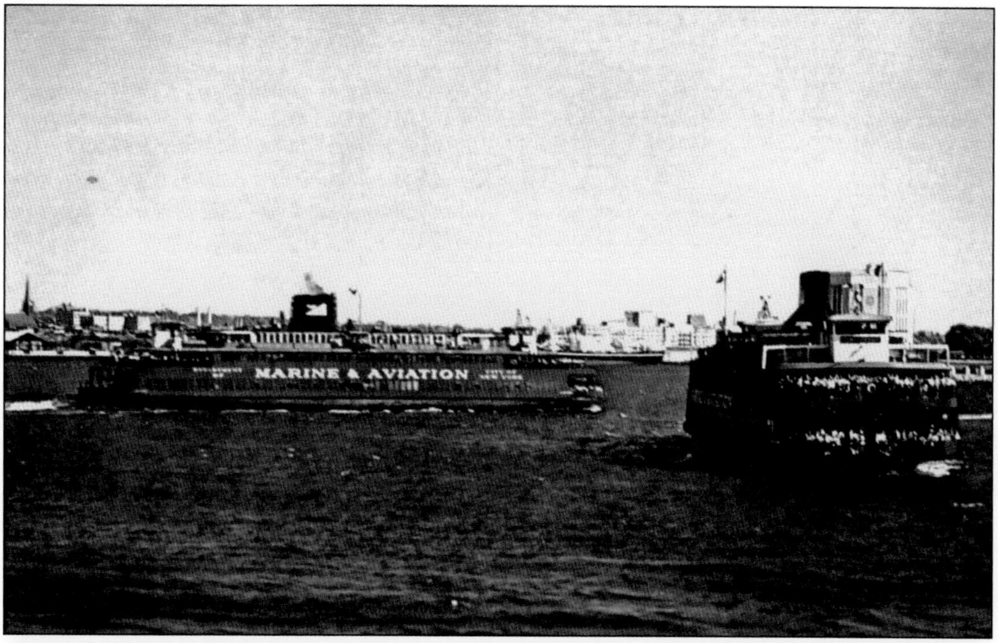

This postcard view shows two ferryboats in the harbor. The caption on the back indicates that the round-the-clock boats carry 26 million people annually on the five-mile trip. (Collection of James G. Ferreri.)

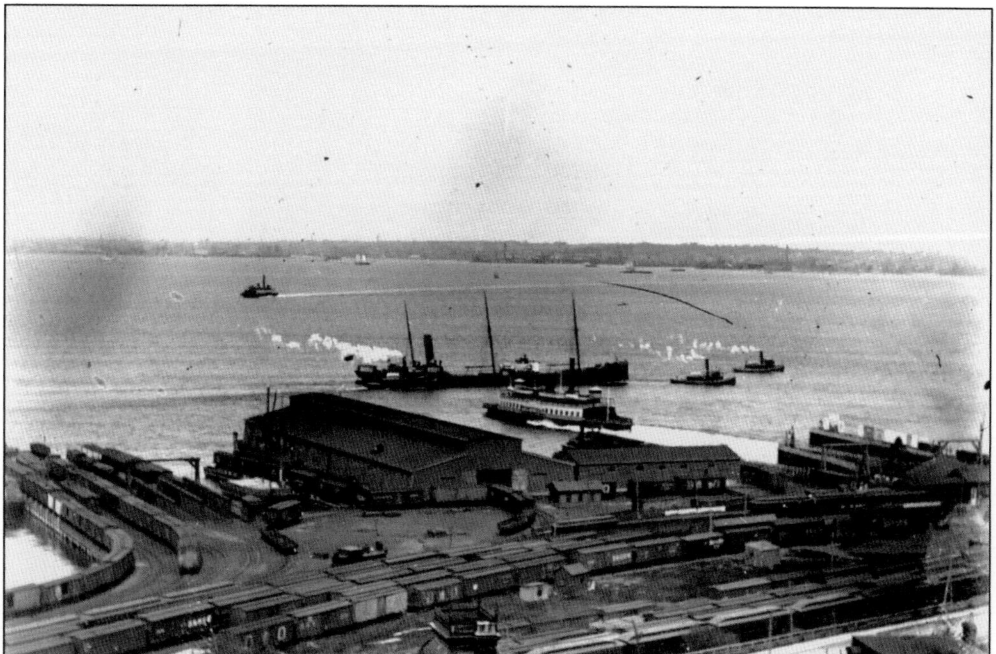

A Staten Island Ferry boat steams into dock near the Baltimore and Ohio Railroad yards in St. George. The photograph is dated 1900 and shows the massive rail system that had accrued by the early 20th century. The shoreline opposite is Brooklyn.

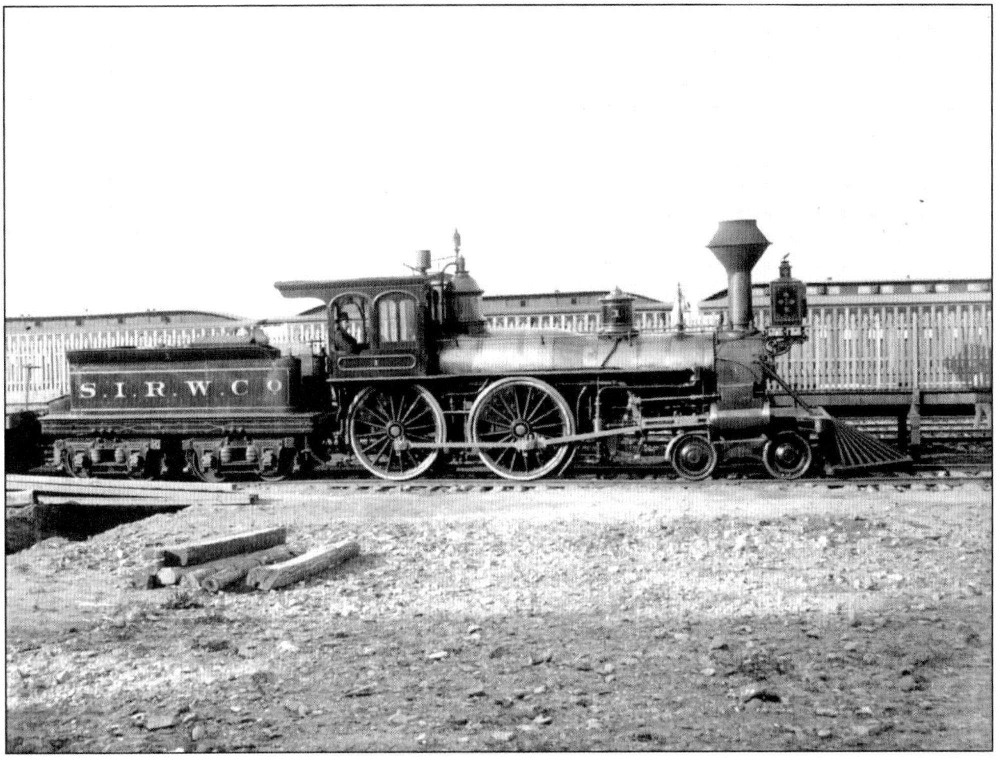

Two early Staten Island rail line locomotives sit at the ready to cross the island. Notice the load of coal behind the engine in the lower photograph. (Collection of David Goldfarb.)

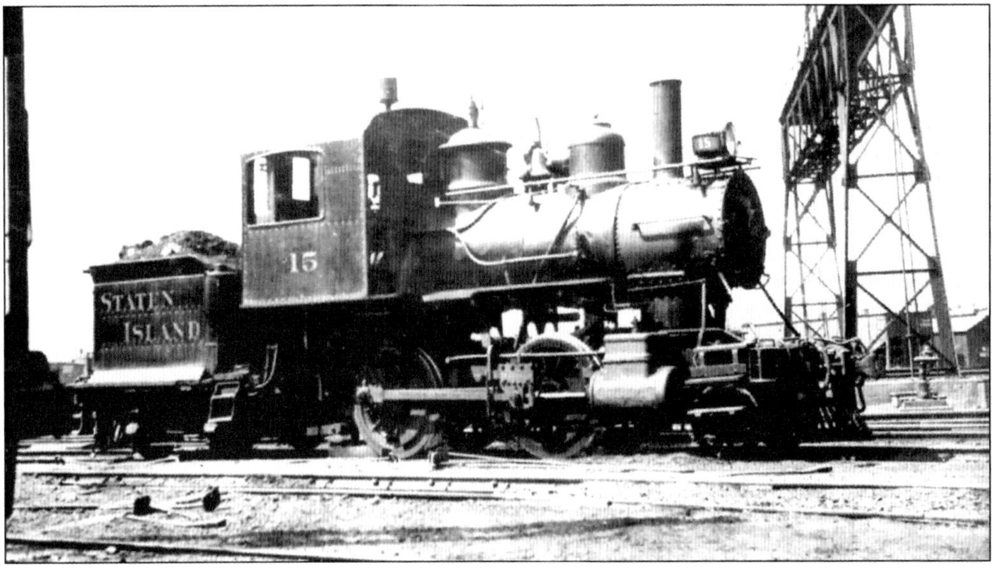

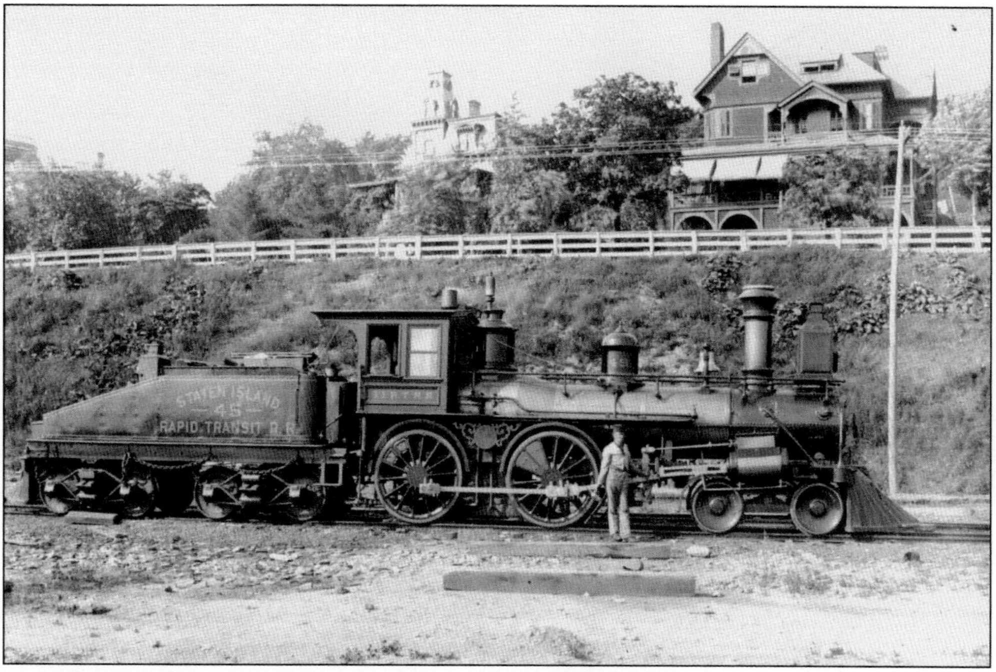

Beautiful shorefront Victorian-era mid- and late-19th century homes that once faced a tranquil beachfront in this picture now face belching locomotives as St. George became the transportation hub of the island. (Collection of David Goldfarb.)

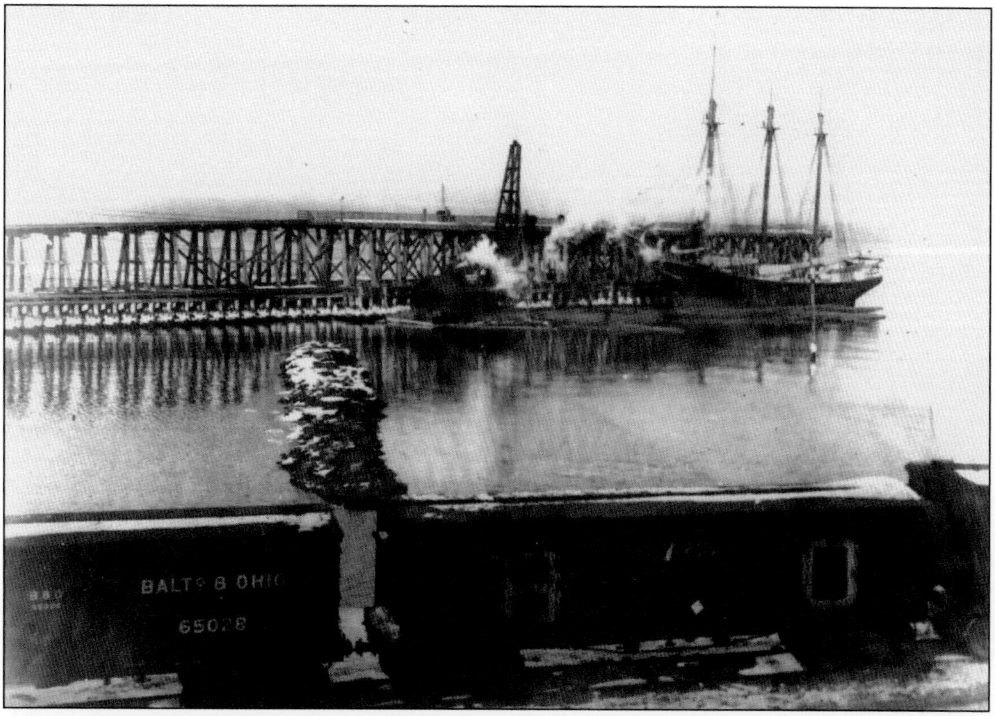

This c. 1900 photograph is annotated "First Coal Dock, St. George." Notice the name painted on the coal carriers is "Baltimore & Ohio Railroad."

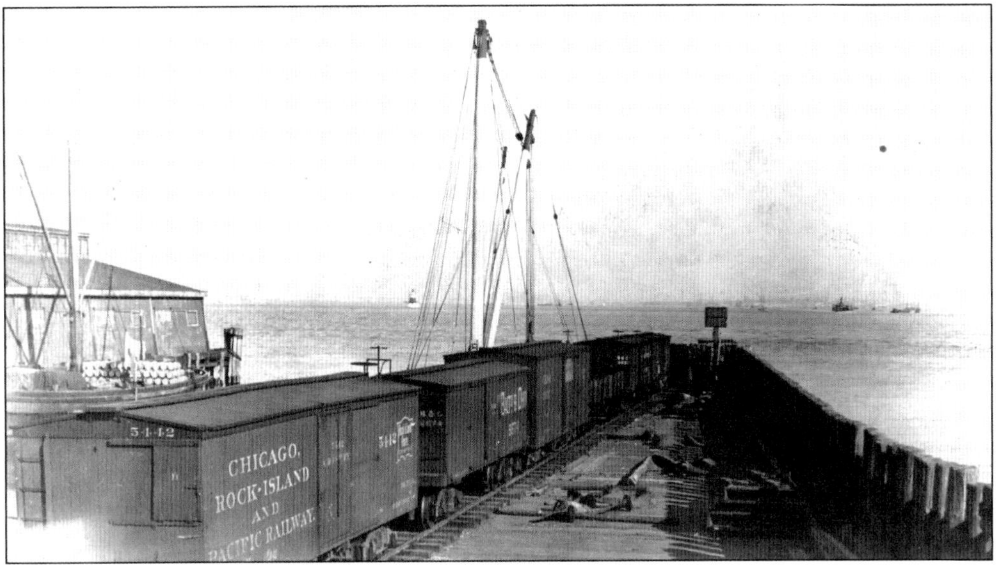

This photograph would be hard to identify except by anyone who has commuted by Staten Island ferry. The railroad cars on the pier and the masts and rigging of the boats almost obscure the small lighthouse to the left of center, visible next to the lines of the mast. Generations of Staten Island commuters can readily recognize this buoy that marks one of the channels in the bay.

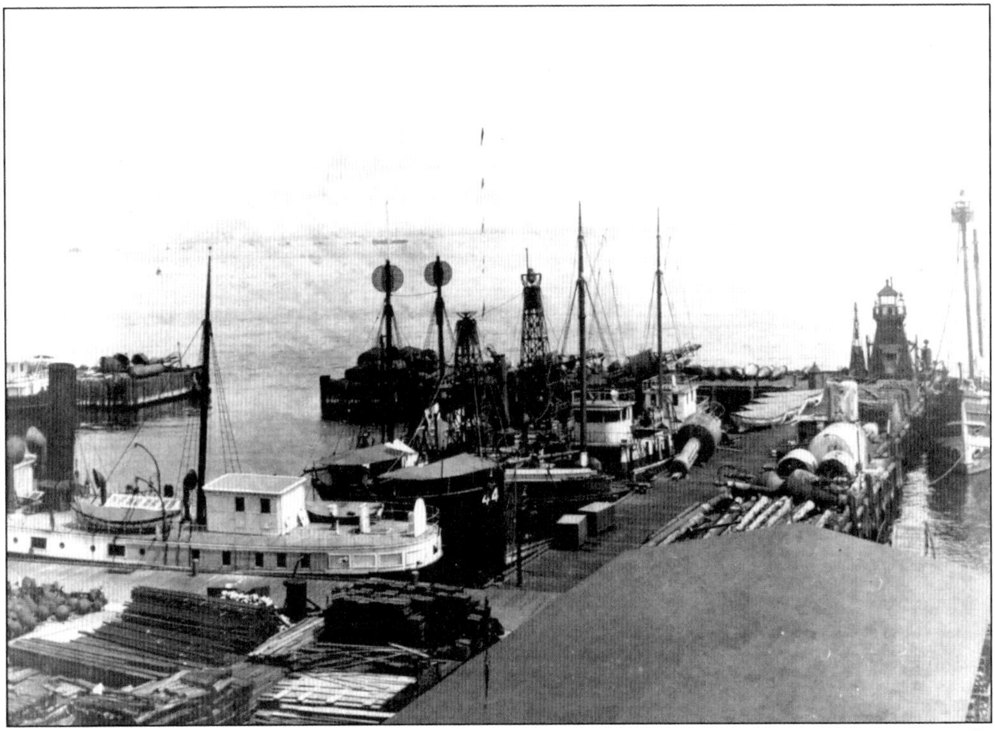

Staten Island's maritime history is well evidenced by this shot of the U.S. Coast Guard's lighthouse depot in St. George. In 1883, a cast-iron lighthouse was built on the pier not as a navigational aid but as a test platform for new oils, lamps, and lenses.

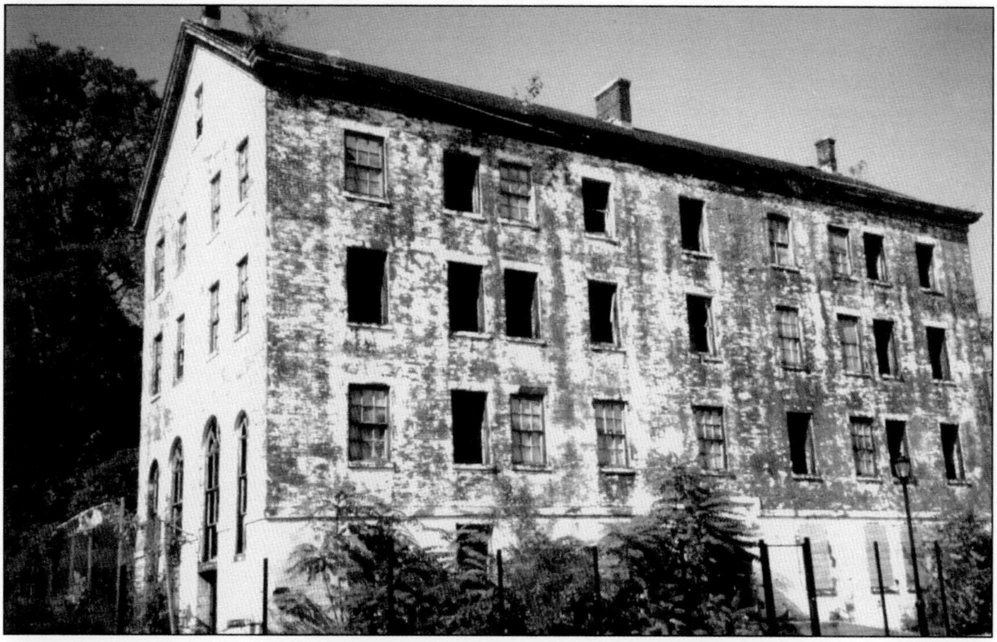

The old lamp shop of the U.S. Lighthouse Depot was constructed as a place to assemble and repair lighthouse lenses, the largest of which stand nearly 18 feet tall and weigh thousands of pounds. The lamp shop was built in 1868. (Collection of David Goldfarb.)

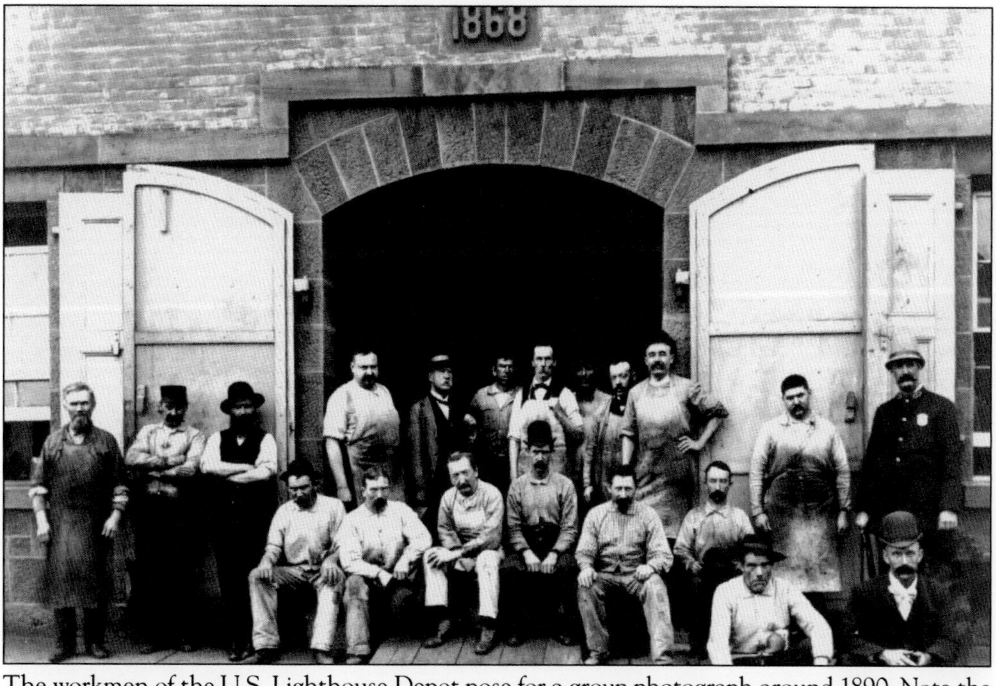

The workmen of the U.S. Lighthouse Depot pose for a group photograph around 1890. Note the construction date above the open doors. This is the oldest building at the U.S. Coast Guard's lighthouse depot, built in 1864, two years after the Light-House Board acquired the land to create the "Super depot." The building was converted to a barrack by the U.S. Coast Guard in the 1940s.

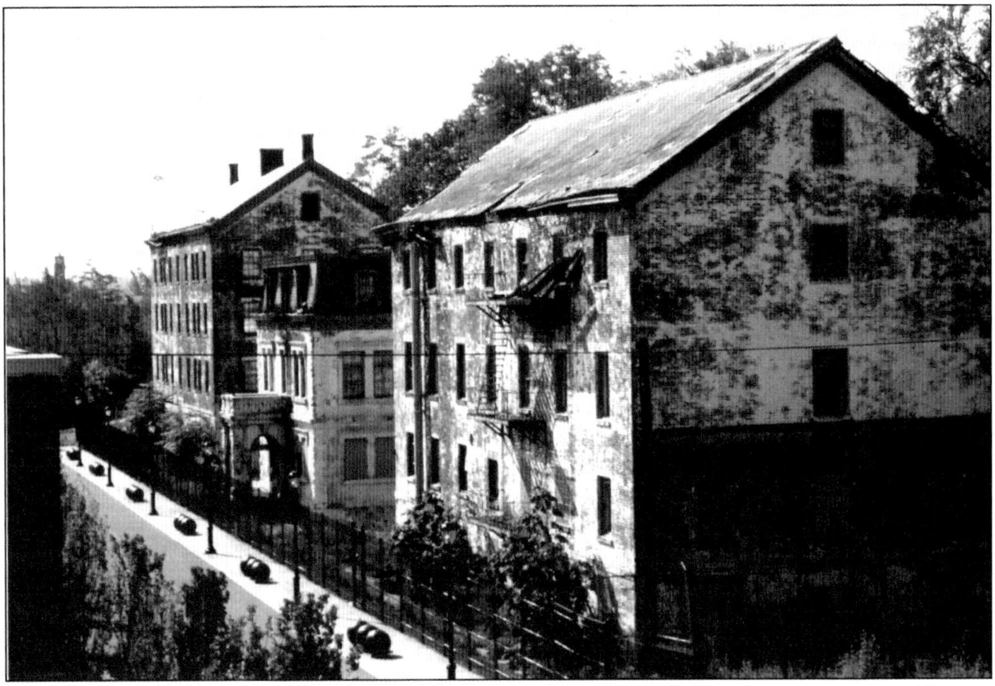

These late-20th-century photographs show the other buildings at the U.S. Coast Guard's lighthouse depot. In the center is the administration building (1869), between the barracks and the old lamp shop. In 1998, the lighthouse depot was selected as the future home of the National Lighthouse Museum. (Collection of David Goldfarb.)

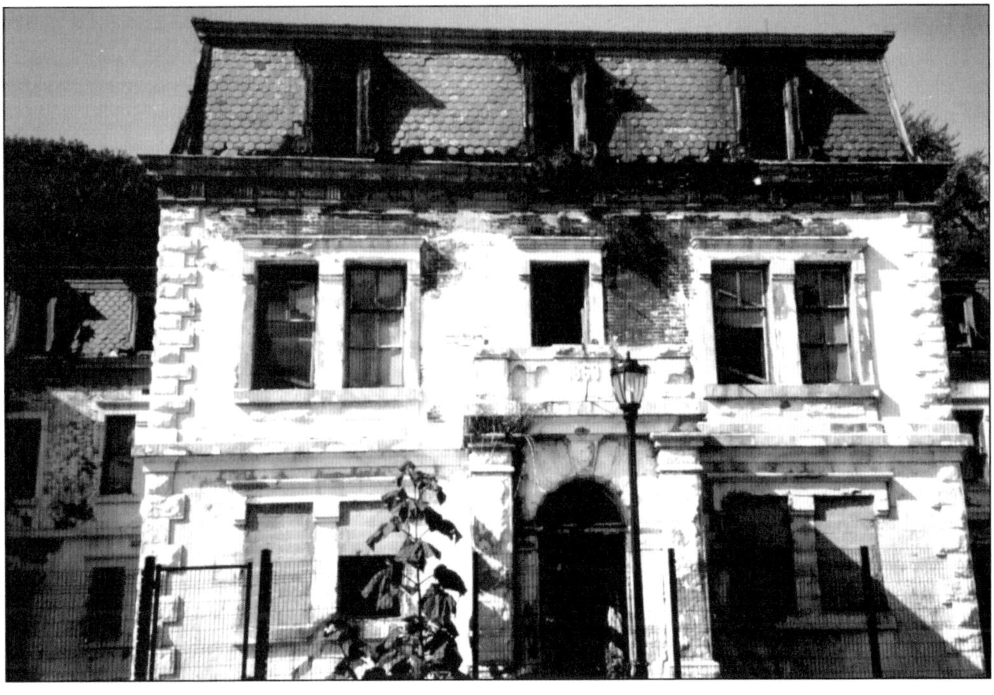

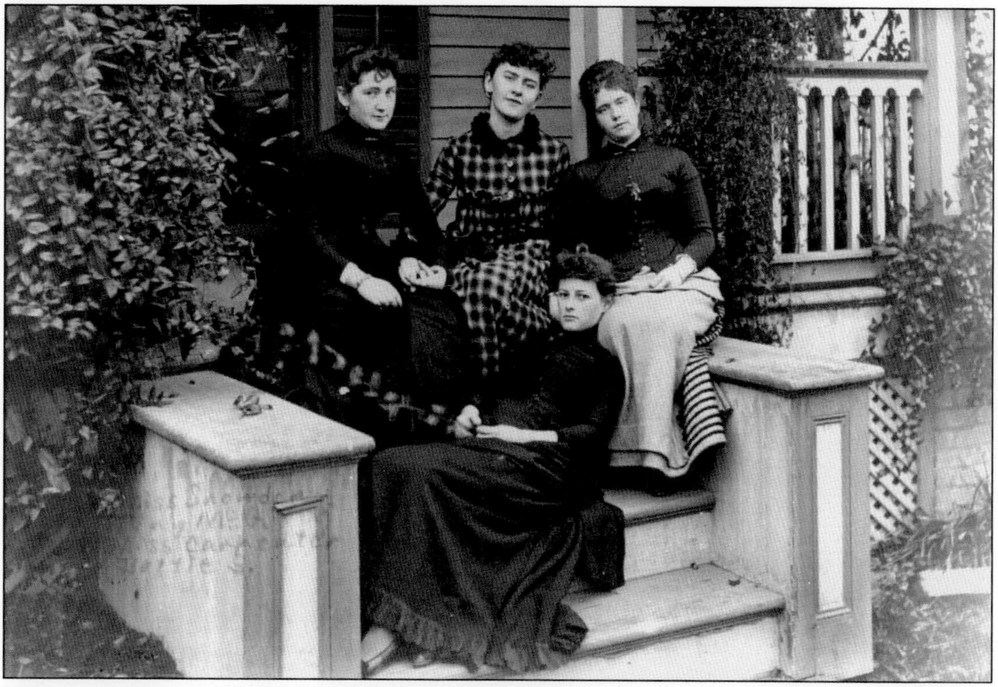

These two photographs were taken by John Millis of Cleveland and show young ladies relaxing on the grounds of the U.S. Lighthouse Depot, which was located on Staten Island due to its proximity to the major port of New York.

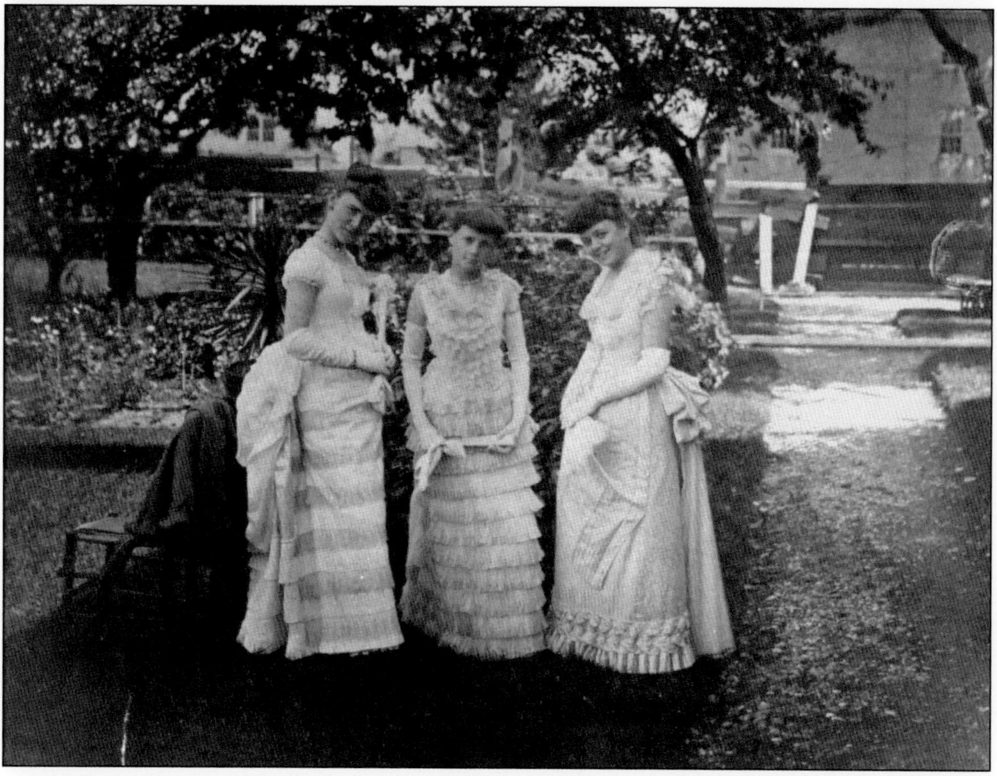

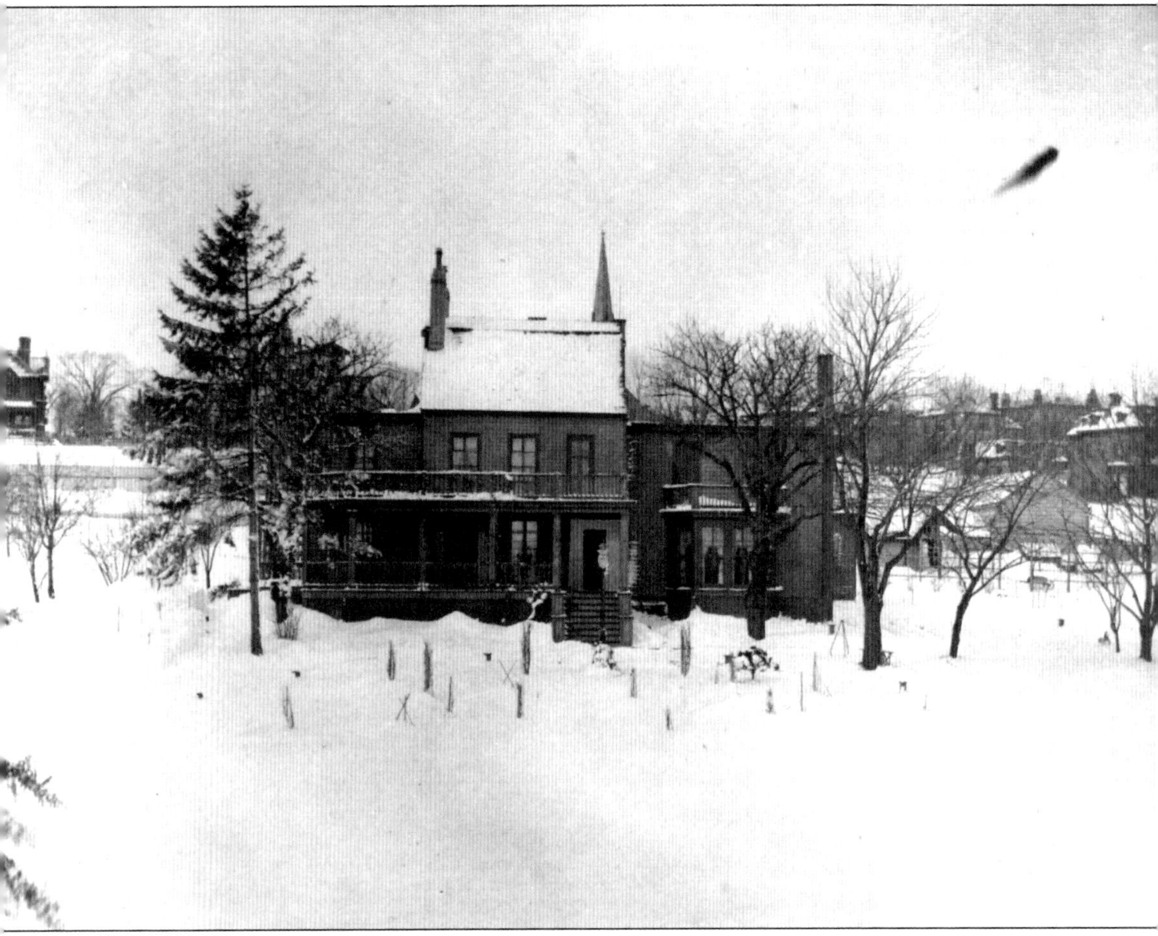

This is a photograph of a building on the grounds of the U.S. Lighthouse Depot taken in the winter of 1888. This building has been demolished.

Seven

Modern St. George

The last quarter of the 20th century saw sweeping changes take place in St. George. After years of decline, a renaissance began as people discovered the convenience of living near the transportation hub with its ease of commuting to Manhattan. Ironically this was one of the major drawing cards for the area for the previous two centuries. Home prices were significantly lower than in Manhattan and Brooklyn, and large Victorian-era homes were scooped up by young urban commuters, determined to save the unique character of both their homes and the area.

The site of the Hotel Castleton became the location of Staten Island's tallest buildings with the construction of the Castleton Towers in the mid-1970s; the two massive, 18-story, brown brick buildings offering the same spectacular views of Manhattan that the hotel guests enjoyed nearly a century before. In 1994, concerned area residents succeeded in their decade-long attempt at securing a New York City Landmarks Preservation Commission Designation for the St. George Historic District.

The first decade of the 21st century has been no less significant in the changes taking place in St. George. In 2000, a stadium opened as the home of the Staten Island Yankees, a minor league baseball team, on land purchased from the Baltimore and Ohio Railroad adjacent to the ferry terminal. Ironically the stadium parking lot was the site of major league baseball in the 1880s. The Staten Island Ferry Terminal received its first major reconstruction since it was rebuilt after the 1947 fire. The multi-million-dollar project created a stunning contemporary structure with glass walls that allows commuters to see the harbor traffic as it passes, and an esplanade was built along the shore from the ferry terminal to approximately Westervelt Avenue at Richmond Terrace. It is on the esplanade that a memorial was built in recognition of the Staten Islanders who lost their lives in the terrorist attacks on the World Trade Center on September 11, 2001.

Recently developers have purchased tracts of land, sometimes bulldozing significant 19th-century homes, in order to build high-rise residential buildings. Plans are underway for a new county courthouse where the municipal parking lot now stands on Hyatt Street between Central Avenue and St. Mark's Place.

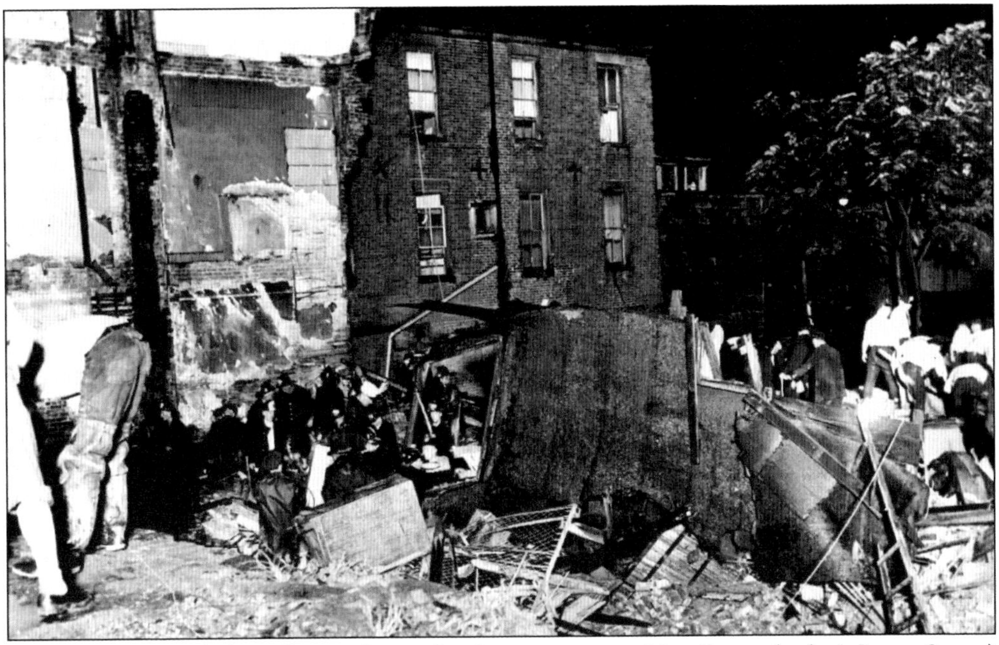

Heavy rains caused the collapse of a six-family tenement on New Street (today's Jersey Street) on August 11, 1937. Some 19 people lost their lives, including police officer Joseph P. McBreen, who attempted to save a child trapped in the wreckage. The tenement site is today the site of the Richmond Terrace Houses, a New York City Housing Project. This is a Wide World photograph from August 12, 1937. (Collection of David Goldfarb.)

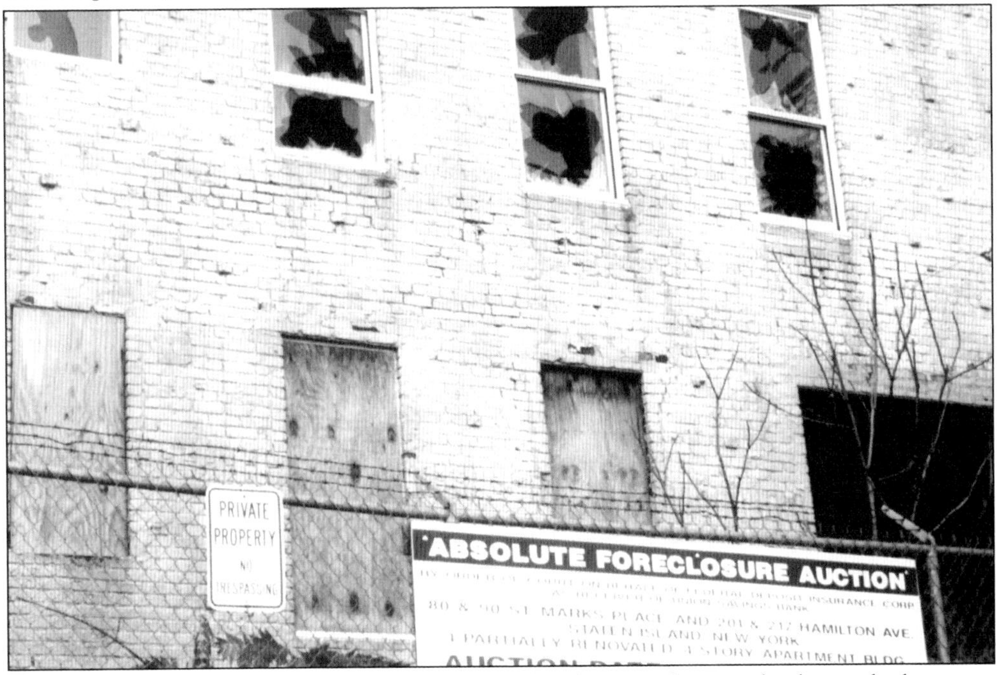

Luxury apartments built behind Curtis High School in the 1920s became derelict in the later part of the 1960s and 1970s. They were later rehabilitated and are once again inhabited. (Collection of David Goldfarb.)

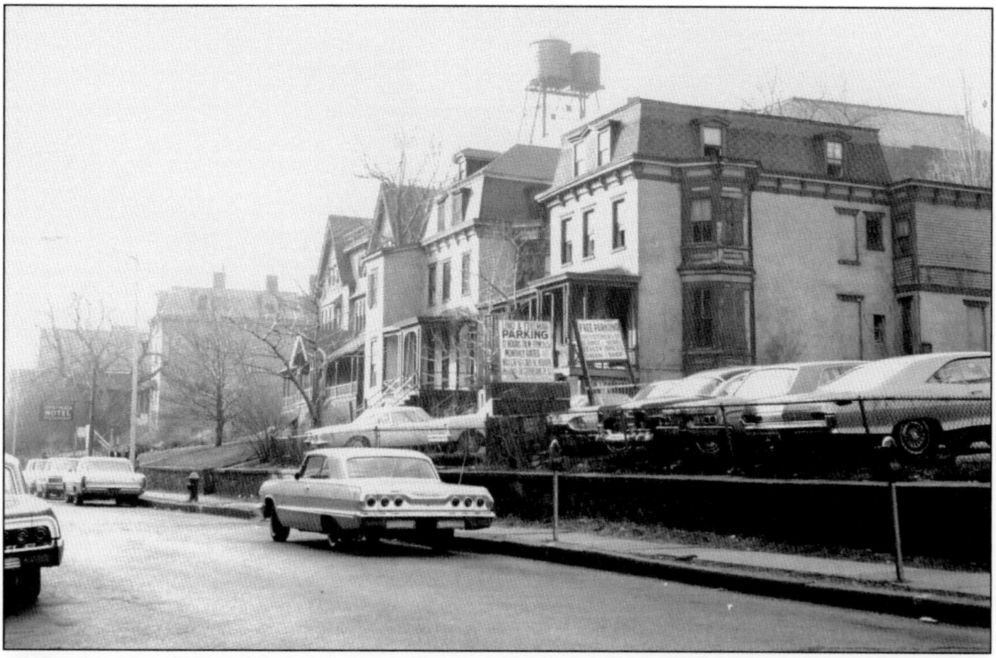

As St. George changed from a town of scenic hotels and imposing Victorian residences to a business and civic center, the grand homes were lost one by one, as seen here along Stuyvesant Place. A parking lot has taken up land where some *c.* 1870 homes once stood. The sign states, "Free Parking for Beauty Salon and Dress Shop." The forth building from the right was the St. George Hotel.

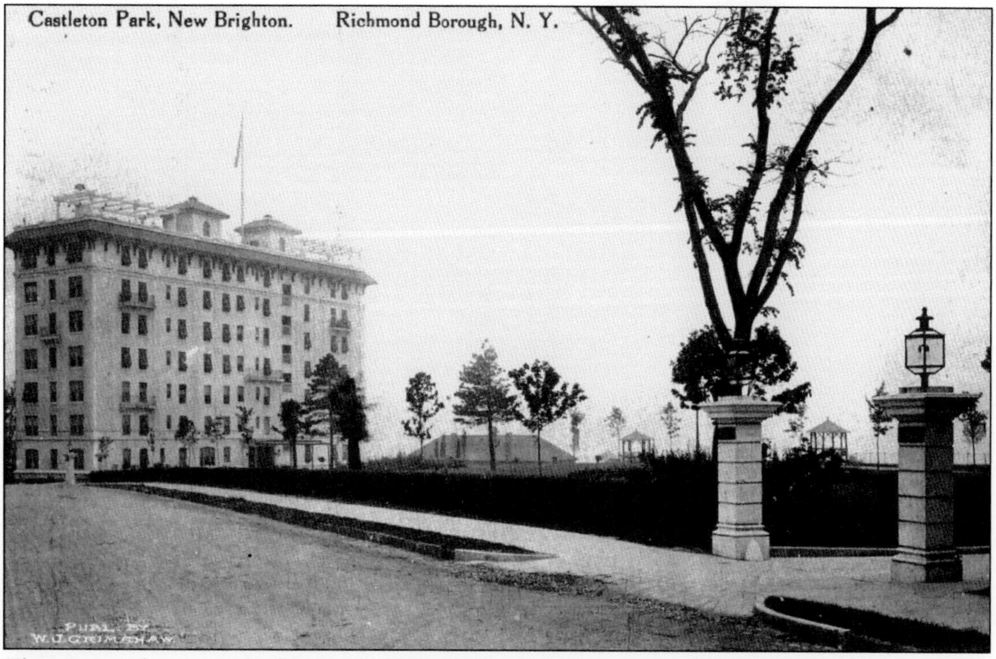

This postcard, postmarked June 21, 1945, shows Castleton Park along St. Mark's Place, which no longer exists. It was the site of the Hotel Castleton that burned in 1907 and is the site of the Castleton Towers apartment buildings today. (Collection of David Goldfarb.)

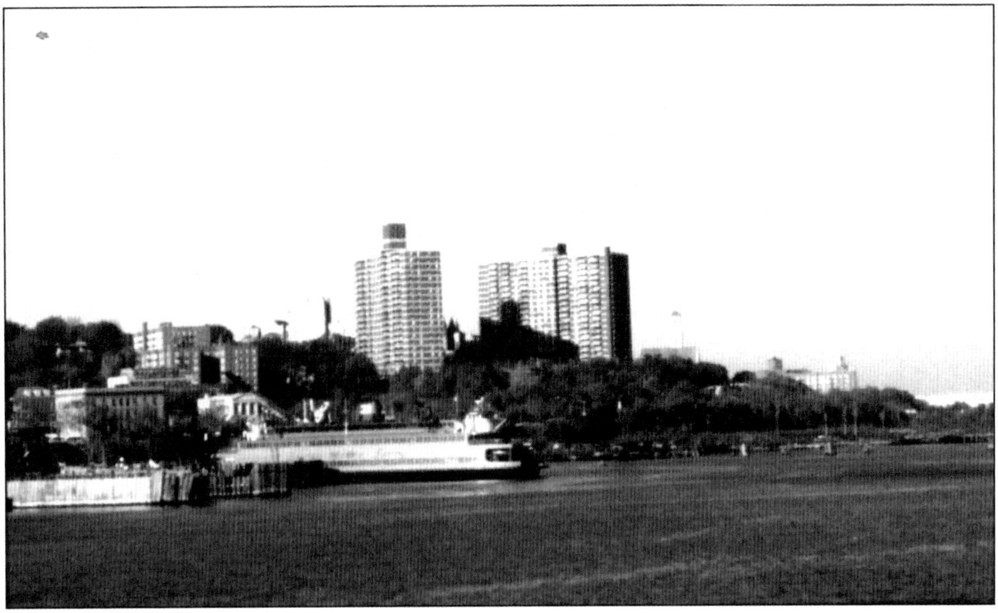

In the early 1970s, the Castleton Towers Apartments were built on the site of the Hotel Castleton. They are the tallest buildings on Staten Island. (Collection of David Goldfarb.)

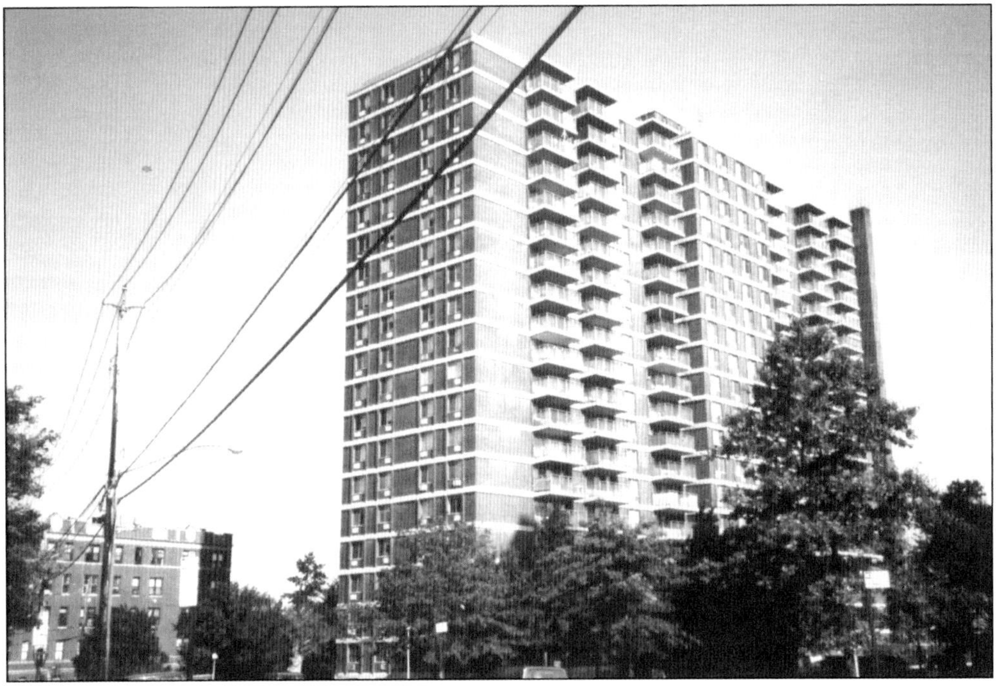

The Ambassador Apartments, at Daniel Low Terrace and Belmont Place, were built in 1932 by architect Lucien Pisciatta in the art deco style. (Collection of David Goldfarb.)

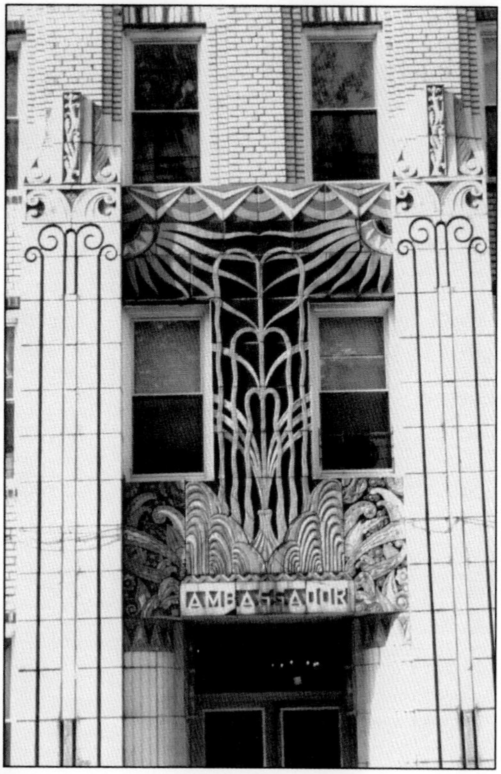

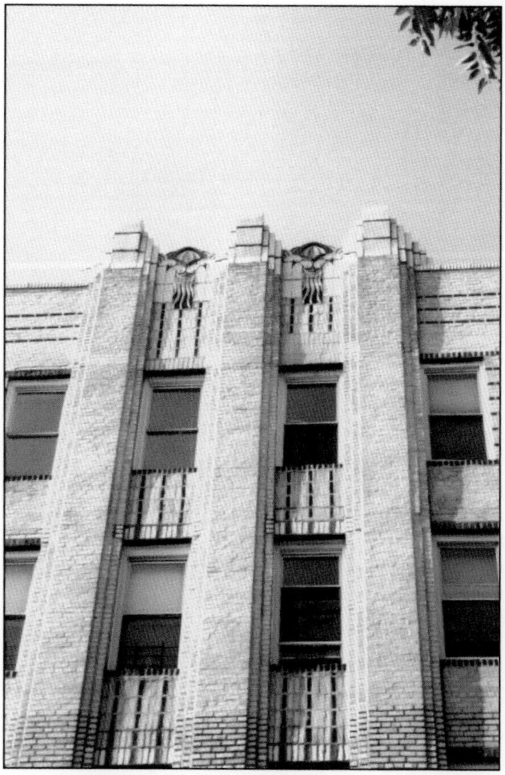

The Ambassador Apartments were the former residence of Paul Newman, Joanne Woodward, and Martin Sheen. According to Sheen, his son Emilio Estevez was born on the living room floor of his apartment in the Ambassador Apartments. (Collection of David Goldfarb.)

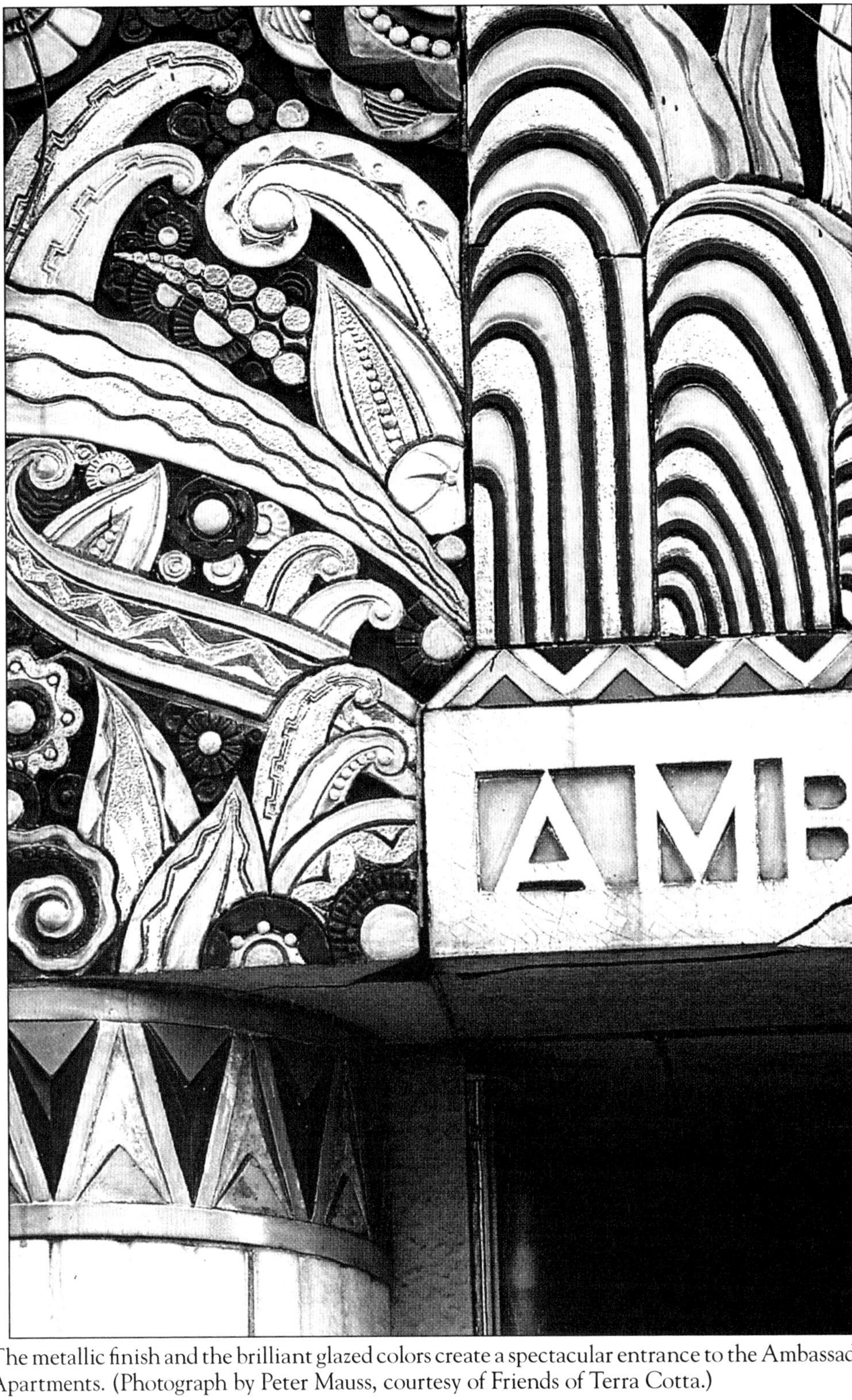

The metallic finish and the brilliant glazed colors create a spectacular entrance to the Ambassador Apartments. (Photograph by Peter Mauss, courtesy of Friends of Terra Cotta.)

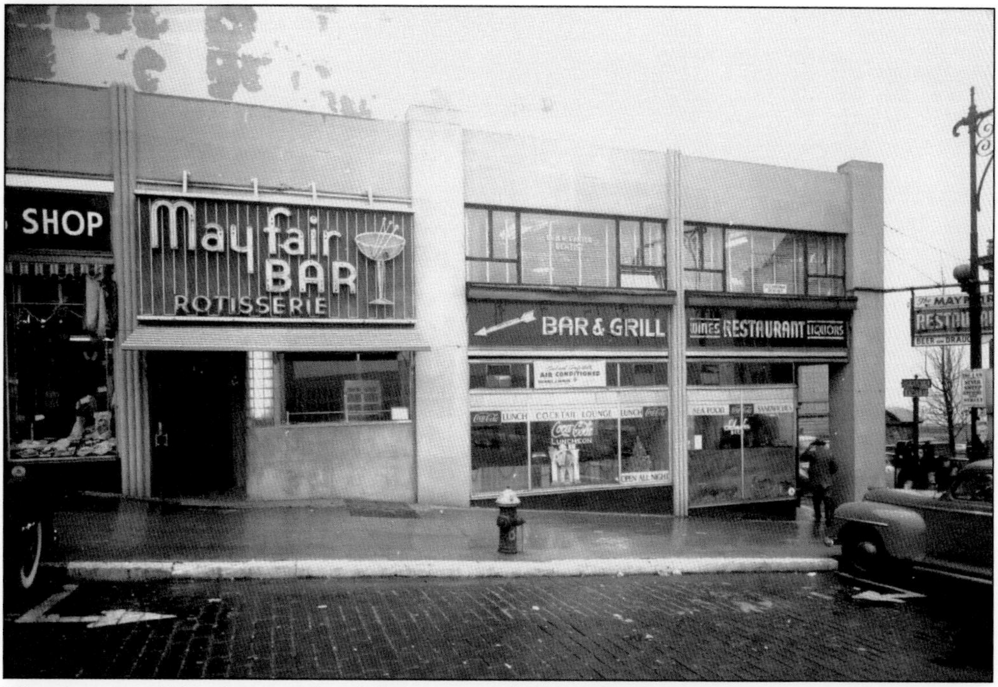

This January 1952 photograph of the corner of Hyatt Street and Stuyvesant Place, directly across from Staten Island Borough Hall, shows the Mayfair Restaurant and Bar, a major island restaurant in its day. Note the signs announcing that the restaurant was "open all night" and that one of its amenities was that it was "air conditioned."

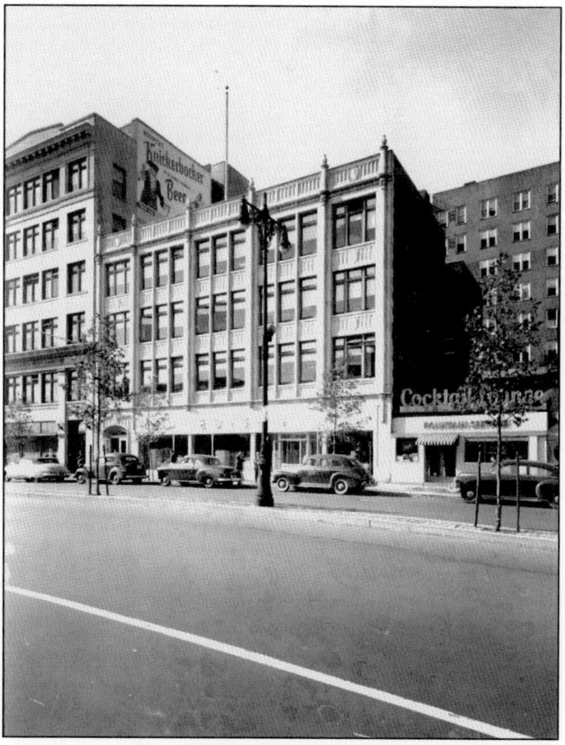

By the time of this 1951 photograph, office buildings have sprung up along Bay Street. St. George was now a bustling business center. The four-story building at the center is the former offices of Con Edison. This building was later used as the technology division of the College of Staten Island and became vacant in the years 1998 to 2000. The taller building to the left was the Title Guarantee and Trust Company, while the St. George Clipper Diner can be viewed at the right.

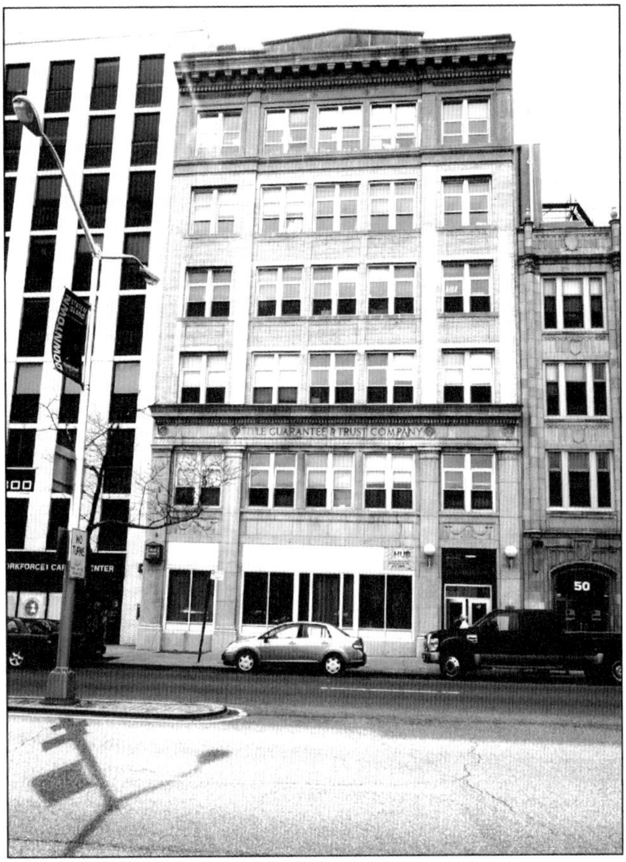

These pictures show the Title Guarantee and Trust Company at 56 Bay Street and the more modern building at 60 Bay Street. (Collection of David Goldfarb.)

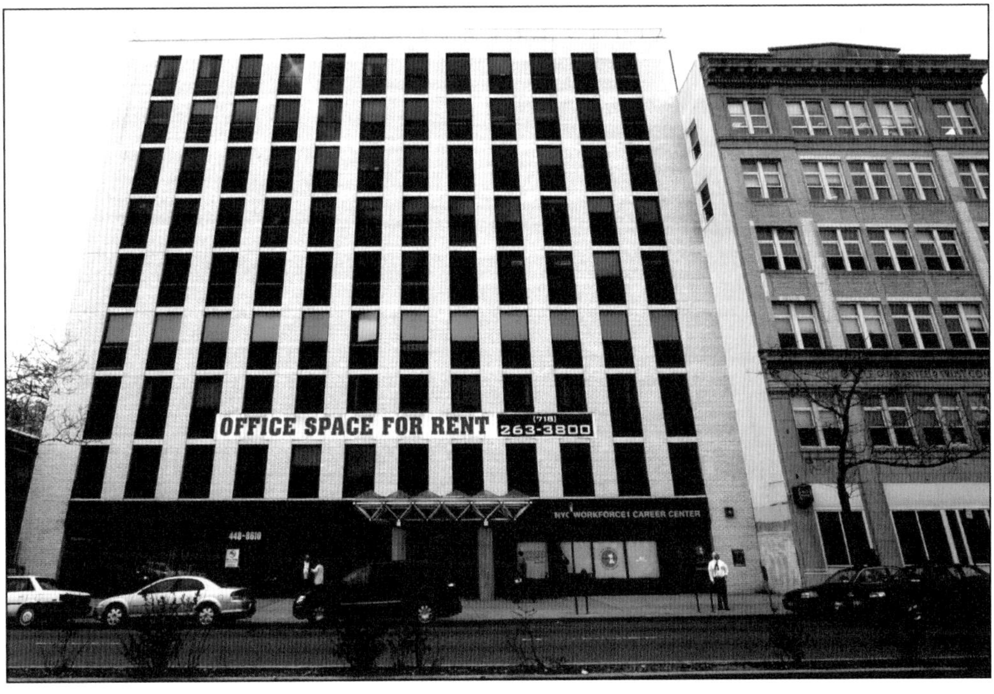

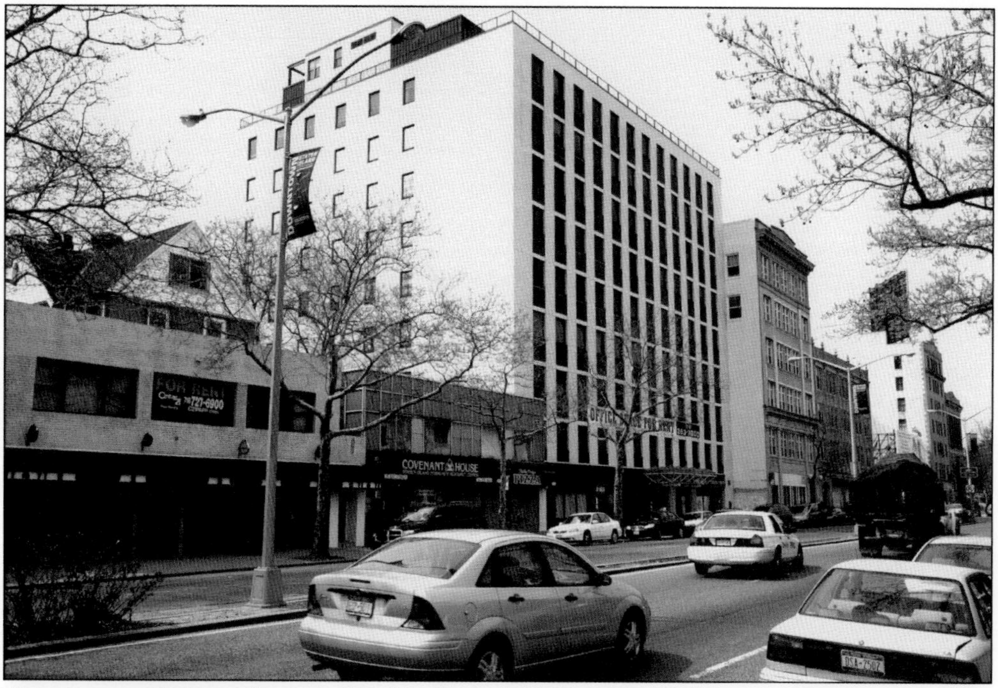

This photograph shows the rest of the block as it looks in 2008. (Collection of David Goldfarb.)

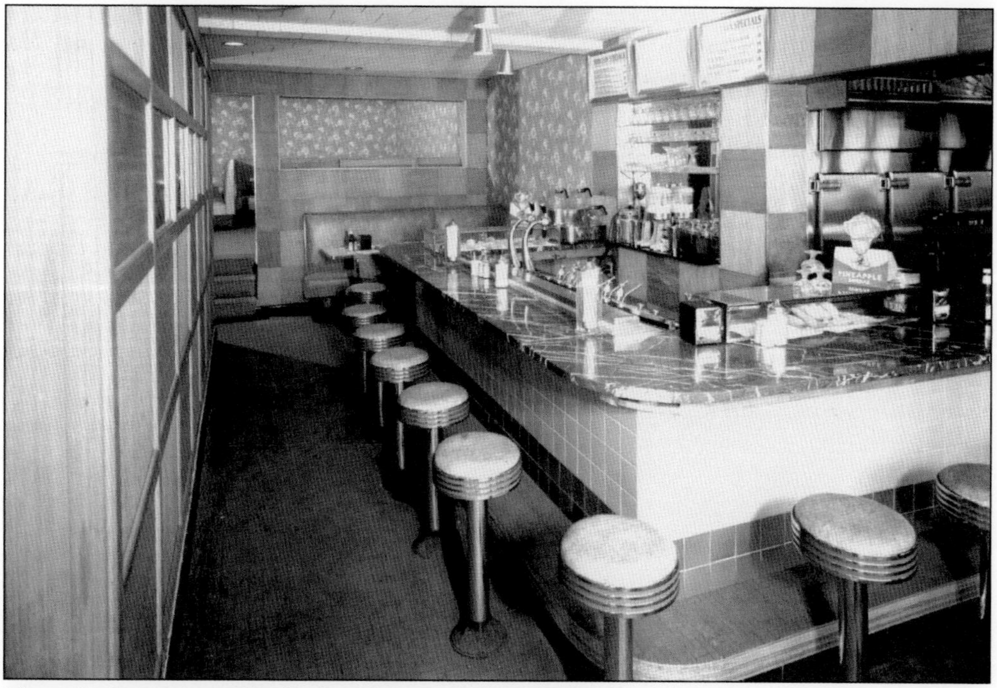

The soda fountain inside the St. George Clipper Diner, photographed on December 14, 1949, boasts all of the best appurtenances for a well-stocked mid-20th-century fountain, including straw dispensers, a milk shake machine, bananas, syrup pumps, and ice cream soda glasses. Note the prices for the fountain specials, none above $1.

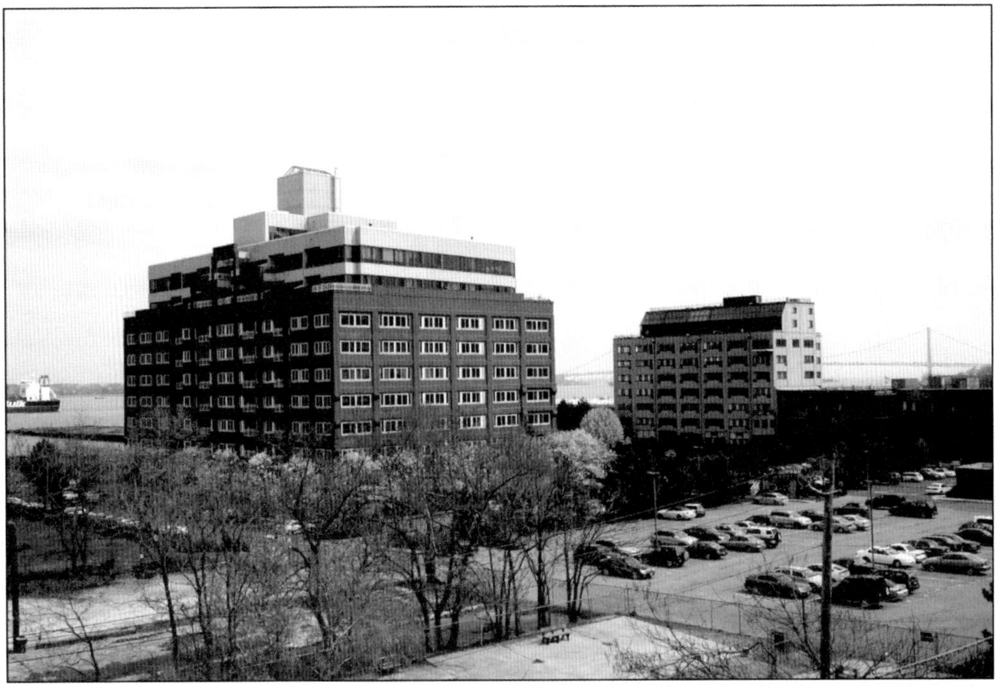

These two images show Bay Street Landing, an adaptive reuse housing development along the eastern shore next to the Staten Island Ferry. The original factory and warehouse buildings of poured-in-place concrete construction were built during the 1930s as warehouse and factory structures along the waterfront. As manufacturing interests continued to leave New York City, the buildings stood empty and derelict until the conversion to loft-style residences took place, construction beginning in the 1980s. The addition of upper floors to the buildings allowed for duplex apartments complete with water and Manhattan views. (Collection of David Goldfarb.)

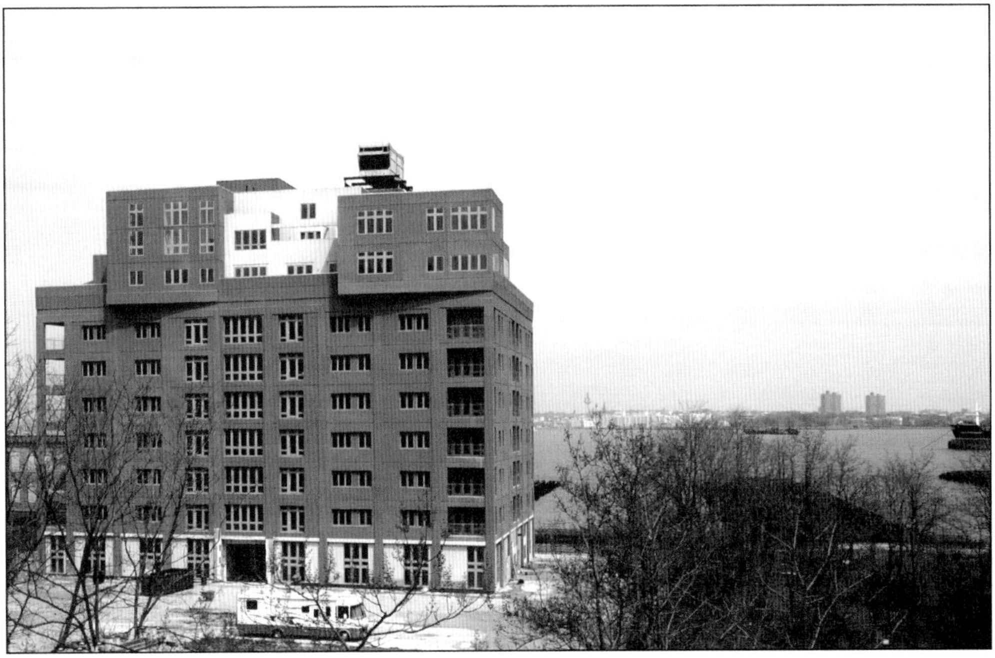

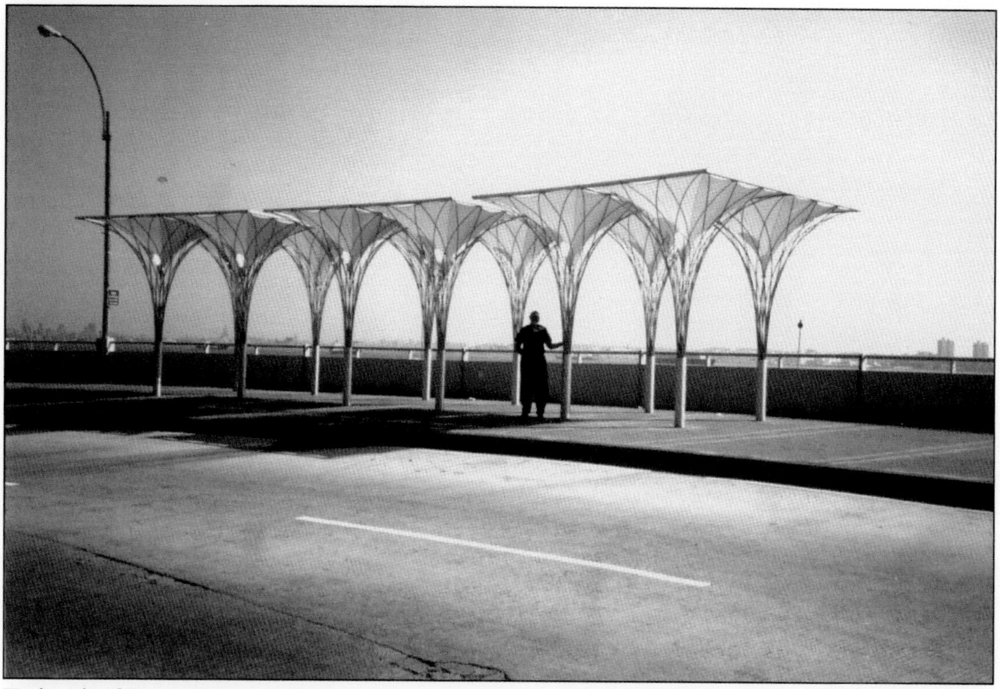

Today the ferry terminal includes art in public places. This sculpture is on the sidewalk alongside the bus ramp. (Collection of David Goldfarb.)

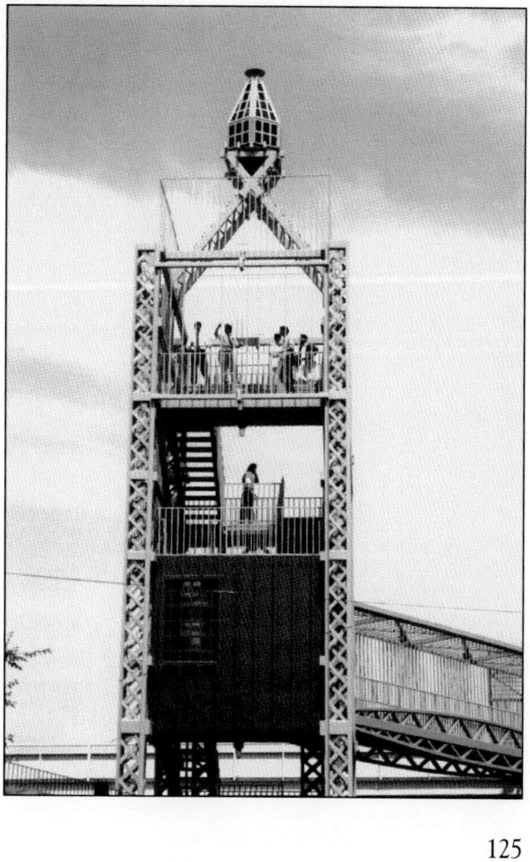

This "folly" today connects the ferry terminal bus ramp to the lighthouse depot. The "bridge," located at the rear, leads to the lighthouse depot. (Collection of David Goldfarb.)

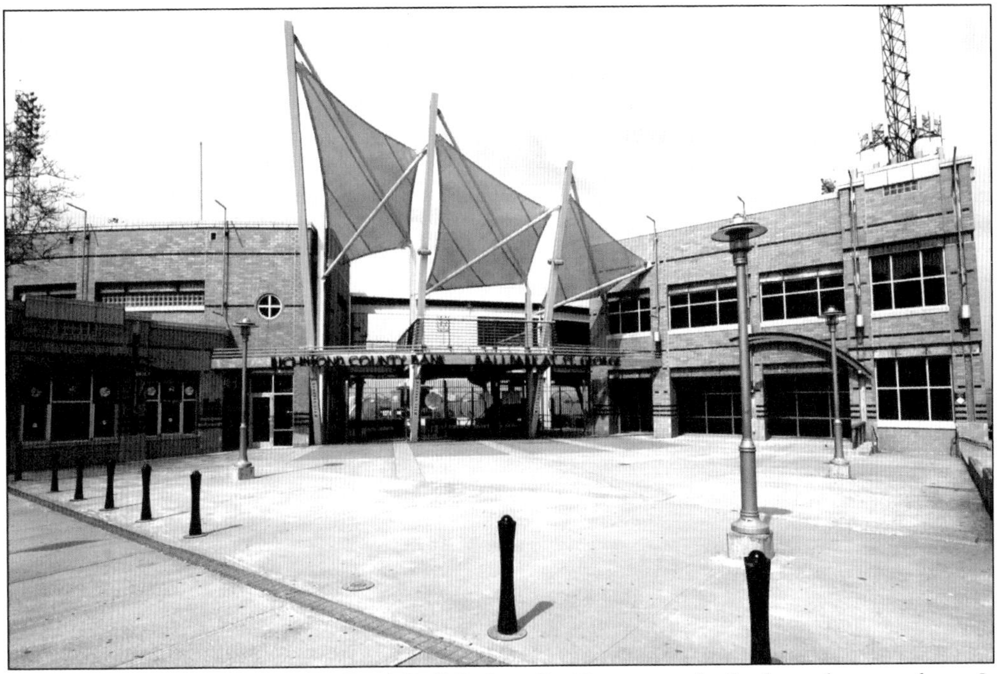

The Richmond County Savings Bank Ball Park at St. George was built along the waterfront. It opened in 2001 and serves as the home field for the Single A affiliate Staten Island Yankees. The stadium seats 7,171 spectators. (Photographs by Daniel K. Goldfarb.)

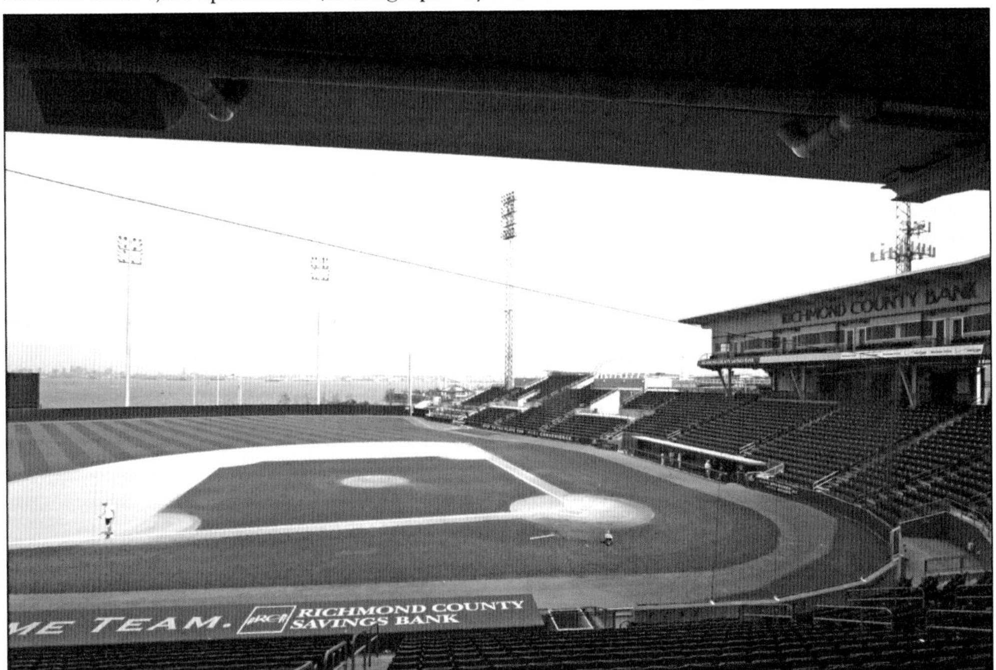

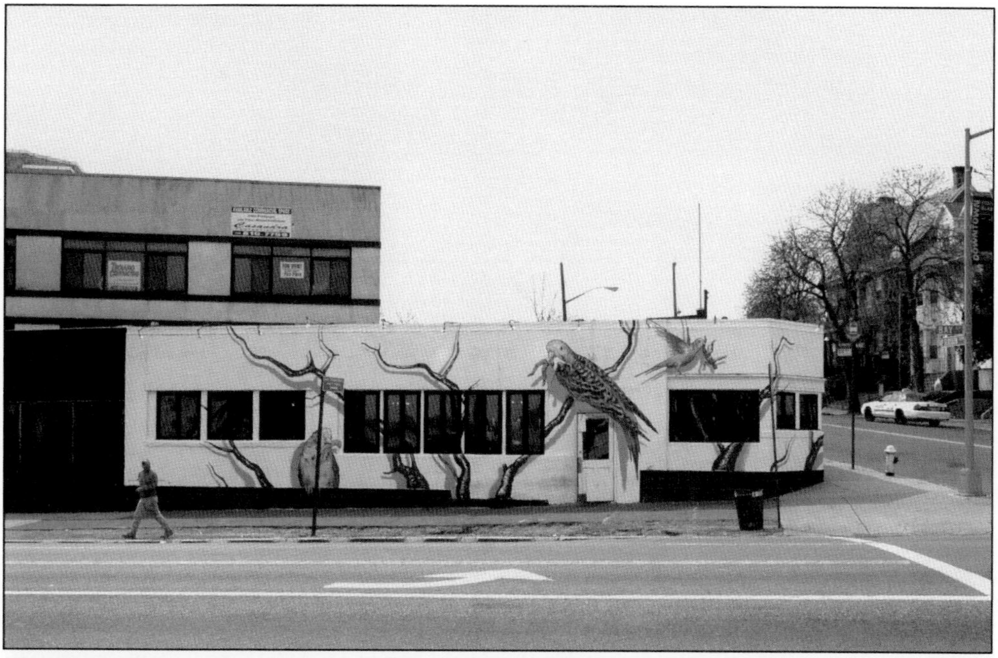

The Cargo Café on Bay Street and Slossen Terrace features unusual wall paintings by Staten Island artist Scott Labado. (Collection of David Goldfarb.)

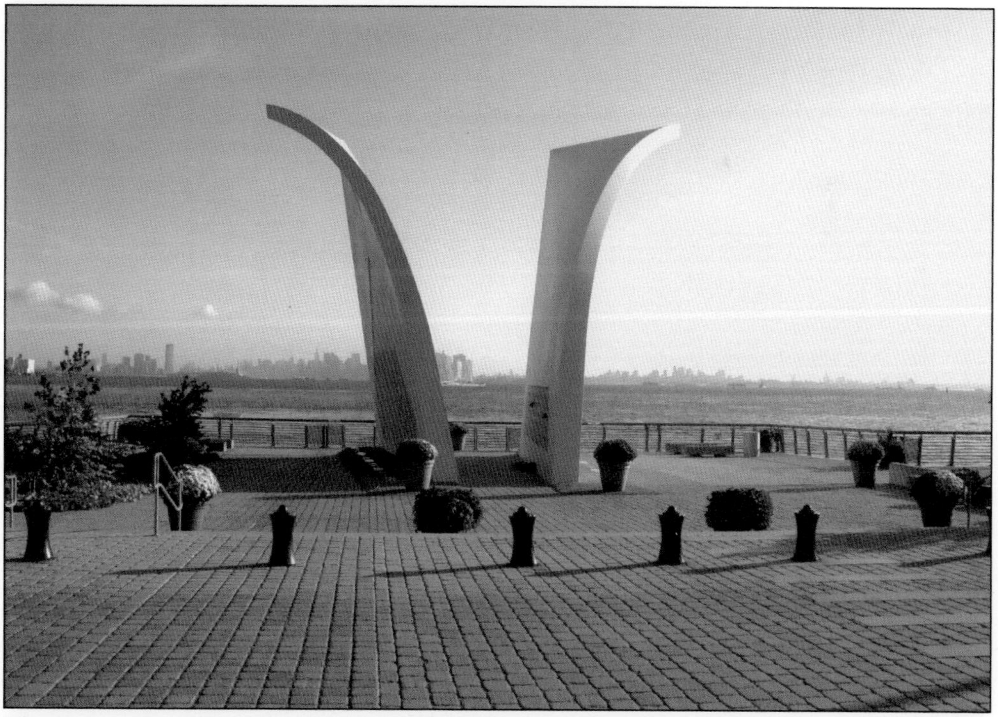

The Staten Island 9/11 Memorial is located along the North Shore Waterfront Esplanade. The site provides panoramic views of New York Harbor, Lower Manhattan, and the Statue of Liberty. The memorial, which has 274 plaques, one for each Staten Islander killed in the terrorist attacks, was unveiled on September 11, 2004, and cost $2.77 million. (Photograph by James G. Ferreri.)